To a very remarkable lady
off on a new adventure

With deepest love
and admiration from
all her children

Christmas, 1970

The Bible Through the Ages

THE BIBLE THROUGH THE AGES

HARRY THOMAS FRANK

CHARLES WILLIAM SWAIN

COURTLANDT CANBY

ASSISTED BY MICHAEL HARWOOD

THE WORLD PUBLISHING COMPANY

CLEVELAND AND NEW YORK

Published by The World Publishing Company
2231 West 110th Street, Cleveland, Ohio 44102
Published simultaneously in Canada by Nelson, Foster & Scott Ltd.
First World printing 1967

Library of Congress Catalog Card Number: 67–29087

Printed in the United States of America

Designed by Edgar J. Frank

CONTENTS

FOREWORD

THE BIBLE IS ONE OF THE enduring and inexhaustible treasures of the world, incomparable with any other book in its importance to human history. For two thousand years men have turned to it as a source of revelation and wisdom, relied upon it for strength and guidance, searched it for historical understanding, sought inspiration and beauty in its words. It has had a major effect in shaping our civilization, and no adequate knowledge of the art, literature, or social codes and institutions of Western man is possible without reference to this Book of Books. Today its creative impact continues, as new translations, renewed study, and wider distribution have made the Bible accessible to men of every station in all parts of the globe.

This unparalleled importance and availability are not matched, however, by widespread acquaintance with the story of the origin and transmission of the Bible. *The Bible Through the Ages* is an effort to tell that story—from its beginnings in the traditions of the wandering Hebrews, through centuries of writing, gathering, copying, and translating, down to the present day. To attempt so vast a task imposes an exacting burden of selection on the authors. The Bible came into being over many generations and has been read, studied, and interpreted over many more. The guiding aim in this book has been to trace the main threads of development, summarizing scholarly contributions in a readable fashion and conveying some of the drama of "a Book in history." It is the conviction of the authors that any reader, whatever his background or beliefs, will be the richer for learning more about the making and meaning of a book that is so vital a part of our shared heritage. It is our hope that many will be prompted by this account to explore the world of the Bible for themselves through further reading and study.

Many individuals have had a part in the preparation of this book. Special acknowledgment is due to Winston G. Potter for his expert contributions to the design and format; to Monroe H. Fabian for his informed and untiring efforts to obtain suitable illustrations; and to Miss Annabel Learned for her invaluable editorial assistance.

SHAPING A TRADITION: DESERT NOMADS TO NATIONAL DESTINY

In the beginning God created the heavens and the earth. The earth was without form and void. . . ."

—Genesis 1:1, 2

THE BIBLE opens on a scene painted in grays and blacks. "The earth was without form and void, and darkness was upon the face of the deep. . . . And God said, 'Let there be light'; and there was light."

Beyond the void and the darkness is the Creator, who speaks and brings order and teeming life out of formless chaos. And the crowning glory of this creation is the making of a creature different from all others, man. Apart from God, man—not merely Hebrew man but *Adam*, literally "mankind"—and the world about him are meaningless; no order can be distinguished, all is "without form and void . . . darkness."

This is the Hebrew vision spelled out in the familiar stories of the first eleven chapters of Genesis: creation, Adam and Eve, Cain and Abel, Noah and the Ark, the Tower of Babel. Together these masterpieces of poetic prose express an understanding of God and of man that underlies the thought of the entire Bible—God's goodness, justice, mercy, and His active relation to His creation; man's freedom and his misuse of it. Except for the brief moment in the Garden of Eden this basic Hebrew understanding of God and of human existence is not idyllic. Here as elsewhere the Bible is starkly, even

I

frighteningly realistic. God sorrows over His creation. And man lives in brokenness, in a clutter of distorted relationships and an outright assertion of self-sufficiency which cut him off not only from his neighbor but also from himself and from God. Only in light of this understanding of the universal condition of man is it possible, according to the biblical writers, to comprehend the particular history of Israel of old, or the "New Israel" of the New Testament.

For a long time scholars have known that legends similar to the stories found in Genesis 1–11 had been told by the peoples living in the Tigris-Euphrates Valley for hundreds of years before they found their way into the Bible. It is from this area, Mesopotamia, that the ancestors of the Hebrews came. In

The massive three-tiered ziggurat at Ur, home of Abraham. Already ancient by the time of Abraham, this temple of the moon god Nammu was the scene of human sacrifice. Excavations (foreground) have revealed a high level of culture that may have been destroyed by a catastrophic flood.

times before writing materials became abundant and before literacy was relatively widespread, oral tradition played a major role in the life of every community. Around campfires and at their sanctuaries the ancient Hebrews rehearsed their own versions of the old Mesopotamian tales. They told the story of the Tower of Babel, probably inspired by the soaring ziggurats of the region. They related the story of Noah's Ark, a Mesopotamian version of which has been deciphered from clay tablets found at Babylon and Nineveh. These tablets tell of the adventures of Ut-napishtim, who built a ship at the command of the god Ea, loaded it with his "whole family and kinfolk, the seed of all living things, the cattle of the field," and rode out a great flood. At Ur and other Sumerian cities evidence has been found of early and widespread flooding which may suggest the origin of this tale. Other stories have been discovered that foreshadow and in some cases parallel their biblical counterparts.

The Hebrews remembered these stories and passed them on from generation to generation. This was not done merely to preserve tribal lore. Through a conscious process of selection, arrangement, and integration they were woven into a uniquely Hebrew unity explaining the meaning of man in light of the marvelous workings of God. For over a thousand years this process went on. Long before it was completed and the stories took the final form in which we now have them (sometime around 500–400 B.C.), the Hebrews had brought together other traditions that spoke of their own beginnings as a people. These reach back into the second millennium, into the Middle Bronze Age, and tell of the wanderings and adventures of the patriarchs, of Abraham, and of Isaac, Jacob, and Joseph.

The Founding Fathers in Israel's History

To UNDERSTAND the place of the patriarchs in history we must move back in time some thousands of years to the first flowering of civilization, which took place in and around the "Fertile Crescent," that arc of well-watered land stretching up from Egypt through Palestine and Syria and then down again into Mesopotamia. Here the first evidences of civilization have been found. Jericho, in central Palestine, the oldest known city in the world, was already a fortified town of some size in 6000 B.C. Civilization matured most rapidly, however, at the two ends of the crescent, in the rich valleys of Egypt and Mesopotamia. Between 4000 and 3000 B.C. the first organized states appeared, with a complex social fabric of kings, priests, warriors, craftsmen, and slaves. Magnificent cities were built, adorned with temples and palaces. The arts flourished and writing was developed.

With the rise of powerful states in Egypt and Mesopotamia the intervening lands, Syria and Palestine, became connecting links, their strong-walled cities subject to the influence of both major powers. It was difficult for these city-states to unite; as with their Greek counterparts later, geography was against it. Palestine, a narrow strip lying between the Mediterranean and the sand, is a patchwork of forested hills, desert, and fertile valleys. It offers no geographical unity in whole or in part. And there was lack of traditional ethnic unity. These cities were always fighting among themselves. Their different backgrounds taught them to distrust one another more than they feared invading armies.

And the armies came: periodically they swept over the land, laying waste the crops, pounding the city gates, pouring over the walls, slaughtering the population, and reducing the houses to smoldering heaps. Archaeological evidence at Shechem, Taanach, Tirzah, and other Bronze Age sites lend mute evidence to the destructive brutality of the time.

The prize sought in this warfare was the lucrative complex of trade routes that crisscrossed the area. Centuries after the Bronze Age the red-rose city of Petra in the south and Palmyra, jewel of the northern desert, gained their

The Bronze Age East Gate at Shechem, showing the effect of an Egyptian battering-ram. Excavators found spear-pierced skeletons lying on the steps in the foreground. This strategic city, visited by Abraham, became a Hebrew shrine at the time of Joshua.

magnificence primarily by tapping this ancient source of revenue. Solomon, too, was not unaware of the benefits to be gained by regulating the trade that passed through his kingdom. This prize, coupled with recurring imperial megalomania, made Palestine a constant battlefield. The armies came, fought, and departed, and they left behind their dead, their wounded, and their veterans. Not only this, but the caravans that made their way slowly over the sands and hills and wadis (dry riverbeds) brought in new peoples, new goods, new methods, new ideas. Before the end of the third millennium B.C. the area was a melting pot of peoples and open to every influence.

Of greater importance than armies or caravans, however, were the mass migrations of seminomads. Between 2300 B.C. and 1500 B.C. waves of people from the north and east moved into the fertile areas of Mesopotamia. Those dispossessed in this region in turn moved southward into Syria, Palestine, and even Egypt. It was probably these people with their great flocks who brought to an end the urban phase of Bronze Age culture in Palestine. Almost all the great city-states disappeared during this time, and the architectural and artistic levels of the later Bronze Age as shown by artifacts so far excavated indicate a cultural decline.

This is the period of the wanderings of the patriarchs recounted in such vivid detail in Genesis 12–50. By the time Abraham set out on his journey from Mesopotamia to Egypt and back to Palestine, Semitic-speaking nomads had long since inundated the settled areas of the Fertile Crescent and had intermingled with the local populations. A Semitic king, the famed Hammurabi of Babylon, who is still remembered for his famous code of laws, had conquered all Mesopotamia and with it the rich inheritance of the world's oldest civilization, Sumer. Among the centers taken by Hammurabi was Mari, a city on the Euphrates at the intersection of two caravan roads. When this site was excavated it revealed a richly decorated palace containing nearly three hundred rooms. This edifice yielded a royal library of over 20,000 clay tablets, which, when combined with those found at Nuzi, Kanish, and other excavated sites in the general area, disclosed startling parallels to the life and times of the patriarchs as set forth in the Bible.

At first reading this resemblance does not appear at all extraordinary—until it is recalled that the traditions of the patriarchs were probably not committed to writing until approximately seven hundred years later. The similarities give independent support for the view that the biblical writers were recording an oral tradition that preserved many authentic features from the days of the patriarchs. Abraham's fear (Gen. 15:1–4) that God's promise would not be fulfilled and that his slave Eliezer would be his heir is understandable in light of the Nuzi texts, which tell us that an adopted slave could inherit his master's property. The background of Sarah's gift of Hagar to Abraham (Gen. 16:1–4) is illumined by texts which show that a childless wife was to provide another woman for her husband in order to produce an heir. Mesopotamian laws of the time forbade the turning out of such a slave mother and her child; this may help to explain Abraham's reluctance to comply with Sarah's wishes regarding Hagar and Ishmael (Gen. 21:8–14).

The somewhat enigmatic story of his attempt to pass off his wife as his sister (Gen. 12:10–20), explained by the biblical writer as owing to fear, may also be partly explained by the suggestion from a contemporary tablet that a wife enjoyed special status if she were also honored with the title of "sister."

Not only are the details of the patriarchal narratives in harmony with what we know of the second millennium B.C., but the general outline of the wanderings and mode of life of these Hebrew ancestors also accords with our extra-biblical evidence. In the Bible they are shown to be seminomads who do little farming and own little if any land. The places where the Bible says they journeyed are the places where seminomads would have wandered in the first half of the second millennium B.C. They roamed the central mountain range from the area of Shechem to the Negeb. But they did not settle in northern Palestine, nor in the Jordan Valley, nor in the plain of Esdraelon. Nor did they penetrate deep or often into the coastal plain. Like herdsmen throughout history, they fought with their agricultural neighbors, often overthrowing cities and destroying their culture. But they were unable to seize and hold large areas where there was a sizable settled population. This picture given by the Bible is receiving increasing confirmation from archaeological research into the Bronze Age.

Yet it must be stressed that in spite of the way in which archaeology has illumined the background of the patriarchal narratives, it has not proved that these stories happened just as the Bible reports them. They are independent accounts. We have no evidence outside the Bible that refers directly to any of the patriarchs, and it is not possible to say with assurance in what century they lived. Not only are there no eyewitness accounts of the travels and adventures of Abraham and his clan; there are few, if any, such accounts of events reported in the Bible until perhaps the time of David's kingdom, certainly none until the Hebrew conquest of Palestine.

What then is the value of these stories of the early ancestors of Israel? And why were they not only preserved, but included among the Scriptures? Their value as objective history is at best only incidental to their original purpose, which was to be *representative history* as remembered by later writers; history as remembered in folklore and celebrated in ritual worship; history as transformed and exalted by an awareness of the purposes of God. The story of Abraham's journey, for example, may well reflect a folk memory of widespread Semitic migrations from an ancestral home in Mesopotamia. This would help to explain why the thought patterns of the Bible owe so much to that region and relatively little to Egypt, with whom the Hebrews had considerable contact later. The stories of Abraham may also reveal something about ethnic origins. They indicate that Israel had a complex beginning and was physically descended from many clans. As late as the Exile, Ezekiel reminded the people: "Your origin and your birth are of the land of the Canaanites; your father was an Amorite, and your mother a Hittite" (Ezek. 16:3). In short, the accounts of Abraham and the other patriarchs may in passing say a great deal about the objective history of early Israel. But the purpose and function of this enormously important cycle of stories has to do with Israel's understanding of itself. And we must leap across many centuries to preview the way this self-understanding took written form in the pages of the Bible.

After the various tribes had been united by Saul, consolidated by David, and glorified by Solomon, numerous customs, traditions, holy sites, folk legends, and individual tribal memories were preserved in the kingdom. Because of significant differences in background, there was no common heritage among the various peoples who made up Israel. Some tribes preserved and cherished memories of a miraculous deliverance from Egypt; others, who had never been in Egypt, shared no such memories. In general the ten northern tribes had more in common with one another than with the two southern tribes, but individual customs and variations of shared tradition were the rule.

A Literature Begins

MUCH LATER, during the period called the United Monarchy that began with Saul, an excited nationalism, coupled with the breakdown of older social and religious patterns, produced a cultural life seldom again equaled in ancient Israel. One expression of it was the gathering together of the religious beliefs, folklore, legends, and traditions of the people into a national epic. The theme of this epic, which centered in the Exodus tradition, was the way in which God had been at work in history to create a people for Himself and to give them a land.

After the division of the monarchy into two kingdoms in 922 B.C., with Israel in the north and Judah in the south, the process continued apace. The diverging national epics—for there were now two of them—reflected the different histories of the two kingdoms, and dissimilarity was heightened by the fact that each epic sought to explain and justify its own national institutions.

Scholars have been able to piece together from the biblical text the probable content of various collections of traditions. In Judah the account took the form of a history from Creation to the conquest of Canaan. At its heart was God's promise to Abraham (Gen. 12:1–3), and the purpose was to trace out its fulfillment. In response to God's call Abraham leaves his homeland behind and goes forth to an unknown future sustained by his faith in the divine promise. Through many vicissitudes and hardships, among the fleshpots of Egypt and through penitential wanderings in the searing desert, Abraham's descendants came at long last into possession of "the land of milk and honey": the Promised Land. Whatever one may—or may not—say of Abraham historically, it is clear that in the theology of the southern kingdom he is understood as the point of Israel's origin. The nation begins with God's promise.

The epic drama of the southern kingdom as reconstructed is called the J Document because it speaks of God as Yahweh (Jahweh in German, Jehovah in English, often translated as "the LORD" in the Revised Standard Version). Viewed from a literary angle this document is structured in three stages corresponding to the three parts of the initial promise. The first part shows how Israel did, in fact, spring from Abraham's seed. The second portion shows how through Joseph, who rose to power in Egypt, the nations are blessed and saved from starvation. Finally, the epic tells how Israel, delivered from bondage, conquers Canaan in fulfillment of the promise of a homeland. The J Document is a prime example of a nationalistic writing. It embodies the pride and aspirations of a people who are, quite suddenly and for the first time, beginning to feel the dignity of power coursing through their veins. The material for this drama (in order to be appreciated fully it should be read as epic drama) was not, however, the creation of the writer. His contributions were selection, arrangement, modification, and style.

At Hebron the Mosque El-Khalil ("the friend") stands above the site of the Cave of Machpelah, burial place of Abraham, "the friend of God." The large stones in the lower half of the wall are remains of a temple built by Herod the Great. Hebron is sacred to Jew, Christian, and Moslem.

In the northern kingdom, Israel, the epic called the E Document (referring to God as *Elohim*) was much less polished than its southern counterpart and its theology less sophisticated. But the scope and purpose were much the same. As might be expected, it stresses the importance of Jacob, a northern hero, rather than Abraham, who was associated with the shrine at Hebron in the south. Indeed, in its nationalistic orientation the E Document speaks of the significance of the shrines and holy places of the north almost to the total exclusion of sites closely identified with the memories of the southern tribes.

In 722 B.C., in its two-hundredth anniversary year, the northern kingdom was destroyed, its population scattered, and its national life ended. But its religious traditions were preserved. The priests at Jerusalem now sought to combine the two streams and once more bring wholeness to the religious heritage of the people. Thus the J and E Documents were blended. This accounts for the occasional presence of two different versions of the same episode in the early books of the Bible, and for the same person sometimes being known by two different names.

In 586 B.C., a hundred and thirty-six years after the dissolution of Israel, the heavy hand of conquest fell upon Judah, and its national life, too, came to an end. Now followed the agonizing years of the Exile in Babylon. During or just after this time the JE material was again edited and combined with a third body of tradition. This latter collection is known as the D Document after the Book of Deuteronomy, the chief contribution of this tradition.

Finally, about 400 B.C. or slightly before, the JED tradition was combined with yet a fourth view of the way in which God had dealt with His chosen people. This last addition of material and editorial reworking was accomplished by priests (hence P Document), whose purpose was to show how, from the dawning of creation, God had been at work to separate and keep holy His people. This the priestly writers seek to make clear by the construction of an elaborate system of ten genealogies which emphasize the racial purity of Israel. The J and E Documents begin their history of Israel with Abraham. But in the P Document Israel begins with the "first man," Adam. One result of this attempt to trace Israel's origin to Adam was to produce another account of Creation (Gen. 1:1–2:4a), which now stands first in the Bible although it was written considerably later than the creation story from the J Document (Gen. 2:4b–24). A second result of this kind of thinking was bluntly to contradict the rest of the biblical traditions regarding Israel's origins.

It is clear from this much simplified overview of a complex process that neither during the time of the United Monarchy (1020–922 B.C.) nor later in the early postexilic period (539–ca. 400 B.C.) do we have a Bible, or even biblical books, with the form and function now known to us. It is possible, however, to see here the beginning of the literary development that produced what we know as the Bible.

This process accounts only for the making of the first five books, the

"Baal of the Lightning," a limestone relief discovered at Ras Shamra (ancient Ugarit), shows the high god of the Canaanite fertility cult with the lightning bolts thought to produce rains for a rich harvest. Writings from Ugarit confirm the antiquity of cult practices assailed by biblical writers from the time of the Conquest until after the period of the Exile.

"Torah" or "Law," and for the story of the conquest of Canaan recorded in Joshua and Judges. The other books of the Old Testament, those known as "the Prophets" and "the Writings," had different origins and paths of development. Their history is the focus of the final section of this chapter and of Chapter Two. At this stage, however, it is essential to return to a formative event in Hebrew history, the Exodus. For the memory of the deliverance from Egypt molded the self-consciousness of Israel as a people, created the sense of religious destiny, and conditioned the literary development of later centuries.

Out of Egypt with a Mighty Hand

MORE OFTEN THAN NOT the wrong question is asked of the Bible. Most people ask, "What happened?" and turn to Scripture for an answer. By now it should be clear to the reader that it is more important, and leads us more nearly to the heart of the Bible, to ask, "Why are these stories remembered and preserved in Holy Scripture?" Nowhere is it more obviously necessary to ask the right questions than in dealing with the account of the Exodus, the touchstone of the promise-fulfillment motif for both the Old and the New Testament.

The story of the Hebrew sojourn in Egypt is woven on the fabric of historical authenticity. Everywhere the subtle hues of the magnificence of the Egyptian New Kingdom clearly shine forth. With a wealth of local color and authentic detail the narrator tells how Abraham's great-grandson Joseph was sold into bondage by his brothers, rose to high power under the Pharaoh, and brought his family clan to live in Goshen, the rich grazing grounds of the eastern Nile delta. Many generations later the Hebrews, now populous but oppressed and enslaved by a pharaoh "who knew not Joseph," were led forth from Egypt in the Exodus under the leadership of Moses.

Yet in spite of its ring of historical authenticity, the Exodus account, like much of the biblical material dealing with the premonarchical period, tends to give a simplified version of a complicated situation. This shows again that the biblical writers were not interested in an exhaustive historical account of their people, but in the thematic tracing out of the dealings of God with their forefathers, and thus with themselves as heirs of the promise.

We know that from an early date many Semitic families, clans, and tribes entered Egypt for trade or because, as we are told of the Hebrew patriarchs, famine forced them to look for greener pastures. It is possible that the Joseph story telescopes the memory of a number of such incursions.

So massive was the Semitic incursion at one point that it became an invasion which overthrew the Egyptian rulers. The Hyksos, apparently a horde of Semitic-speaking, chariot-driving tribesmen, overran the "Land of the River" about 1700 B.C., and ruled it and parts of Asia, including Palestine, for about 150 years. It was perhaps during this time that Joseph rose to power under

Apis, the bull god of Memphis, capital of Lower Egypt during the time of the Exodus. The cobra projecting from its head is the royal symbol of Lower Egypt. This fertility deity calls to mind the Hebrew worship of "the golden calf of Egypt" at the foot of Mount Sinai.

A rare miniature sphinx portrays a Hyksos king shaking an Egyptian captive by the ears. The head-dress shows that the Hyksos, like other foreign rulers, sought to imitate Egyptian ways.

one of these pharaohs—more sympathetic to a "sand-dweller," as the Hebrews in Egypt were called, than a native king would have been. After the Hyksos were driven out, Egypt entered upon its second pinnacle of high civilization. The New Kingdom reached its zenith under Rameses II (1290–1224 B.C.). He is probably the "pharaoh who knew not Joseph," and the one on whose treasure cities the Hebrews slaved. It would then have been Rameses who is reported to have said to Moses and Aaron, "Rise up, go forth from among my people, both you and the people of Israel; and go, serve the Lord, as you have said. Take your flocks and your herds, as you have said, and be gone. . . ." (Exod. 12:32).

And the Hebrews went. Away from the rising cities they went; over the fertile grazing lands into the burning desert and then across the waters to safety at last. The Egyptian records make no mention of this event, possibly because it was their habit to record only great accomplishments and military victories. Perhaps, too, it was just not very important from an Egyptian point of view. A large number of slaves and their families had got away—a matter of some seriousness, but no disaster. After all, there were plenty of people to be pressed into labor gangs.

From the Hebrew outlook it was something else again. They remembered the harshness and bitterness of their plight under the Egyptian yoke, their groaning and crying out under the whips of their harsh taskmasters. They recalled the might of Egypt—magnified a thousandfold as compared with their own weakness. In short, they remembered their hopelessness.

"Sing ye to the Lord, for He hath triumphed gloriously; the horse and his rider hath He thrown into the sea" (Exod. 15:1). The Hebrews had escaped! Miraculously the might of Egypt had been stayed from falling upon them in their flight. Fear, degradation, and slavery were in the past. "The Lord brought us out of Egypt with a mighty hand and an outstretched arm. . . ." (Deut. 26:8; *et al.*).

Life and hope snatched from the jaws of despair and death—this is what the Hebrews understood the Exodus to be, and this is what they recited over and over again in their memories and their worship. "A wandering Aramean was my father," said the Hebrew as he approached the altar with the first fruits of his land laid across his hands, "and he went down into Egypt and sojourned there, few in number; and there he became a nation, great, mighty, and populous. And the Egyptians treated us harshly. . . . Then we cried to the Lord the God of our fathers, and the Lord heard our voice. . . ." (Deut. 26:5–7). Remember, says the preface to the Ten Commandments, "I am the Lord your God, who brought you out of the land of Egypt, out of the house of bondage" (Exod. 20:2; Deut. 5:6). Even down to our own day the Exodus theme remains at the heart of Jewish and Christian thought and ritual. The central festival of Judaism is the Passover, the Haggadah for which begins: "Why is this night different from all other nights?" The answer of the father opens: "Slaves were we to Pharaoh in Egypt. . . ." In the Christian sacraments of baptism and the Supper there are overtones of the Exodus theme. In passing through the waters and into newness of life the

The statue of Rameses II in the outer court of the temple at Luxor dwarfs the figure of Queen Nefertari at his side. This stern, ambitious "Pharaoh of the Exodus" built massive temples at Karnak and Abu Simbel, and used Hebrew labor to rebuild great treasure cities of the Delta.

Christians, like the Hebrews of old, confess that God has acted to redeem the hopeless and to bring life out of death. In these and other ways the Exodus memories have served as constant reminders to God's people that the meaning of their community and the basis of their responsibility lie in the fact that they have been redeemed from slavery.

When the Old Testament was completed, the writers had devoted a historically—but not theologically—disproportionate amount of space to the account of the Exodus. This story is dominated by the figure of Moses: "slow of speech and slow of tongue," but for all that a visionary and a stern leader. He is the precursor of the prophets; indeed, the Deuteronomist sees him as the ideal prophet. He staggers under the weight of responsibility and complains to God that his shortcomings make him inadequate for the tasks to which he has been called. Here is the prototype of Isaiah and of Jeremiah.

But there is another side to his character. His fearsome spirit kept the eyes of his followers fixed on the goal of the Promised Land when their courage failed in the wilderness. "Would that we had died by the hand of the Lord in the land of Egypt," they murmured, "when we sat by the fleshpots and ate to the fill; for you have brought us out into this wilderness to kill this whole assembly with hunger" (Exod. 16:3). The voices of empty stomachs could not compel him to turn back. Many years before as a fugitive from Egypt he had seen, in the wilderness of Midian near Mt. Sinai, a vision of the Lord in a burning bush. With unshakable awareness of the purposes of God seared into his heart, he now steadily led his cantankerous and complaining people toward that sacred place, toward Sinai, the Lord's mountain. Here, even while his people below were reveling in worship of the golden calf of Egypt, the vision was renewed. Here, in one of the most sacred moments in Hebrew memory, Moses received the Ten Commandments and sealed a covenant between the Lord and the Chosen People. The Lord had acted decisively in delivering them from Egypt and had graciously revealed Himself to them in the Law that was now given. In response the people, through Moses, bound themselves to Him forever. This was the covenant, and it created a people.

The importance of the covenant idea can hardly be exaggerated. Indeed, so important is it to Christian thinking that the Christian Bible is divided into the Old Covenant and the New Covenant ("testament" is Latin for "covenant"). To the Hebrew mind the covenant arose out of an act, out of the initiative, of God. In sovereign freedom, He bound Himself to this people in a relationship characterized by *hesed*. This word, often translated as "mercy" or "loving-kindness" or as "steadfast love," could perhaps be better rendered as "covenant loyalty." It means that God is merciful over and above the requirements of justice, and that the people's faith must move beyond the mere letter of the law.

God had saved His people. To the Hebrews their salvation was an undeniable historical fact; it was already achieved. It did not come about as a part of the bargain. The people pledged themselves in gratitude to God with a pledge as absolute as had been their own deliverance from Egypt. This, however, was no *quid pro quo* arrangement. The covenant was no legal instrument binding two independent parties together. Indeed, far from entering into a relationship with God as an independent entity, the people *as a people* had no existence apart from their election by and covenant with Him. Here, in fact, the nation Israel was constituted. According to the prophets it was neglect of this basic relationship that eventually led from tragedy to tragedy and from disaster to disaster. In their higher moments the ancient Hebrews were aware that they were not a race, nor a single tribe, nor a nation in the sense that other peoples might be so. They understood that what gave Israel its unity, drive, aim, meaning—what gave form to its institutions, shaped its ethics, and determined its world view—was its sense of being chosen by God and in covenant with Him.

Law is a vital part of covenant, and a considerable part of the Old Testament is law. Most of the Hebrew laws are found in the first five books of the Bible and like the books themselves are traditionally ascribed to Moses. There is little doubt that some form of law did accompany the ancient covenant.

Sinai, the holy mountain of the wilderness, is sacred in the memory of Jews and Christians. In the Monastery of St. Catherine (below), built there in the fourth century A.D., *the famous* Codex Sinaiticus, *one of the most important biblical manuscripts, was found in 1856.*

This is probably enshrined in the Ten Commandments and the nucleus of a group called the covenant code (Exod. 22:22–23:34). But all biblical laws were not given by Moses, and in fact they do not all or even mostly come from his time. Many are much later.

The form and much of the content of these laws show again the Hebrew dependence upon northern neighbors for their general framework of thought. No one has yet established any connection between Hebrew and Egyptian law—precisely because no one has yet been able to show that the Egyptians had a continuing body of law or found it necessary or desirable to commit their laws to writing. The Pharaoh was the living embodiment of the law; there was neither place nor need for a written code that would continue from one generation to another. But many have shown that the laws and legal practices of the Mesopotamians profoundly influenced the Hebrews. From early times the people who lived "between the rivers" wrote down their laws. There are Babylonian laws from about 2050 B.C., the code of Ur-Nammu. Hammurabi's celebrated code dates from about 1700. There are extant Assyrian laws of about 1100. And the Hittite treaties, dating from the thirteenth century B.C., may have served as the model for the Hebrew covenant form.

It is possible, of course, that the Hebrews were influenced by a kind of general pattern of law in the ancient Near East rather than by any specific set of laws. Perhaps they were informed both by a general ethos and by specific codes. It is difficult to know. At any rate, it is striking that both the Hebrew Law and the Code of Hammurabi address themselves to the same issues and often in almost the same terms. "If an ox has gored a citizen while going along the road, and has occasioned his death, there shall be no penalty attached to the case," says the Code of Hammurabi. "But if the offending ox belonged to a citizen who has been notified by the authorities of its propensity to gore, and he has not removed its horns, or has not tethered the ox, and that ox gored a man of citizen status occasioning his death, he shall pay a half-mina of silver." "When an ox gores a man or a woman to death," says Exodus 21:28, "the ox shall be stoned, and its flesh shall not be eaten; but the owner of the ox shall be clear. But if the ox has been accustomed to gore in the past, and its owner had been warned but not kept it in, and it kills a man or a woman, the ox shall be stoned, and its owner shall be put to death."

The similarities between Hebrew law and others of the region and time are great. But the differences are equally great. The peculiar covenant context of Hebrew society gave their laws a unique cast. Some laws may have dealt with man's civil responsibilities and some with his duties toward the shrine and the cult, but all alike were religious laws, for law was a part of the covenant. This context helps to explain the twofold thrust of Hebrew law. It was among the most severe in the ancient world. There were, for example, extreme punishments for crimes against God, such as idolatry and blasphemy; and there were similar punishments for crimes against God's people, such as murder, usury, and incest. At the same time, it was in general more merciful than any

Detail from the stele containing the Code of Hammurabi, the most famous and influential collection of laws in the ancient Near East.

other of its time. It protected the widow, the poor, the orphan, the oppressed, and even the enemy. It mitigated the practice of flogging and with one exception (Deut. 25:11–12) forbade the bodily mutilation that was common practice among Israel's neighbors. It was also lenient in its exemptions for military service, and the *lex talionis*, "an eye for an eye and a tooth for a tooth," which occurs in the Bible in all its crudeness, is modified in the laws to make clear that such a statement was viewed as a principle of proportionate compensation and not as a literal guide to practice.

Among the Hebrews, particularly during the postexilic period when the biblical materials were reaching a form recognizable to us today, there was a tendency to ascribe certain kinds of writings to ancient and venerated leaders. Because of this the Psalms were associated with David, the Wisdom Literature with Solomon, and the Law with Moses. Just as it is now apparent that David is not the author of all the Psalms, nor Solomon of all the Wisdom, so it is clear that all Hebrew law did not originate with Moses. One of the primary evidences for this is the simple fact that most of it reflects a settled, agricultural, and urban society, not a nomadic, desert background. It was only after the death of Moses that the Hebrews abandoned their desert ways and settled in Canaan. The dramatic story of the conquest of the "promised land" is told in the Books of Numbers, Joshua, and Judges.

The Promised Land

THE JOURNEY to Canaan was a long one. According to the sacred narrative it began when the children of Israel, well marshaled by Moses, left Sinai bound for the Promised Land. Encamping at the oasis of Kadesh in the Negeb they sent spies northward into Canaan. "We came to the land to which you sent us," they reported; "it flows with milk and honey. . . . Yet the people who dwell in the land are strong, and the cities are fortified and very large. . . ." (Num. 13:27–28). There was a division among the people. Some were fearful and wished to retire to the desert; others, more bold, pressed for immediate entrance into the land. At length a small number did attack, but were repulsed. The Hebrews withdrew to the wilderness around Kadesh, where for forty years they lived the life of seminomads, a mode of life which was then already ancient and which continues down to our own day. At last, around 1225 B.C., they moved east around the hostile kingdom of Moab and camped on the Plains of Moab on the eastern side of the Jordan near the place where it empties into the Dead Sea. On the heights of Mt. Nebo, Moses, having glimpsed the fertile Jordan Valley and the Promised Land beyond, died. His mantle fell upon Joshua, a man of courage and military ability. Almost at once he urged the people across the Jordan, where they reduced Jericho and in a lightning campaign conquered most of the rest of Canaan.

This, in brief, is the story told in the books of Numbers and Joshua. Like the account of Israel in Egypt, it is a coherent dramatic narrative built around the exploits of individuals. But once more it is a compilation of traditions, which many years later were cast into the form of an epic to dramatize the emergence of the Hebrew nation under God.

There is a very different story of the conquest in the first chapter of the Book of Judges, which is supported by certain passages in Joshua and by mounting archaeological evidence. According to this account the conquest of the land was hardly a blitzkrieg. On the contrary, it spanned several centuries, with occasional pitched battles. This last is particularly important to note, for it means that we do not have to accept exclusively either the Joshua or the Judges account, but may understand that both reflect something of what was a many-sided affair.

By combining the two accounts we are able to understand, too, that the conquest was not solely the work of those Hebrews who took part in the Exodus from Egypt. The migrations told of in the patriarchal narratives were a small part of a larger movement in the early second millennium. A number of people of the same stock as the Hebrew patriarchs settled in the land. Later, a similar group came into the country, but were not able to make the transition so well from seminomadic to agricultural life. These people settled in the central hill region, became freebooters and bandits, and wreaked havoc upon

Shepherds in the Syrian desert today have a mode of life not unlike that of the patriarchs of Israel. The loose-flowing garments, goat-hair tents, and fierce independent spirit of the seminomads have changed little since biblical times.

The Masabah, or Sacred Stone, at Shechem is thought to be the shrine where Joshua renewed the covenant following the Hebrew conquest. Discovered early in the twentieth century, the Masabah was restored in 1962. Mount Gerizim, site of the Samaritan temple (see page 64), is in the background.

the lowland farmers and towns. These may have been the "Habiru" mentioned in the Amarna letters—communications from vassals in Palestine to Pharaoh Amenophis IV (Akhenaten, 1370–1353). These documents indicate that Palestine, nominally under Egyptian control, was in fact in a state of anarchy and that the Habiru had taken over the central part of the country, including the important city of Shechem. If the Habiru did make common cause with the invading Hebrews more than a century later, it would explain how the Hebrews were able to put their main shrine at Shechem when there is no evidence that fighting took place in that area.

In the south it is probable that certain tribes, entering directly from the southern desert, gradually penetrated the lower part of the country. There are also indications that the northern tribes, perhaps Asher, Zebulon, and maybe others, subdued northern areas in some independent fashion. Joshua's invasion of the western highlands with the Hebrews from Egypt more than a century later (according to the first account, shortly after the death of Moses) seems to have been the occasion for bringing together a number of diverse but nonetheless related groups in the name of the Lord. This new unity, based upon a common religious allegiance and cemented by loyalty to a central shrine (eventually Shiloh), probably explains the thrust of the great covenant ceremony described in Joshua 24. Out of a background of differing practices and shrine loyalties the various tribal leaders gathered at the ancient city of Shechem nestled in the valley between towering Mts. Gerizim and Ebal to reach a basis for some sort of cooperation. Joshua, speaking forthrightly, set out his position and that of his followers: ". . . As for me and my house, we will serve the Lord." The others agreed and pledged their loyalty. The covenanted faith in God thus formed the basis for unity, and those tribes which had not heretofore been a part of the covenant under Moses swore their allegiance at the sacred stone of Shechem.

This unity was religious; it was not economic, nor social, nor military. Yet it may well account for the archaeological evidence which indicates the destruction of a number of Canaanite cities during the thirteenth and twelfth centuries B.C. The holy war to secure the Promised Land was undoubtedly in many of its aspects as bloody and brutal as the Book of Joshua depicts it. But this campaign was not, as the writer of Joshua seems to understand it, the whole story; the conquest was long and drawn-out, and by no means a purely military struggle.

The Canaanites who were in the land are generally known to the popular mind through the portrait of them drawn by the writers of the Old Testament, who speak in indignant generalizations of "the abomination of the Canaanites." They are stigmatized by the whole of the biblical tradition—writers, poets, prophets, editors, the lot. This is not the mere residue of hatred after a military campaign, but the result of centuries-long conflict between Canaanite and Hebrew culture and religion. The Hebrew outlook, as we have seen, derived from a seminomadic desert background and came into conflict with the Canaanite view based upon settled agricultural life. To the

The Canaanite snake goddess (left) dates from before the Hebrew conquest; the figure of Astarte (right), consort of Baal, is a fertility-cult object from Judah during the period of the Divided Monarchy.

seminomads with their strict desert ethic the society into which they had come seemed a combination of idolatrous practices, intemperate use of wine, sexual license, and a social structure that led to human degradation. Those Hebrews who were faithful to the covenant neither understood nor tolerated the religious fertility rites of the Canaanite shrines, and their understanding of clan brotherhood did not permit them to accommodate easily to an economic system in which a man, in order to gain much, risked all and could end up an indentured slave.

This conflict of cultures in which the Hebrews resisted and eventually eradicated some Canaanite practices, such as human sacrifice, did not however end in the supremacy of everything Israelite. The final result was more of an amalgamation. Some Canaanite practices did disappear, and undoubtedly some Hebrew practices likewise. But at last, in the realm of religion at least, the remaining Canaanite customs became adapted to Hebrew usage and the festivals were purified and subsumed into the worship of the Lord.

The Hebrews were not victorious in all things; if they eventually won the religious struggle, they lost the social and economic one. This was mainly due to the advanced state of Canaanite urban society. The size and wealth of the cities, the sophistication of their culture, their genius in the plastic arts, as revealed by recent excavations, are astonishing. Hazor in the north, one of the mightiest of Canaanite cities, covered over twenty-six and a half acres enclosed within massive walls, towers, and gates. Its population in the late Bronze Age (ca. 1300 B.C.) is estimated to have been greater than that of Jerusalem at the time of Jesus. Its houses were well built, with drainage systems, and adorned with pottery from Cyprus and Greece. The principal temple closely resembled that built many years later in Jerusalem by Solomon. And at Megiddo and Beth-shan, the Canaanites had palaces and temples whose magnificence challenged the splendor of Hazor.

Yet all was not luxury. The Canaanite kings, tough fighters, were constantly at war with one another or with a foreign foe. They commanded formidable fleets of chariots, the tanks of their day, and their well-trained

A late twelfth-century B.C. *ivory fragment from Megiddo depicts the splendor of a Canaanite king campaigning in war. Seated outdoors on a cherub throne, he is served food (left), serenaded (center), and presented with Hebrew captives (right).*

warriors were protected by breastplates and other armor. It seems incredible that the Israelites, a relatively poverty-stricken people just settling down in their crudely built villages, could have overthrown such large, prosperous, and well-defended cities. They did so by the timeless tactics of the guerilla fighter: infiltrate, hit, and run—fight only where the troops and weapons of your superior enemy are least effective. The Hebrews even succeeded in destroying the garrison of the splendid city of Hazor, which they then captured and burned to the ground. Several decades later, on its flattened ruins a rude little Hebrew settlement sprang up. The site, as one archaeologist describes it, consisted of nothing more than "rubble foundations of tents and huts, numerous silos dug into the earth for the storage of pottery and grain, and crude ovens." What better comment on the difference in cultural level could there be than the contrast between this humble village and the magnificence lying buried beneath it?

Heroes of Israel

AFTER the initial incursion into Canaan there was a long period of anarchy. The Hebrews had succeeded in upsetting some centers of power and stability, but not in replacing them. Slowly the tribes formed themselves into a loose religious confederation, an *amphictyony* not unlike those developed from time to time by the Greek city-states. The focal point was a shrine, in the case of the Hebrews the shrine at Shiloh. But this centralization and the common religious foundation it provided did not bring stability. The Hebrews were not able to inflict crushing blows upon their many enemies or even to stop fighting each other. During this period the tribe of Benjamin was almost obliterated in intertribal warfare. Nonetheless, although the confederacy did not provide the needed political unity, the Hebrews were gradually forsaking their nomadic ways, learning to farm and to build, and embarking upon trade. All these things they learned by the time-tested way of the Canaanites.

Religiously united, the Hebrews were otherwise fragmented. When an enemy fell upon one of the tribes, loyalty to the central shrine, unsupported by economic and political ties, was not strong enough to rally the others to its defense. Local leaders inspired by the "spirit of the Lord" rose to meet the challenges. These military leaders were called "judges." One of the most interesting was a woman whose exploits are celebrated in the Song of Deborah (Judg. 5), one of the oldest poems in the Bible. The Canaanites had attacked in the great, fertile northern valley of Esdraelon, and with their chariots seemed assured of carrying the day. But it was not to be. In a bloody battle the Hebrews upset the mighty foe. Even Sisera, the Canaanite general, though he escaped from the battle, died while resting, when a woman who pretended to be friendly drove a tent peg through his head.

The kings came, they fought;
  then fought the kings of Canaan,
at Taanach, by the waters of Megiddo;
  they got no spoils of silver.
From heaven fought the stars,
  from their courses they fought against Sisera.
The torrent Kishon swept them away,
  the onrushing torrent, the torrent Kishon.
March on, my soul, with might!
          —Judges 5:19–21

So proclaims the Song of Deborah. It was not the stars, however, that won the battle. It was the mud. The river Kishon, following a heavy cloudburst, overflowed its banks and mired down Sisera's nine hundred chariots and

A relief from the temple of Pharaoh Rameses III at Medinet Habu celebrates his victory over the "Sea Peoples," or Philistines. The defeated sailors fled eastward and settled along the coast of what became known as Palestine, the name being derived from "Philistine."

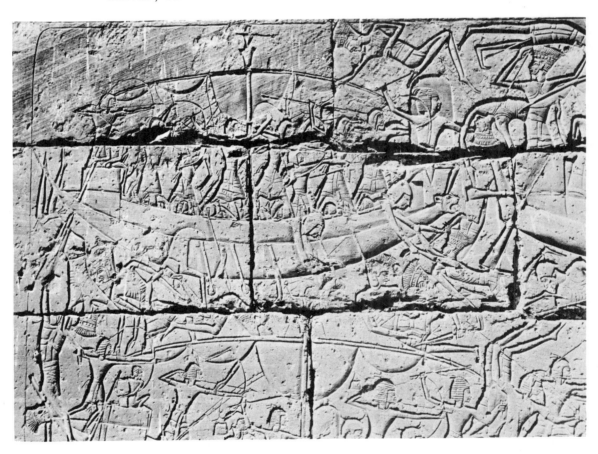

heavy infantry, and the more lightly armed and mobile Hebrews swarmed over them. The writer of this hymn of victory underscores his faith that the God who had brought them into the land made the very elements help them, so that it might be preserved in their hands.

The chaotic situation in Canaan was not unnoticed by the states and peoples east of the Jordan: Moab, Edom, Ammon, and the nomadic Midianites. Tempted by the mounting anarchy, they made dangerous raids which were checked from time to time and from place to place by various local judges, among them Ehud, Jephthah, and the more famous Gideon. The Midianites, whose camels allowed them to strike far from their bases, swept almost to the Mediterranean while the terrified Hebrews huddled in mountain caves. But by far the worst threat came not from the east but from the southwest. The Philistines, those "Sea Peoples" who had settled along the southern coast about the time the Hebrews were breaking into the western highlands, a warlike folk with a high level of culture, soon clashed with the Hebrews, for both intended to subjugate Canaan. It was a long and bitter contest, and from it Israel emerged as a nation.

Also emerging from this struggle were many folk tales and the prototype of the folk hero—Samson. At one stage in the development of the tradition about Samson he probably symbolized the ineffective Hebrew resistance to the Philistines. But as he finally appears in the pages of the Bible he is the precursor of Saul and the prefiguration of David. The Hebrew national epic magnified Samson's patriotic fervor and his divine calling. His exploits with the Philistines—not to mention those with women—served to emphasize his strength and his cunning. The nature of his birth, his devotion to God, and the manner of his death underlined the ultimate source of his strength.

These stories about Samson are but a few of the rustic tales which the writers of the nationalistic epic infused with the spirit of the awakening Hebrew state. For all that, the pristine freshness and superlative artistry of the stories comes through. However the epic writers may have sought to make of him the prototype of a national hero, Samson has remained for all the ages what one scholar has called "a sort of irresponsible and uncontrollable Till Eulenspiegel or Peer Gynt."

"Give Us a King"

THE PERSONALITY that dominated the scene during the later Philistine wars was very different indeed. Samuel, a devoted man of God, judge and prophet all in one, had been dedicated as a child at the shrine at Shiloh. In his maturity he became the nominal head of the confederation, and it fell to him to rally the tribes against the Philistine thrust, for the Sea Peoples challenged on a broad front, menacing all the Hebrew tribes. Samuel sought in vain to unite his people against their common foe. His sons, whom he wanted to succeed him, were no leaders. The people demanded a warrior to guide the campaign. So Saul, a popular hero because of his recent victory over the Ammonites, when he delivered the city of Jabesh-Gilead from siege, was anointed the first king over Israel. Whether Samuel meant to anoint Saul as king for life or only as a "judge" for the duration of the emergency is a moot question. Saul understood that he was king. Moreover, it was patently obvious to all who wished to see that the confederation was simply powerless to carry on concerted economic, social, or military action unless it could develop a strong centralized government.

Saul was a transitional figure in Israel, half-king, half-chieftain. He was apparently a magnificent young man, tall, strong, gifted in battle, and, as a member of the weak and geographically central tribe of Benjamin, acceptable to all the tribes. Constant warfare prevented his consolidation of the monarchy and the establishment of a royal city. In the end he alienated the religious leaders and laid the land open to the victorious Philistines. Yet his achievements were monumental—chiefly in two areas: to begin with, he united the tribes of Israel in common cause for the first time, and secondly, he established the institution of monarchy in Israel. If he himself did not succeed in either area, at least he made beginnings that were firm and far-reaching.

The biblical judgment on Saul is harsh, and little is said of his accomplishments: "So Saul died for his unfaithfulness; he was unfaithful to the Lord in that he did not keep the command of the Lord, and also consulted a medium, seeking guidance, and did not seek guidance from the Lord. Therefore the Lord slew him, and turned the kingdom over to David the son of Jesse" (I Chron. 10:13–14). Saul, the anointed one who slipped from the Lord's hand, is constantly compared, overtly or subtly, with David, the Lord's champion. Close examination of the apparently considerable material devoted to Saul reveals that the stories about him are really about David. Apart from the account of his anointing (I Sam. 11:14–15), all the narratives dealing with Saul show him in decline and David rising steadily toward the throne. When the writer of Chronicles addresses himself to Saul's reign he only adds from tradition the story of his death; the accounts of the history of Israel given in Psalm 78 and in the hymn in the apocryphal Ecclesiasticus 44 make no mention of him. He is not referred to in the New Testament. His name was virtually removed from the sacred history of Israel. Musicians and artists through the ages have maintained this juxtaposition of Saul and David. Handel's first great oratorio, *Saul*, opens with the chorus, "How excellent is thy name, O Lord," proclaiming the youthful vigor of the first king of Israel. But attention is immediately turned to David, who is praised for quelling the foes of Israel and defeating fierce Goliath in battle. As a subject for art, David has been celebrated, while one looks long to find a painting or sculpture glorifying Saul, who virtually disappears from art just as he does from the biblical record.

All the same, there is a certain sympathy in the way biblical writers speak of the suprapersonal working out of his guilt; it is, as one scholar says, "the fate which overtakes one from whom God has turned away." Saul, king forever in Gilgal, hangs lifeless upon the walls of Beth-shan. And the course of events which led from the coronation shouts at Gilgal to the Philistine jeers at Beth-shan was determined by forces which Saul did not set in motion. Oedipus, Macbeth, Boris—celebrated tragic figures—each was responsible for bringing to life the internal and external forces that eventually combined to destroy him. Not so Saul, one of the truly tragic figures of the world's literature.

King David

"THUS SAYS THE LORD OF HOSTS, I took you from the pasture, from following the sheep, that you should be prince over my people Israel; and I have been with you wherever you went, and have cut off all your enemies from before you; and I will make for you a great name, like the name of the great ones of the earth. . . . So David reigned over all Israel; and administered justice and equity to all his people" (II Sam. 7:8–9; 8:15). David the king, once a bold shepherd lad, "ruddy and comely in appearance," emerges from the biblical record as the antithesis of Saul. The first king of Israel was victim to the Philistine juggernaut; but David met, blunted, and in the end destroyed it. Never again was the Philistine knife at the Israelite throat. While the rejected and superstitious Saul worshiped other gods and sought out a medium to know what the future held for him, David was zealous for the Lord and desired nothing more than to build a magnificent house of worship in which to place the Ark of the Covenant. As Saul's name gradually disappears from the annals of Israel the figure of David becomes dominant in Old Testament and later Hebrew thinking.

The accomplishments of this remarkable monarch were legion. Not only did he defeat the warrior Philistines, but he struck in all directions and subdued one neighboring area after another. Thus within a few years after the disastrous defeat of Saul's army by the Philistines on Mt. Gilboa, which left the Hebrews prostrate and seemingly defenseless, the Israelites found themselves in control of an empire. David's successful war of succession against Saul's surviving son gave stability to the royal house, and his capture of the Jebusite city of Ophel (Jerusalem), which he turned into a capital for the empire, further strengthened the new-found power of the Hebrews. Powerful nationalism was heady wine for a people who only a few months previously had looked forward to the bleakest of futures.

David's kingdom was made up of diverse elements. The confederation of tribes was based upon a religious unity of covenant faith which overlay a large number of local traditions. The series of events that led to David's accession had shown that this foundation as it was would not support a nationalistic structure. The people who now found themselves a unified and

Scenes from the life of David in a twelfth-century A.D. Bible illumination show him being anointed by Samuel, defending his sheep against a bear and a lion, facing Goliath, and playing the harp before Saul. At lower right his piety and prayerful dedication are emphasized, as they are in the Book of Chronicles.

powerful nation began to ask about their roots, their heritage—about what made them not merely a nation but also a people. A unified national epic made up and enriched by a diversity of traditions began to take shape, and the loom on which this vast fabric was woven was the covenant faith, for this the tribes shared in common. One of the most important patterns in the epic is enshrined in the cultic ritual found in Deuteronomy 26:5–9. This passage, a part of the Festival of First Fruits, tells how the Hebrews who went into Egypt fell into hopeless bondage, only to be delivered by their God, who entered into covenant with them and gave them a land. This enshrines the core of the sacred memory around which were gathered the traditions and literature of a unique people, and here is the heart of the process which eventually issued in the collection we know today as the Bible.

The figure and personality of David have captured the imagination of artists in every age, especially during the Renaissance and Baroque periods. Above is Bernini's masterful statue of David facing Goliath.

There is no evidence that David contrived to produce such an epic. On the contrary, it appears that various persons in various places had come to the realization that the time had come for writing down the traditions and bringing some order out of the chaos of competing claims to authority. Further, the process seems not to have got into full swing until the advent of Solomon. But David's political sensitivities and religious convictions would have combined to assure his support for such undertakings.

That David was a man who combined high abilities with religious conviction can be seen in what happened to his status in the subsequent history of Israel. He is transformed from a person into a symbol, and becomes the spotless holy king who with his sons rules not merely Israel, but the "kingdom of God." He becomes a symbol of the promises of God and of hope for the future redemption of Israel. Judaism may understand its adherents to be "Sons of Abraham," but its identifying mark is the "Star of David." And Christians, who understand themselves to constitute a "New Israel," see Jesus as the Davidic Messiah who fulfills the promises of God and offers salvation to all men.

Much of the credit for this transformation falls upon the writers of the books of Chronicles. They present David as a deeply religious, wholly blameless person who was a perfect king and in all things at all times zealous for the cause of his God. What the Chroniclers have probably done, of course, is to set forth in written form the view of David that came to life with effective power in the period when the monarchy had disappeared and Jews not only had no national freedom, but had few hopes of attaining it. In such a time the symbol of Hebrew greatness, which has been and is to come when God's promises are fulfilled, became David the great king. There is in the Chronicles portrait no suggestion of intrigue, much less of adultery or murder.

But if we turn to what is perhaps the oldest and still one of the finest pieces of literary portraiture in the world, II Samuel 9–20, there is quite another picture. The idealized view of David in Chronicles does not begin to render the magnificence of the man in the way the somber splendor of the secular history does. In this "court history of David," apparently the work of an eyewitness, the full spectrum of human emotions may be seen. The king, a warrior and musician who is a legend in his own time, full of graciousness and kindness, is also capable of the basest kind of self-concern. He is saint and sinner, moralizer and adulterer, savior and murderer, a man of joy and a man of desolation. He dances before the Ark of the Covenant in wild ecstasy, and as a broken old man mounts the stairs to a room of grief-filled solitude, crying out as he goes, "O my son Absalom, my son, my son Absalom! Would I had died instead of you, O Absalom, my son, my son!"

Those who appear in these stories—Saul, Nathan, Bathsheba, Joab, Amnon, Tamar, Absalom, even minor characters like Shimai and Barzillai—are products of portraiture of the first rank. But over all is the commanding David, the figure who stands like a colossus astride all Hebrew history, the man who gave to Israel the ideal of kingship by which all monarchs after him are both judged and sustained. David—from whom flows the concept of the Messiah. David—who stands out not merely in valor, wisdom, and righteousness, but also in guilt. David—father of his country, and failure as father to his sons.

The historian of the rise, reign, and near fall of David does not deliver value judgments, but he does not fail to communicate to the sensitive reader the idea of a nemesis that pervades all. Even the end of the matter, the anointing of Solomon, hardly allows the reader to catch his breath. Too much as been revealed of the realities, not merely of an ancient Hebrew monarch, but of life itself.

His carefree days only a dim memory, the ancient king tottered toward death. He had lived too long, done too much, and paid a high price for his personal failings. Death was a welcome friend. Shortly before the end, in deference to Bathsheba, David had Solomon, their son (but not his eldest), anointed king.

The Price of Glory

UNDER SOLOMON the pastoral kingdom of Israel became a full-fledged oriental monarchy. With the potential inherited from David he completed his father's work. City life flourished, the courtier and the merchant grew rich, the arts and learning had their devotees, and king's men replaced the local councils as the old tribal boundaries were abolished and new administrative districts set up. Solomon brought the kingdom to the pinnacle of splendor, crowning it with the glorious and majestic Temple and royal palace at Jerusalem. It is said of Augustus that he found Rome a city of brick and left it a city of marble. Much the same may be said of Solomon and Jerusalem.

Compared with the portraits of Saul and David, however, the biblical picture of Solomon is lifeless. There is, in fact, no consistent account of him or of his reign. What we do have points to an eastern despot who secures his position by ruthlessly disposing of his opposition, then settles down to the work of glorifying his reign, his kingdom, and himself. All is done in the grand manner, with extravagant flair.

That Solomon was an able administrator seems beyond question. He used all the resources of Israel to build up the largest foreign trade the Hebrews ever had. From the port of Ezion-geber at the head of the Gulf of Elath he sent spice fleets along the eastern coasts of Africa—one result of which was

The ruins of the vast stables at Megiddo, Solomon's great northern fortress, hint at the splendor of his reign. A flourishing trade in horses and chariots was but one feature of prosperous commercial expansion during the Solomonic era.

This ninth-century B.C. basalt stele describes the campaign King Mesha of Moab waged against Israel and Judah. Israel is called "the land of Omri" after a king of historical importance who is given scant notice by the religious writers of the Bible.

the popularity of monkeys as household pets among the rich of Israel. He received the Queen of Sheba on a trade mission and amazed her with the enormity of his wealth. In the desert behind Ezion-geber he had copper and iron mines, and erected a large smelting refinery. In the north at Megiddo recent excavations have revealed the kind of buildings he built to facilitate his extensive trade in chariots and horses. And he gave Hiram, king of Tyre, whole cities in exchange for material and craftsmen to build the Temple and his palace. But the true measure of his importance may be seen in the fact that he took as wife one of the daughters of the Pharaoh of Egypt, while not giving a daughter in return.

For all this, from our point of view in the present volume the most important feature of Solomon's reign was the awakening of intellectual forces under the impetus of rampant nationalism. This accelerated and brought to fruition the creation of the national epic begun under David. And with this the literary period of the production of the Bible began (see above, pp. 7–10).

Solomon's enemies harassed him (I Kings 11:14 ff.), but no one went to war with Israel while he sat on the throne. This was partly owing to the weakness of other states, but weakness is relative and Solomon was a man who found peace through strength. He ruled in supreme splendor, in pomp and majesty, not unlike the absolute monarchs of Egypt or Tyre. Yet in spite of all his power, or perhaps because of it, he did not have the vision to realize the vital importance of the religious foundation of Israelite kingship. David's success as king had been based upon his profound grasp of this fact. His son did not understand it. Among other things he introduced the worship of foreign gods into Jerusalem. Just south of the Mount of Olives is the hill upon which he built shrines for the gods of his foreign wives. To this day it is called "the Mount of Offense." Hence, in the opinion of the prophets, his accession saw the kingdom enter on the dangerous road of abandoning obedience to the Lord in favor of a position of unchallengeable human power and worship of non-Hebrew deities.

He further aggravated the situation by exacting heavy taxes and putting Hebrew and non-Hebrew alike into forced-labor gangs. There is evidence that in these matters he tended to favor Judah, the largest and richest tribe—and, incidentally, his own. This could only lead to disastrous consequences. At his death the religionists combined with those oppressed by his civil policies to bring down the Solomonic throne when his son tried to mount it. Young Rehoboam was headstrong. When the elders of the ten northern tribes waited upon him with requests for a more lenient regime than his father's, the pleas were arrogantly rejected. The result was the secession of the northern half of the kingdom in 922 B.C.

There were now two Hebrew states, the northern called Israel and the southern called Judah. The causes for this disruption lay far deeper than the policies of Solomon and the arrogance of his son. North and south had different histories. They were probably settled separately, at different times and in different ways. The northern kingdom, much larger than Judah and potentially much richer, was geographically as well as culturally wide open to the influence of its neighbors, particularly the Phoenicians, those Canaanite mariners of the northern coast. Located in its barren hill country, little Judah was more conservative, especially in religion. It was also more homogeneous and more stable, and continued to live under a single dynasty (David's) until its extinction in 586 B.C. By contrast Israel, during its two centuries of existence, had nine dynasties and nineteen kings.

A House Divided

THE BOOKS of Samuel and Kings, the backbone of the "Histories," deal with the United Monarchy in fifty-nine chapters. This period covers less than a century. But the history of the Divided Monarchy, four times as long, is covered in only thirty-five chapters. Such imbalance is sure to produce major omissions when viewed historically. For instance, there is bare mention (thirteen verses: I Kings 16:16–28) of Omri, one of Israel's greatest kings, who founded the elegant northern capital at Samaria about 885 B.C. His conquest of Moab is not mentioned at all, though recent excavations and the study of rich Assyrian records and of the Moabite Stone—erected by Mesha of Moab about 850 B.C. to commemorate his successful revolt against Israel— have done much to fill out the historical picture. From these we know that long after his death Israel was referred to as "the land of Omri."

The biblical historians pass over Omri because his religious influence, however bad, paled in the light of what came after him. That he married the heir to his throne, Ahab, to Jezebel, the daughter of the priest-king of Sidon, was a matter of some seriousness. But her actions when she subsequently became queen in Israel commanded the almost undivided attention and scorn of biblical writers. She was a willful woman, a born autocrat, who intended by royal patronage to shift the people's allegiance from the Lord to Baal-melkart, high god of the Phoenicians.

In this hour of danger a great prophet arose in Israel. Elijah, a stern, rugged, and somewhat mysterious man, opposed the incursion of Baal worship with a tenacity fully equal to that of Jezebel herself. Ahab, caught between the contrary demands of his unrelenting queen and the fierce prophet, could do little more than watch hopelessly as the conflict took shape. The account of this struggle is preserved in the books of Kings in at least two traditions which are woven together to form a unified picture of Ahab's reign and that of his son and grandson. Most important is a collection many call the "Elijah cycle" (I Kings 17—II Kings 2), a recitation of events in the prophet's life, overlaid with the legendary accretions in natural stories told of a hero, in this case one who fought fearlessly to preserve the worship of the Lord.

Elijah was able to force the issue, and in a face-to-face confrontation caused the destruction of the priests of Baal following a contest of fire on Mt.

Carmel (I Kings 18:17–46). But he was unsuccessful in bringing down Jezebel and was obliged to flee the wrath of the vengeful queen. The death of
Ahab and the accession of Ahaziah strengthened her hand. Although Elijah
continued his opposition, in the end he passed on his struggle against royal
patronage of foreign deities to Elisha—less of an individualist but no less a
man of action—who touched off a full-scale and violent revolution.

Elisha's champion, the brutal Jehu, was proclaimed king by his army, and
not only put to death the ruling king, Jehoram, Ahab's grandson, but also
Jezebel, and by a stroke of fate the king of Judah, who happened to be
visiting Jehoram. Moreover, in a blood bath reminiscent of the reign of terror
of the French Revolution, he put to death anyone who had any connection
with the Omrides. A century later the prophet Hosea speaks of the Jehu
revolt as a dark stain on Israel's history (Hosea 1:4).

If the revolt settled for a while the country's internal difficulties, it did
nothing to relieve her external woes. Assyria, raiding in ever greater strength,
forced Jehu to pay tribute. When the Assyrians had gone, Damascus opened
almost fifty years of war upon Israel, bringing her close to ruin and ravaging
Judah as well. Both kingdoms were rescued when the Assyrians attacked
Damascus. But then Israel turned on Judah in a senseless conflict. War, it
seemed, had become a way of life.

Finally, early in the eighth century, peace came. Assyria was in decline,
and Israel and Judah, able to turn their energies elsewhere, did not assault
one another. The peace of these small nations depended on the momentary
weakness of large powers to the north; it could not last. Yet for a brief flicker
of time quiet returned and with it prosperity, and that in abundance. But this
prosperity was not for all, nor even for many. The upper classes, aping
Phoenician sophistication, lived in extravagant luxury, while the lower classes
were increasingly exploited and slipped ever deeper into debt and degradation. There was no middle class. Graft and extortion were rampant; only the
man with money could get "justice" in the courts; idleness and alcoholism
walked hand in hand; religion had become perfunctory, devoid of ethical
content.

Prophets and Kings

THE EXTREMITY of the situation produced a reaction. The great ethical
prophets of the eighth century, Amos, Hosea, Isaiah, and Micah, rose up
to address the Word of God to their contemporaries. Amos and Hosea, from
whom came the first more or less complete books of the Bible, preached in
the northern kingdom, Israel, while Isaiah and Micah, whose writings also
survive in the Old Testament, raised their voices in Judah, the southern
kingdom.

Amos, a southerner prophesying in the north, was the first of the literary prophets—those whose words were written down either by themselves or by their immediate followers. And in Amos' case these were sarcastic, biting words, full of scorn for those who emphasized the privilege of the covenant rather than its responsibilities. In the same breath he could speak of decadent women, "cows of Bashan," and of the Lord God, "maker of the Pleiades and Orion," against whose majesty he saw their unworthy lives. In a crescendo of wrath he voices God's hatred of empty ritualism and social injustice and calls for repentance: "I hate, I despise your feasts, and I take no delight in your solemn assemblies. . . . I will not accept them . . . I will not look upon [them] . . . I will not listen [to them]. But let justice roll down like waters, and righteousness like an everflowing stream" (Amos 5:21–24). The true worship of the living God was, in Amos' eyes, to *do* justice, not merely to admire it.

Hosea, Amos' younger contemporary, had essentially the same message, but he was from the northern kingdom. Thus his words were filled with compassion for his nation, which he compared to an unfaithful wife who is

A detail of the Black Obelisk of Shalmaneser III celebrates his victory over Israel in 841 by depicting King Jehu kneeling in submission.

still loved. By such imagery Hosea sought to call his people back to a proper covenant relation with God, before it was too late—to remind them of the purity of their former faith and of the hope that lay in repentance. It was to no avail. The people looked only at what they thought was their special privilege—and saw God's honor and power tied to the existence of their petty kingdom. "Is not God in the midst of us?" they said. "No evil shall come upon us."

Assyria, the sleeping giant of Mesopotamia, awoke in 745 B.C. and once more cast hungry eyes southward. This time the two little Hebrew kingdoms could hardly hope to escape. Opinion polarized; war and peace parties struggled for power. In Israel four kings were assassinated within ten years, and immorality and pleasure-seeking grew at a frantic pace. Time was growing short. The Assyrian raids of earlier days had now become planned campaigns, spearheaded by a mighty military machine, adept at siege and using brutality as deliberate policy. To this had been added the practice of deporting conquered peoples and settling their homelands with strangers.

General uproar broke out among the smaller states of Syria-Palestine. What to do? Where to turn? How could the Assyrian be held off? Pekah, king of Israel, and Rezin, king of Damascus, decided that coalition was their best hope. Naturally they wanted Judah to join them, since it would be dangerous to have on their flank a neutral who was a potential enemy. But Ahaz, newly anointed king of Judah, preferred an independent route to safety. Whereupon Pekah and Rezin invaded Judah from the north with the intention of removing him from the throne and putting in his place one more sympathetic to a coalition policy.

As the Aramean-Israelite army closed in on Jerusalem, Isaiah, one of the towering figures of the Old Testament, counseled Ahaz to stand fast, to depend upon God for deliverance, and to recognize that the nations ranged against him were nothing more than "smoldering stumps." A few years before, in the year of Uzziah's death (742), Isaiah had been called to his prophetic office in a vision that impressed upon him both the awful holiness of God and the depth of the nation's sin (Isa. 6:1–13). While he sounded many of the themes of Amos and compared Judah to a luxurious and well-tended vineyard that produced no grapes, Isaiah combined this with a call to trust in the infinite mercy and power of God.

This prophet was high born and had easy access to the monarch. For fifty of the most perilous years of Judah's existence, he advised and often opposed official government policy. Ahaz, the first king Isaiah served directly, wavered in the face of his difficult position. In the end, however, he rejected Isaiah's counsel and appealed to Assyria for help against Pekah and Rezin. The price was heavy. Tiglath-pileser of Assyria placed a tribute upon Judah which for all intents and purposes surrendered its independence. Isaiah, handing over a record of his words to his disciples (Isa. 8:16–18), withdrew from the scene for twenty years.

Whatever the religious shortcomings of Ahaz' policy, it was for the moment politically successful. In 732 Damascus fell before the plumed Assyrians, and shortly thereafter a puppet king, Hoshea, was placed on the throne of the greatly diminished kingdom of Israel. This last king of Israel, foolishly believing Egyptian promises of aid, rebelled against Assyria. After heroically withstanding a three-year siege, the Israelite capital Samaria fell to Sargon II in 722/1. By the Assyrian monarch's trumphant reckoning, 27,290 captives were deported to Upper Mesopotamia and Media. Their places were taken in Israel by Babylonians, Hamathites, and others who, intermarrying with the remaining Israelites, became the Samaritans, henceforth despised by Judah for being of mixed blood. In Mesopotamia the Hebrews were scattered and lost their identity. The fabled "ten lost tribes of Israel" disappeared from history's view.

The southern border of Assyria was now the northern border of Judah. For well over a century the country somehow survived, a hooked fish vainly struggling. Spasmodic rebellions alternated with periods of abject submission; there were bitter internal conflicts between pro-Assyrian and pro-Egyptian

A Babylonian inscription from Nineveh portrays the storming of Lachish by Sennacherib. The victory over this fortified outpost city of Judah was achieved by means of bows and arrows, staves, and siege ladders.

parties. The northern cloud hung dark over the land; nothing was normal.

Around 714 the Philistine city of Ashdod, backed by Egypt, proposed to Hezekiah, the new king of Judah, that he join in a revolt against Assyria. Hezekiah had made Jerusalem, already one of the strongest fortresses in the area, even stronger by constructing a rock-cut tunnel to increase the city's water supply and enhance its chances of withstanding siege. This twenty-seven-hundred-year-old tunnel, a remarkable engineering feat, is still in use today. It is seventeen hundred feet long, has an average height of six feet, and is two and a half feet wide. It has a fall of seven feet. In 1880 a truant schoolboy chasing a ball in the tunnel discovered an inscription nineteen feet from the mouth. It was a contemporary account of its construction (see color plate, p. 41).

Against Hezekiah's preparations for war Isaiah counseled peace. This prophet who had opposed subjection to Assyria now opposed revolt against Assyria. He carried his appeal directly to the public and appeared in the streets of Jerusalem barefoot and clad only in the loincloth of a prisoner of war. This, said Isaiah, would be the fate of Egypt, upon whom the Judeans were considering pinning their hopes! Hezekiah wisely decided against joining with Ashdod, and when that city, waiting in vain for Egyptian aid, was destroyed by the Assyrians, Judah averted disaster.

Meanwhile another prophet was heard in the streets of Jerusalem. Micah, a man of humble origins from the village of Moresheth-gath in southwestern Judah, vehemently attacked the wealthy nobles and corrupt officials for their oppression of the poor and their failure to dispense impartial justice. He went beyond Isaiah and even beyond Amos in forecasting doom not merely for the society but also for sacred Jerusalem and inviolable Zion. The people's response, that he should be quiet, that "one should not preach of such things; disgrace will not overtake us" (Mic. 2:6), only served to confirm the prophet's view of the hopelessness of the situation. Yet for Micah all hope was not lost. Although Zion would be plowed as a field and Jerusalem become a heap of ruins, God's covenant with David would stand. From Bethlehem a Davidic prince would rise to usher in an age of peace (Mic. 5:2–6).

In 705 B.C. Sargon died, and long-suppressed hatred of the Assyrians burst into flame. This time Judah was a leader in the rebellion. Isaiah bitterly opposed it, calling the rulers of Jerusalem "scoffers" and predicting that those "who go down to Egypt for help and rely on horses, who trust in chariots because they are many and in horsemen because they are very strong, but do not look to the Holy One of Israel" (Isa. 31:1) were headed for sure and complete disaster. Such attacks earned him the scorn of the nation's rulers. Following his earlier pattern he wrote down his words for his disciples (Isa. 30:8) and withdrew. When the rebellion ended in 701 with the nation on the edge of ruin, the conduct of people who had barely escaped with their lives convinced the prophet that the only hope lay in the path of destruction and the survival of a "righteous remnant."

Once more we hear of Isaiah. Sennacherib, Sargon's son, marched south to

A fresco of the third millennium B.C. (below) depicts bull-worship at Mari, a city in the land of the Hebrews' ancestors. Priests wore special feathered garments to induce the presence of the gods as they proceeded to the sacrificial altar. Bull-worship, common in the ancient Near East, was later encountered by the Hebrews in bondage in Egypt. Their hardships in the desolate wilderness—not unlike the Judean wasteland surrounding the Monastery of St. George (above)—led some to revert to Egyptian practices by worshiping the Golden Calf.

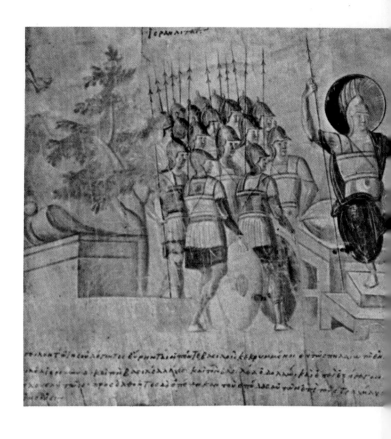

For centuries after their conquest of Canaan, the Hebrews fought the attacks of foreign armies and the lure of foreign gods. A scene from the famous Joshua Roll of Alexandria (above) shows enemy soldiers killed before a victorious Joshua. But the fertility cult of Israel's Canaanite neighbors was a persistent threat to Hebrew faith: a rare temple model from the time of King Saul (top left) displays the fertility symbols of a serpent (on lower level) and birds (held by the priest). The Siloam Inscription (below) tells how King Hezekiah built an aqueduct to ensure Jerusalem's water supply when Sennacherib of Assyria threatened siege. Sennacherib commemorated his victory at the Hebrew city of Lachish in a plaque (left) at his palace in Nineveh. A century later (596 B.C.) the Hebrews were conquered by Babylonia; they remained in exile until freed by Cyrus the Great, founder of the Persian Empire, whose splendor is reflected in the gates at Persepolis (lower left).

The Ezekiel Scroll from the early third century A.D. (right) is one of the oldest manuscripts of the Old Testament. The Prophet Ezekiel constantly warned the Hebrews against foreign gods by reminding them of God's condemnation of their forefathers for following "the idols of Egypt." The Egyptian religious preoccupation with dreams and the afterlife is shown below in a wall painting of the hawk god Horus bestowing immortality.

crush still another Judean revolt. Overrunning the country, he took forty-six walled cities and shut up Hezekiah in Jerusalem, "like a bird in a cage" he said on his victory monument. The capstone of this glorious campaign was to be the capture of Jerusalem. Isaiah, who felt that Assyria as an instrument of God's judgment had overreached herself, counseled Hezekiah not to surrender the apparently doomed capital. God, who had delivered the people from the hopelessness of Egyptian bondage, was about to rescue them again. Contrary to Micah's view and to his own earlier position, Isaiah now believed that Jerusalem would be defended by God and that the people should stand fast. "Like birds hovering," said Isaiah, "so the Lord of hosts will protect Jerusalem" (Isa. 31:5).

A clay tablet found at Babylon includes the rations decreed for King Jehoiachin, captured and exiled by Nebuchadnezzar.

The city stood firm. It did not fall. What caused the Assyrian army to withdraw on the brink of victory we shall probably never know. The biblical historian merely tells us that "the angel of the Lord went forth, and slew a hundred and eighty-five thousand in the camp of the Assyrians; and when men arose early in the morning, behold, these were all dead bodies. Then Sennacherib king of Assyria departed, and went home, and dwelt at Nineveh" (II Kings 19:35–36). Many scholars have suggested that plague broke out among the encamped army.

Hezekiah now came to terms with the Assyrians, terms which allowed him to institute a drastic religious reform. His son Manasseh, however, reverted to Ahaz' policy and for half a century was a loyal Assyrian vassal. He restored pagan rituals, erected Assyrian altars in the Temple, and like his grandfather even offered one of his own sons in a fiery sacrifice to the god Moloch. Peace and prosperity were the fruits of his policy, and he was harsh toward any opposition, particularly the prophetic party, from whom little is heard during his reign. But those loyal to the Lord were not completely inactive. During this time they were at work combining their own J narrative with the northern E tradition to which they had fallen heir after the destruction of the northern kingdom. This compilation and rewriting of the Hebrew epic furnished, as we have seen, the substance of much of the early portion of the Old Testament. Its leaven was provided by the prophets, those inspired teachers whose flights of poetry and keen ethical insights raised Old Testament writings to heights it had seldom known before.

This literary effort had its voice and conscience in the prophets, but its theology and ideals were also expressed and preserved in writings by unknown scribes and priests. One such writing was a book of law found during the reformation of Josiah in 621 B.C. When the godly Josiah came to the throne he destroyed the shrines built by his predecessor and ordered the Temple to be cleaned and restored. In carrying out the king's wishes, the priests "found" in the Temple the Deuteronomic scroll for which they claimed the authority of Moses, no less. This work, which forms the core of the Book of Deuteronomy, furnished the tone and framework for a reworking of the Hebrew epic. Internal evidence indicates that it was probably written by priests shortly before its "discovery," perhaps even during the reign of Manasseh. In any case, Josiah, much moved, had it read aloud to the assembled people, and it was adopted in solemn covenant as the nation's guide. For the first time among the Hebrews a written document endorsed by priests, prophets, king, and people had been elevated to the status of Holy Scripture. By adopting the Deuteronomic Code, which in reality is not a code at all, but a sermon reflecting the ethical purposes of the prophets, the nation had been restored to the status of a religious community, bound together by covenant.

In 612 B.C. occurred one of the pivotal events of ancient history. Assyria the invincible was suddenly destroyed by Babylon. The Hebrews were wild with joy. "The Lord takes vengeance on his adversaries and keeps wrath for his enemies," sang the prophet Nahum, "Ninevah is laid waste, who will bemoan her?"

But Judah did not rejoice for long. The defeat of Assyria increased, rather than relieved, the difficulties of this small Hebrew nation. New international rivalries raged and Judah was again threatened. In the turmoil Josiah was killed. His second son, Jehoiakim, placed on the throne by Egypt, was forced

One of the famous "Lachish letters" is a military communiqué written on a potsherd and revealing the growing desperation of the Hebrew commander under siege by Nebuchadnezzar.

to submit to a triumphant Babylon. Jeremiah, like Isaiah before him counseling passive vassalage, was called a traitor and suffered scorn for his unpopular opinion. There was revolt, and Jerusalem soon found herself under siege by Nebuchadnezzar, tougher than any Assyrian who ever stood before her walls. In the spring of 597, after three months of siege, Jehoiakim's successor, the eighteen-year-old Jehoiachin, surrendered the city. He, his mother, and many high officials along with enormous booty were taken to Babylon. His uncle, Zedekiah, was placed on the throne.

With valor, determination, and the will to fight all mixed with a good deal of unwise appraisal of the situation, the Judeans once more rebelled. We have only literary evidence of what Nebuchadnezzar did to Jerusalem itself, but his fury is clearly revealed in the excavated ruins of the outpost citadel Lachish. There archaeologists have found that the masonry of the inner walls had consolidated into a chalky white mass streaked with red, and had flowed in a liquid stream over the burnt road surface and lower wall, below which were piled charred heaps of burnt timbers. The latter were fuel brought by the Babylonians to feed the blaze that consumed the town. In a guardroom of the gate the famous Lachish letters were found, messages hastily scratched on bits of broken pottery and sent to Lachish from neighboring outposts during the last agonizing days of the siege: "May the Lord grant that my lord should hear good tidings . . . we are watching for the signal stations of Lachish . . . we are no longer receiving signals from Azekah."

In various stages of desperation Jerusalem held out for a year and a half. Zedekiah tried to surrender the city, but Nebuchadnezzar refused the offer. In July 586 the walls were breached and the Babylonians poured in to take their vengeance. Zedekiah escaped only to be captured; brought before the victorious king, he was made to witness the execution of his sons and then blinded, put in chains, and dragged off to Babylon, where he died. A month later the walls of Jerusalem were pulled down and the torch put to the city.

"The Lord," says Jeremiah in his Lamentations (4:11; 5:1), "gave full vent to his wrath, he poured out his hot anger; and he kindled a fire in Zion, which consumed its foundations. . . . Remember, O Lord, what had befallen us; behold, and see our disgrace!"

A PEOPLE OF THE BOOK:
THE HEBREW BIBLE

O GOD, the heathen have come into thy inheritance; they have defiled thy holy temple; they have laid Jerusalem in ruins," lamented the psalmist as he surveyed the wreckage of the Babylonian victory and the degradation of the Exile. "We are become a reproach to our neighbors, a scorn and derision to them that are round about us. How long, Lord? Wilt thou be angry forever?" The ways of the Lord were mysterious and incomprehensible to His chosen people, who such a short time before had rested secure in the belief that no disaster could overtake them and that their kingdom, like their God, was from everlasting to everlasting. But now catastrophe had swept away their national life, overturned the altars of their faith, and taken their leaders into a faraway land.

The Exile was the watershed of Hebrew history. Behind those who trudged, shackled, into an uncertain future lay humiliated Jerusalem: glorious Zion—now capped by the blackened ruins of Solomon's once splendid palace and Temple. And buried within the Temple rubble were the remains of the Holy of Holies, probably entombing the remnants of the Ark of the Covenant along with the broken hopes of thousands. Ahead lay Babylon—frightening, overpowering, bewildering. "How can we sing the Lord's song in a foreign land?"

A century and a half earlier the Hebrews of the northern kingdom had been taken away to Assyria, where they were scattered, lost their identity, and disappeared from history. Was this to be the fate of the southern kingdom? The shrines, institutions, practices, and beliefs through which they had traditionally understood their meaning as a people were gone. Judah as a national entity had ceased to exist. Yet out of this hopelessness a phoenix arose—out of the Exile came one of the most sublime and enduring religions of man: Judaism.

Voices of Hope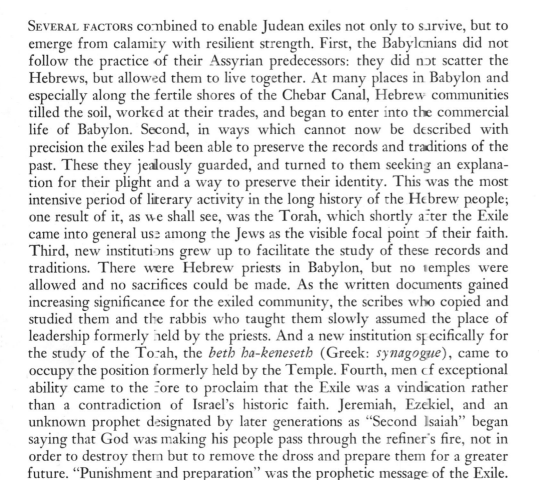

SEVERAL FACTORS combined to enable Judean exiles not only to survive, but to emerge from calamity with resilient strength. First, the Babylonians did not follow the practice of their Assyrian predecessors: they did not scatter the Hebrews, but allowed them to live together. At many places in Babylon and especially along the fertile shores of the Chebar Canal, Hebrew communities tilled the soil, worked at their trades, and began to enter into the commercial life of Babylon. Second, in ways which cannot now be described with precision the exiles had been able to preserve the records and traditions of the past. These they jealously guarded, and turned to them seeking an explanation for their plight and a way to preserve their identity. This was the most intensive period of literary activity in the long history of the Hebrew people; one result of it, as we shall see, was the Torah, which shortly after the Exile came into general use among the Jews as the visible focal point of their faith. Third, new institutions grew up to facilitate the study of these records and traditions. There were Hebrew priests in Babylon, but no temples were allowed and no sacrifices could be made. As the written documents gained increasing significance for the exiled community, the scribes who copied and studied them and the rabbis who taught them slowly assumed the place of leadership formerly held by the priests. And a new institution specifically for the study of the Torah, the *beth ha-keneseth* (Greek: *synagogue*), came to occupy the position formerly held by the Temple. Fourth, men of exceptional ability came to the fore to proclaim that the Exile was a vindication rather than a contradiction of Israel's historic faith. Jeremiah, Ezekiel, and an unknown prophet designated by later generations as "Second Isaiah" began saying that God was making his people pass through the refiner's fire, not in order to destroy them but to remove the dross and prepare them for a greater future. "Punishment and preparation" was the prophetic message of the Exile.

Four main bodies of tradition were preserved, reworked, and added to by the exiles. These included cultic laws; a new theological history from creation to Sinai; another historical collection covering the period from the conquest to the destruction of the kingdom; and the sayings and writings of the prophets.

Arab children on the banks of the Euphrates River south of Babylon, where the Hebrews in exile "sat down and wept when we remembered Zion."

The priests, momentarily denied their normal function in Israel's cult but looking forward in hope of its restoration, devoted their efforts to the collection and codification of the ritual laws of the people. The body of law that resulted from this labor is present in the Bible in two forms. One portion, narrative in form, was a *midrash*, or historical commentary, on the Pentateuch, which had been begun under David and Solomon and was at this time reaching the form in which we have it. One result of this rewriting was the addition to the Genesis account of a second story of Creation (1:1–2:4a), which, while preserving something of the emphases of the earlier account (2:4b–24), underlined the origin and importance of Sabbath observance. As we shall see, emphasis on Sabbath observance was one of the main elements in the successful effort by the exiles to maintain their identity and create a new focus for their faith. The other section of cultic material was juristic, giving specific commandments and prohibitions. The eventual result of this part of the exilic priestly undertaking was the inclusion in Holy Scripture of such ancient materials as the rituals for Passover, the Day of Atonement, and other holy days; instructions for the building of the Tabernacle, directions for the organization of the priesthood and for acceptable forms of ritual and sacrifice, laws on clean and unclean things, and numerous miscellaneous customs. Like the narrative section of the priestly writing, the juristic part was brought up to date to show its relevance for the contemporary life of the Jews.

These writings were not completed during the Exile. The body of priestly writings continued to develop and did not take final form until the Persian period, perhaps sometime around 400 B.C. But the exigencies of the Exile had already marked these compositions with certain emphases which they retained, and which are found not only in the Pentateuchal writings (Genesis through Deuteronomy), but also in much of the prophetic writing that came from exilic and postexilic times. There was stress upon certain externals which became means for setting Israelites apart from the surrounding culture and thus preserving their unique identity. Among the most important were Sabbath observance, circumcision, and ritual cleanness. Isaiah and the priestly writer of Genesis saw the Sabbath as a perpetual sign of the covenant through which Israel knew herself to be Israel. Circumcision too was understood as a sign of the covenant. Since it was not practiced by the Babylonians, as it had been by most of Israel's neighbors, it also served to set the Hebrews apart. Ceremonies of ritual cleanness, strongly emphasized in the law codes and by the exilic prophet Ezekiel, further served as a visible sign of the unity of the Hebrew people at a time when their traditional symbols had disappeared.

The scholarly consensus today is that these emerging legal writings were being combined at this time with the priestly theological history of the events from Creation to Sinai. Thus the Pentateuch, now containing the traditions of the northern and southern kingdoms plus the ancient cultic laws, was beginning to take the shape in which we know it today.

At a later time still another large body of material was added to this work. Deuteronomy, so new and yet so important to the Hebrews, was reedited during the Exile. Additional material, some of it reworked from ancient sources, was added. When this was united with the rest of the Pentateuchal writings—probably early in the Persian period if not during the Exile itself— the Deuteronomic writers edited the entire Torah, as the first five books of the Bible came to be known.

The Deuteronomists' contribution to the Scriptures was not confined to these tasks, monumental though they were. They were responsible for the preservation and for much of the current form of the Deuteronomic historical corpus (Joshua through II Kings), which is essentially a history of the

A papyrus scroll, rolled, tied, and sealed, and a scribe's palette from a fifth-century B.C. Hebrew community on the Island of Elephantine, near Assuan in Upper Egypt. The Elephantine Papyri show that after the destruction of Jerusalem in 586 many Jews not exiled to Babylon scattered to other parts of the world, forming the communities of the Dispersion. The papyri are written in Aramaic, indicating the early decline of Hebrew as a living language. They include letters appealing to Bagoas, governor of Judea, and Sanballat, governor of Samaria, for funds to restore the Hebrew temple destroyed by local priests of the god Khnum.

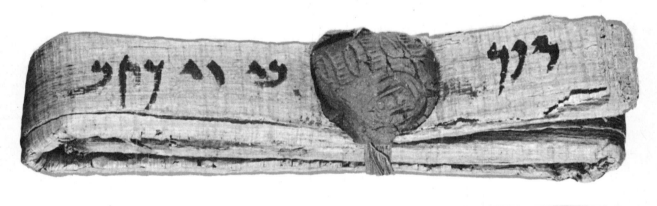

settlement of the land and of the kingdoms. When this material was edited, during the Exile, it was done from a special perspective. The disaster of 721, which had destroyed the northern kingdom, and that of 597–586, which had brought the southern kingdom into exile, were events of vast theological meaning. Far from contradicting Israel's historic faith, these events vindicated it. Israel, unfaithful to the covenant, had seen God reject its nationalistic expressions and now felt the heavy but just wrath of God upon the people. The severe judgments this writer brings to bear upon the rulers of the two kingdoms are made on the basis of one criterion: how faithful were these kings to the worship and demands of the Living God of Israel?

A further vindication of Israel's faith is set forth in the fourth major body of writings and traditions: the sayings of the prophets. The destruction of the kingdoms and even the desecration of the Temple did not offend God or affect His nature. On the contrary they glorified Him. This is what Amos, Hosea, Isaiah, Micah, and others had been saying for years. They had been constantly telling the people that God was not tied either to Israelite nationalism or to the cult. The final catastrophe of 586 lent credence to such views, for which these stalwart preachers had suffered so much in the past. At the same time their understanding of God's way with man moved to the center of Hebrew thought.

The Prophetic Assurance

THIS WAS the twilight time of prophecy. The Hebrews were rapidly moving to the view that the authentic voice of religious authority was to be heard in the written and not the spoken word. This was one of the significant shifts in thought that produced Judaism. For Judaism as for Christianity the written word is the authority, and "the voice of the prophet is heard no more in the land." This is the direction in which thought was moving in the Exile as prophecy began to wane in its long service to Israel. But what a glorious twilight! Three of the greatest of all the prophets come from this time.

Jeremiah and Ezekiel were older than Second Isaiah, the famous "Unknown Prophet." They were important figures at the beginning and first part of the Exile, while Second Isaiah appeared near the end, when it was becoming increasingly clear that the time of restoration was almost at hand. Jeremiah had actually been active in Judah as early as the reign of Josiah (640–609) and the greater part of his work was done before the Babylonian siege and victory. In many ways he may be compared with Hosea and Amos. He rails against the unscrupulous who prey on widows and orphans—against those who desert their God to serve other gods, and those priests and prophets who, while claiming to serve God, are misleading the people. Like Isaiah he holds a high view of the importance of the Temple, and counsels the kings to accommodate themselves to the demands of the Babylonians in order to preserve the sanctuary intact. But like Micah he sees the pollution of the holy place and the growing darkness as Israel prepares to pay for its unfaithfulness. Yet for all his similarities to his predecessors, Jeremiah was unique among the prophets. All felt the failure of their task keenly, but in no other does the unity of the man and the prophet break down as in Jeremiah. He performed his prophetic task with unrelieved faithfulness; yet there was no time in his life when he was at ease, much less at rest, in the prophetic role. Constantly this sensitive and vulnerable man questions the ways of God, argues with God, complains to God. There is never a word of thanksgiving, but always the awareness of his prophetic failure. Among the "personal laments" of Jeremiah, those remarkable writings in which he lays bare his soul, is the following revealing passage.

> O Lord, thou hast deceived me,
>   and I was deceived;
> thou art stronger than I,
>   and thou hast prevailed.
> I have become a laughingstock all the day;
>   every one mocks me.
> For whenever I speak, I cry out,
>   I shout, "Violence and destruction!"
> For the word of the Lord has become for me
>   a reproach and derision all day long.
> If I say, "I will not mention him,
>   or speak any more in his name,"
> there is in my heart as it were a burning fire
>   shut up in my bones,
> and I am weary with holding it in,
>   and I cannot.
>   —Jeremiah 20:7–9

In addition to these glimpses into Jeremiah's inner struggles, the biblical record preserves a kind of Boswellian view of the prophet. The narrative of his faithful friend and scribe, Baruch (Jer. 37–45), traces his grim sufferings from imprisonment to imprisonment until his final, apparently forced exile in Egypt. The cause of much of Jeremiah's suffering was his conviction that the Babylonian king, Nebuchadnezzar, was God's instrument and that tiny Judah was destined to be brought under his sway. When the besieging army encamped about Jerusalem, and every Hebrew was being urged to give his last ounce of effort to save the city, Jeremiah's conviction took the form of urging the troops not to fight and advising those in high office to surrender the city as quickly as possible. As might be expected, such behavior under these conditions met with strong hostility. On at least one occasion friends had to intervene to save his life.

In spite of all—the hostility of his countrymen and the siege of the enemy—he survived. After the Babylonian victory he was treated kindly by the conquerors, as indeed were most of his fellow Hebrews. In this first conquest of Jerusalem the Babylonians sought to make Judah a loyal subject. The leaders who had favored a policy of resistance were taken into exile and Zedekiah placed on the throne as a client king. The intent of the Babylonians was to remove potential leaders of revolt. What they succeeded in doing, however, was to remove almost all men of vision, common sense, or character. Into this situation extremists immediately stepped, among them prophets who proclaimed that God would intervene at any moment to restore the dignity and power of Judah. These ideas and voices Jeremiah opposed with the full power of his scathing denunciation. As a part of his opposition he wrote a letter to those who had been taken away, expressing the inevitability of total Babylonian victory and advising them to make a place for themselves in their new land.

> Build houses and live in them; plant gardens and eat their produce. Take wives and have sons and daughters; take wives for your sons, and give your daughters in marriage, that they may bear sons and daughters; multiply there, and do not decrease. But seek the welfare of the city where I have sent you into exile, and pray to the Lord on its behalf, for in its welfare you will find your welfare.
>
> —Jeremiah 29:5–7

At the same time this advice was being offered, intrigue was compounded by intrigue in Jerusalem. The result was the total destruction of the Judean state and a series of new deportations. After the second and final siege of the city (586) Jeremiah went to live near or perhaps with Gedaliah, the Jewish governor appointed by the Babylonians, at the village of Mizpah northwest of Jerusalem. Apparently the siege had made the latter no longer suitable as a capital. From Mizpah he either went or was taken into Egyptian exile by a group of Jewish nationalists who murdered Gedaliah and the Babylonians who served with him.

Of the last days of Jeremiah's life we know little. He seems to have continued to work among the Hebrews in Egypt, but in the end his path trails off into the misery that had followed him all his days. His departure for Egypt meant the loss to the Hebrews, at a crucial moment in their struggle for survival, of one of the most sensitive, brilliant, and conscientious men they ever produced.

Many of the exiles took Jeremiah's advice, but found it increasingly difficult to maintain their identity. Babylon offered an exciting and cosmopolitan atmosphere to the provincial Jews. Many succumbed and were amalgamated and lost. It was a land of wealth, splendor, and high culture, as it had been many centuries before under Hammurabi. Nebuchadnezzar, the conqueror of Jerusalem, was a vigorous ruler who glorified his reign and far outstripped Solomon in the magnificence of his building program. He surrounded the city of Babylon with double walls, pierced by the massive Ishtar Gate; adorned it with broad avenues, quays, temples, and palaces; and capped the whole undertaking with the fabulous Hanging Gardens. He encouraged the arts and trades, and made it possible for the Jews to take part in the life and culture of the country. In this atmosphere many put down roots and gave up plans of returning to Judah. Some became religious apostates; others, like Nehemiah years later, remained faithful Jews but entered into the mainstream of Babylonian life.

Psalm 137 expresses the feelings of a minority: "By the waters of Babylon, there we sat down and wept, when we remembered Zion." These traditionalists dreamed of the return to Jerusalem and the rebuilding of their Temple, where they might once more offer the prescribed sacrifices. For all their lenience, the Babylonians would permit no Hebrew shrines or sacrifices. "How shall we sing the Lord's song in a foreign land?" How? the religious ones echoed—How?

The prophet Ezekiel had an answer. The issue, not only for those who longed for the restoration, but perhaps more importantly for those who had found a home in Babylon, was the danger of losing their distinctive character. This was the central issue for those who preserved and were reworking the traditions of Israel. So great was the danger of falling away from the ancient religion of their fathers that the Hebrews, in their attempt to preserve it, brought about a major change in the religious structure. In this process Ezekiel played a prominent part; he has rightly been called "the Father of Judaism."

His way had been prepared by the Deuteronomic reforms, which had eliminated local sacrificial shrines and infused Hebrew religion with the spirit of the prophets; and by Jeremiah, who had spoken of the "individualization" of the covenant and had taught the early exiles that God could be worshiped anywhere, even in exile. Yet, like any other religious genius, Ezekiel did much more than repeat the counsels of his predecessors. He was a priest who had apparently been taken into exile along with Jehoiachin in the deportation of 597. From his new home in Chebar he followed events closely. When news came of the destruction of Jerusalem he spoke out against the city and her inhabitants in much the same way as his contemporary Jeremiah had done earlier. But he also revealed his double attitude toward the city. On the one hand he saw her as utterly depraved, deserving the fate that had befallen her. On the other hand he saw her as cleansed, and looked forward to the restoration of worship of the true God in her midst. The overthrow of shrine and nation was brought on because the people made themselves "unclean," because they offended against the sacred ordinances and judgments of God. As Ezekiel reviewed the history of Israel it was clear to him that the Exile was an inevitable outcome and that it vindicated the faith of those who understood the nature of God.

But the Exile was not for him a permanent situation. While he did not share with the false prophets the belief that it would end momentarily, he did look forward to the restoration of Jerusalem and threw his considerable energies into preparation for that time. The situation of the exiles made it impossible to carry on a prophetic ministry in the style of classical Hebrew prophecy as seen in Hosea and Amos. It was not enough for him to condemn or pronounce. Diatribe and threat, so common in Ezekiel's early preaching, practically vanish after the events of 586. Moreover, preaching itself no longer had its former importance. Ezekiel's prophetic message is expressed in carefully thought-out written form. As a result, the image of him that has come down to us is one of rational aloofness, of detachment from the circumstances in which he lives and about which he writes.

Yet he is far from indifferent to his times. He argues and debates with his fellow exiles and constantly holds up to their attention the deserved punishment that has befallen them and the restoration that lies ahead. In the striking imagery of the Valley of Dry Bones (Ezek. 37) he combines the two themes with an immediacy that has made this vision one of the great passages in biblical literature.

Ezekiel is not a traditional prophet. He is priest and theologian, visionary and builder. The emphases that appear in other literary activities of the Exile find heightened expression in his writings. Foreign elements in religion and life have brought the Hebrews to their sorry plight; they must be eliminated. The Jews are a holy people. Sabbath and circumcision must be observed and ritual cleanliness must become a way of life. If it was now impossible to perform the old Temple sacrifices, it was not impossible to stress the Law, which was after all equally ancient and an equally revered token of God's revelation of Himself. Covenant and Law were two sides of the same thing. Therefore, readings from the Law, with prayers and the singing of psalms, became the focal point of the Hebrew community.

The sacrifices were not forgotten. Ezekiel, looking forward to the return, showed interest in the regulations for the priesthood and drew up detailed plans for a new Temple in Jerusalem. All this strongly affected postexilic Judaism. When the time came, the Temple was rebuilt, the sacrifices restored, and the priesthood regulated along lines laid down by Ezekiel. But they did not regain their central place. During the Exile the curling smoke of the sacrificial fire had been replaced by meditation upon the Law. Now at the heart of the community stood the Law, the synagogue, and the rabbi. In his concern for the preservation of Jewish identity, of a distinctive character within an alien culture, Ezekiel wrought more than he realized. "Ezekiel gave us the Law," the early rabbis repeatedly emphasized. "Ezekiel gave us the Law."

In the Exile Israel had become a people of the Book.

About 550 B.C. Cyrus the Persian, a vassal king of the Achaemenians in southern Iran, launched a series of brilliant campaigns which resulted almost at once in the isolation of Babylon from her allies, and in 539 brought about the destruction of this once-mighty empire. The rise of this new power had an electric effect upon the Hebrew exiles, and the decade preceding the actual fall of Babylon was for them a time of intense theological activity. The feeling grew that the long-expected restoration of Jerusalem and of the

Davidic state was close at hand. This was encouraged by awareness of Cyrus' policy toward subject peoples. He not only permitted them to keep their religious and cultural ties, but admonished them to be zealous in maintaining them.

Second Isaiah so called because his writings were appended to those of Isaiah of Jerusalem, addressed himself to the hopes and fears of his people near the end of their sojourn in Babylon, and in so doing gave a reinterpretation of the history and meaning of Israel. He agreed with those who saw the coming of dawn at the end of the long dark night. In prose unsurpassed for its poetic quality, Second Isaiah assured the captives that their sins were forgiven and that their God, the everlasting living God, would restore them to their land.

> Comfort, comfort my people,
>   says your God.
> Speak tenderly to Jerusalem,
>   and cry to her
> that her warfare is ended,
>   that her iniquity is pardoned,
> that she has received from the Lord's hand
>   double for all her sins.
>
> A voice cries:
> "In the wilderness prepare the way of the Lord,
>   make straight in the desert a highway for our God.
> Every valley shall be lifted up,
>   and every mountain and hill be made low;
> the uneven ground shall become level,
>   and the rough places a plain.
> And the glory of the Lord shall be revealed,
>   and all flesh shall see it together,
>   for the mouth of the Lord has spoken."
>
> A voice says, "Cry!"
>   And I said, "What shall I cry?"
> All flesh is grass,
>   and all its beauty is like the flower of the field.
> The grass withers, the flower fades,
>   when the breath of the Lord blows upon it;
>   surely the people is grass.
> The grass withers, the flower fades;
>   but the word of our God will stand for ever.
>
> —Isaiah 40: 1–8

The prophet did not stop with affirmation of his belief; he surprised all by pointing to the agent of God's will: Cyrus, destroyer and builder of empires, was none other than God's "anointed"! The course he was causing events to follow was that ordained by God to carry out His purposes in history. Over against the strain of pessimism among those who were tempted to embrace the gods of Babylon and Persia because of the momentary ascendancy of these nations on the scene of world history, Second Isaiah asserted the controlling activity of God over all history. The gods of the Babylonians and of the Persians, said Isaiah, are "no gods," images of wood or stone. The God of Israel is the only god; "there is no other." He who had power to create man and the world surely has the power to restore Israel to Jerusalem and to call the peoples of the earth to gather around His holy city to behold His glory. God had made this people Israel in redeeming them from the hopelessness of Egyptian bondage. Now a new Exodus was about to take place. God Himself would lead them back to Zion, where through their sufferings they would become "a light to the nations," bringing the good news of God's redeeming love to all men.

"For you shall go out in joy," the prophet told the redeemed of the future, "and be led forth in peace; the mountains and the hills before you shall break forth into singing, and all the trees of the field shall clap their hands."

Return to Zion

"ALL THEIR POPULATIONS I assembled and restored to their dwelling places," boasts Cyrus on his famous cylinder. The Book of Ezra (6:3–12) still preserves the edict allowing the Jews to return to Judah, carrying the sacred vessels of the Temple and permission to build a new edifice for them. After long preparation several caravans set off across the desert for Palestine. At this moment, however, no mountains or hills broke forth into singing, nor did the trees of the field clap their hands. Trials and disappointments made the return a period of bitterness and of narrowing horizons. Doubt and even cynicism replaced the buoyancy of Solomon's Golden Age, the self-satisfaction of the later monarchies, and the hope of the Exile. The prophetic voice gave way to the earthly wisdom of Proverbs, the scepticism of Ecclesiastes, and a restricted interpretation of the Law. Nehemiah and Ezra, building upon the work of Ezekiel, sought with brilliance and courage to help the people maintain their ancient faith in light of their new situation. But as hopes for the restoration of the Davidic kingdom began to fade, some began to dream of another, far-distant kingdom, a kingdom not of this world, while others drew the cloak of their Scriptures closely about them and settled down to live in alien cultures.

Strange as it may seem, we know less about this Persian period of Hebrew history (ca. 539 B.C.–ca. 330 B.C.) than about any other after the twelfth century B.C. Our lack of knowledge is owing, on the one hand, to a scarcity of documents, and on the other, to confusion in those that do survive. There are, for example, almost no dated Jewish materials from the fourth century, and those from the century before confront the scholar with almost insurmountable difficulties.

The main source of information about early postexilic Judaism comes from "the Chronicler," writer of the books of Ezra and Nehemiah and of I and II Chronicles. This is one of the two major blocks of written material that survive from this time. The other is the completed Torah, to which we shall turn in a moment. The Chronicler meant to provide a history of the Hebrews from Adam to Cyrus, and his motive may be gleaned from the Greek title of his work: *Paraleipomena*—that is, "omitted things." It may be that he wanted to provide a supplement and addenda to the history as found in the books of Samuel and Kings. It was St. Jerome (see Chapter Four) who spoke of the work as "the chronicle of the whole of sacred history" and thus inspired the name that two of the books and their author bear in Protestant Bibles.

Some think the Chronicler had "a complete lack of historical sense." Some speak of his work as having suffered "serious dislocation after leaving his hands." The difficulties involved in understanding the dating of his work may be seen in the fact that scholars are not even agreed as to whether Ezra or

The Jerusalem Isaiah Scroll from Qumran, opened to Isaiah 40:2–28, consists of seventeen parchment sheets sewn together and rolled. Because respect for the sacred written Scriptures led pious Jews to discard old and tattered copies, few such ancient scrolls of the Old Testament have survived.

Nehemiah came first. But while precision in detail is lacking, the Chronicler's work helps us to see that the history of immediate postexilic Judaism can be divided into three periods: from the return to the rebuilding of the Second Temple; the time of the work of Nehemiah and Ezra; and the period "under the cloud." For the latter there are no contemporary records, but inferences may be drawn by comparing the situations at the beginning and at the end of that time. This period is particularly important for the development of the Bible. When Judaism emerges once more into full light there is a threefold distinction in the written traditions: Torah, Prophets, and Writings.

The first phase of postexilic Judaism saw the return of the deportees. After over half a century in Babylon, a rich land full of opportunities, only a small minority were willing to hazard the difficult journey and the uncertain future. For those who did go, it was a holy crusade. "When the Lord restored the fortunes of Zion," sang the pilgrims, "we were like those who dream. Then our mouth was filled with laughter, and our tongue with shouts of joy" (Ps. 126:1–2a). The dream was soon shattered. So thorough had been Nebuchadnezzar's vengeance that Judah still lay ravaged, depopulated, and poor. The Hebrews' ancient enemies, Edom, Moab, Ammon, and even the Philistines, were hostile to their return. The Samaritans, who worshiped the same god as the Hebrews but were considered racially unclean, proved actively troublesome. When the Jewish leaders curtly refused their help in rebuilding the Temple, the Samaritans in pique sought to block the work, and the enmity between them continued into New Testament times. Yet in spite of all, Sheshbazzar, leader of the returned exiles, succeeded in laying the foundations of the holy sanctuary.

But the Temple was not to be completed for many years. The little Jewish community huddled around Jerusalem was too small and poor to support such an undertaking. Moreover, the attempt to establish Zerubbabel, grandson of the last king, Jehoiachin, failed. He vanished from recorded history. With him went hopes for continuation of the line of David on the throne. Further, some of those who had begun to prosper soon put religious considerations and aspirations at the lower end of their scale of priorities. The prophet Haggai pled with those who dwelt in "paneled houses, while this house [the Temple] lies in ruin" to "consider how you have fared" and to give first place and effort to completion of the shrine. Under his urging and that of his contemporary Zechariah, the Second Temple, the "Temple of Zerubbabel," a modest building, was finally completed. In March 515 B.C. the hills around Jerusalem resounded with psalms and prayers of thanksgiving as smoke rose from the sacrificial fire, and the Temple of the Lord was dedicated.

The major objective of the exiles had been accomplished. Holy Zion had been cleansed, and upon its brow stood the rededicated sanctuary of the Living God. If the glory of this building shrank into insignificance beside the remembered splendor of Solomon's edifice, the devotion of the priests was no less pure, and the prayers of the people no less sincere than those of others who had worshiped on this hallowed ground.

The new Temple gave to those who had returned and to the Jewish communities scattered throughout Judah a focus and a new sense of unity. But it did not provide them with protection nor change their status as vulnerable islands in a hostile sea. Judah remained a weak province under the shadow of a malevolent Samaria. Perhaps even more important, the walls of Jerusalem remained as Nebuchadnezzar had left them: blackened, broken, tumbled. From any direction, at any moment, enemies—and there were many—could sweep into the unprotected city. Worst of all, money and leadership were lacking to correct these things. As the high priest approached the new altar for the first time and the people's song of thanksgiving became a paean of joy, the question before them was not one of prosperity, but of survival.

The Temple and the Law

JUDAISM is the monument of Nehemiah and Ezra. It was their energy and vision that brought about the transformation of ancient Judah and turned it into a Jewish community which after them continued to grow and gain strength along the lines they had set out. To measure the accomplishment of these two extraordinary men we must see the condition into which the postexilic community had fallen. And for this picture we are indebted to the prophetic books of Obadiah, Joel, and Malachi.

Obadiah is an indictment against Edom, which had seized a part of Judah's territory after the debacle of 586 and continued to deal treacherously and maliciously with the Jews. Joel and Malachi, on the other hand, show us the internal situation. Joel takes the occasion of a natural disaster—a plague of locusts—to call upon the people to repent of their ways, throw off their religious apathy, and gather for a great fast of repentance and lamentation. Malachi, who probably wrote about a generation before Nehemiah came to the land, likewise condemns the community for its religious apathy. He paints a vivid picture of a people merely going through the motions of worship, offering an insincere performance of ritual which reflects their loss of faith in God and in their own future. Thus, when Nehemiah, cupbearer to the king of Persia, arrived in Jerusalem as governor in 445 B.C., he found a community living under the continuous threat of foreign hostility, and the more serious threat of spiritual and moral disintegration from within. Disillusionment, laxity, and moral decay—these were the building blocks the people offered him. To them in return he offered the catalyst of himself: his unbounded energy, his love for Israel, his faith in God.

Artaxerxes, the Persian king, had granted permission for the rebuilding of the city walls, and Nehemiah felt this to be his most pressing task. The Bible preserves the vignette of his moonlight inspection of the ruins three days after his arrival (Neh. 2:11–16). Soon he mustered all the Jews of the area, and work began. At first the neighboring peoples only scoffed, but as the project progressed their words turned to sabotage and it became necessary to arm the workers. "So we labored at the work, and half of them held spears from the break of dawn till the stars came out" (Neh. 4:21).

Fifty-two days later, on October 2, 445 B.C., enough of the wall was finished to make the city secure. Although it took over two more years to complete the battlements, Nehemiah had scored a brilliant initial success. But his work had hardly begun. Once the city was safe he turned his manifold talents to the dire economic situation of the province. During the remaining eleven and a half years of his first term as governor he sought to correct economic abuses by levying just taxes and trying to eliminate the usury that was rampant. Severe measures were needed. Moving with customary disregard for his personal popularity, he forced wealthy citizens to cancel the debts of the poor, and set an example by relinquishing his claim to payments due him as governor.

This was a man of firm conviction—some might even say intransigence. Once his course of action was determined, he moved with decision. His far-reaching economic policies had already made him unpopular with an influential group; but he did not stop with these reforms. He had been reared in a strict Jewish tradition and more and more became convinced that a thorough religious reform was required to put the tiny province on a sound footing. His many enemies—political, social, religious, economic, and personal—joined forces. Their attempts to disgrace him, to murder him, or to remove him in some other way show that modern international spy stories are replays of old, old tunes. Sanballat, governor of Samaria, was his inveterate opponent. The weak province of Yehud (the Persian name for Judah) had been dominated by the latter's influence, and he meant to regain his former sway. He sought to prevent the construction of the walls of Jerusalem by interfering with the supply of goods, then by luring Nehemiah from the city with the intention of killing him. These measures failing, he threatened to accuse him of treason before the Persian king. When Nehemiah called his bluff on this, Sanballat set to work through his son-in-law—a member of the high-priestly family, no less!—to undermine Nehemiah's work from within.

All failed. By personal courage, resourcefulness, and faith in the rightness of his cause Nehemiah carried through his political and economic restructuring of the Jewish community. One of the most significant achievements of his first term as governor was to persuade many Jews living in outlying areas to move to Jerusalem in order to repopulate it and garrison the newly rebuilt walls.

But before he could carry out his new policies Artaxerxes recalled him. The king, deciding that his cupbearer had much overstayed his leave, did what Nehemiah's enemies had failed to achieve. Immediately upon his departure those who had opposed his reforms moved to regain their former power. The priests were in the vanguard, contributing to religious laxity by encouraging usurious friends to ply their trade in Temple quarters reserved for sacred purposes. To their dismay they learned within less than two years that

Nehemiah had induced the king to make him governor of Yehud for a second time.

During his new term of office Nehemiah was determined on nothing less than a full-scale campaign against religious laxity. His first act was literally to throw the priests' friends and their effects into the street. In their place he established honest treasurers to make sure that tithes were not only paid, but used to support the Levites who administered the Temple. With characteristic firmness he ordered the city gates shut on the Sabbath so that merchants could do no business. When they set up their tables outside the walls he drove them away.

The policy for which he was most criticized in later years was that of forbidding intermarriage with non-Jews. When he discovered that children of such marriages could not speak Hebrew he flew into a rage, cursed, and assaulted those near him. It was then that he made the people take an oath in the name of God to refrain from such alliances, saying to them, "You shall not give your daughters to their sons, or take their daughters for your sons or for yourselves" (Neh. 13:25). He even forced the high priest's grandson and his Samaritan wife, the daughter of Sanballat, to flee, and called down a curse upon them for defiling the priesthood and the covenant.

Nehemiah was trying to set up a standard for membership in the Jewish community. It had two aspects, one dealing with birth, the other with loyalty to the Temple. Citing the Deuteronomic law (Deut. 23:3 ff.), he prohibited intermarriage and took a census of the people based upon genealogy (Neh. 7:5–69; Ezra 2), to emphasize the importance of being able to trace family ancestry through Jewish forbears. Some scholars think that the Book of

A relief from the royal treasury at Persepolis shows the Persian monarch Darius I receiving an official visitor whose gesture signifies deference and honor. Directly behind Darius stands the crown prince Xerxes, followed by palace guards and attendants bearing the insignia of office.

Ruth, a hauntingly beautiful love story of a Moabitess and a Jew, was written at this time as a protest against his policies. The fact that the story is set in a background of the time of the Judges does not rule out the possibility that it was, in fact, just such a protest from the postexilic period. If this understanding of Ruth is correct, then like the later Jonah and Job it expresses strong dissent from the prevailing views of its era.

The second phase of Nehemiah's standard was loyalty to the Temple and the worship it represented. We have seen that he took measures to insure payment of tithes to the Temple and to abolish commercial activities on the Sabbath. He also organized regular religious services there and demanded support of the people for them. Thus while his accomplishments were mainly political, this was not the whole story. He not only built ramparts of stone around Jerusalem, but also erected a wall of exclusiveness around the Jewish community. The constant threat of loss of identity through cultural assimilation and religious syncretism, which had hung over the Hebrews ever since their entrance into Canaan, was here squarely met by Nehemiah, who sought in this way to preserve the ancient spiritual heritage. Yet for all his efforts, the religious reforms were not completely successful. Somehow his emphasis was misplaced. While he gave importance to the Law, his major concern was

An aerial view of Persepolis, magnificent capital city of the Persian Empire, where Nehemiah rose to the high rank of cupbearer to King Xerxes.

with the Temple; yet the Temple no longer occupied its former place in the people's religion. During the Exile the written traditions had taken on primary significance.

Ezra began with that fact. Toward the end of Nehemiah's second term as governor, probably around 428 B.C., this Jewish priest living in Babylon secured permission from the king to investigate and regulate religious matters among the Jews in Palestine. When he set off on his journey to Jerusalem he was accompanied by a group of Babylonian Jews he had persuaded to return and by a number of scribes who were experts in interpreting the Law. He had in his possession a copy of the Law itself, which he meant to be the instrument for structuring the religious life of his people.

The dating of Ezra's activities is not made clear by the Chronicler and it is now impossible to trace his footsteps with precision. But the major outline is apparent. Shortly after his arrival in Jerusalem, in connection with the Feast of Tabernacles, he mounted a wooden pulpit in one of the main squares of the city and, flanked by the scribes who had accompanied him, read aloud from the Law from daybreak until noon. The effect was remarkable. Men wept in the streets. Priests asked for private instruction, and the festival which was to begin the next day was held in accordance with this Law. The readings, accompanied by interpretation from the scribes, continued for the duration of the seven-day festival. On the eighth day the climax was reached: there was a solemn ceremony of covenant renewal. The people confessed their sins, pledged themselves to the covenant in a solemn oath, and heard Ezra, acting as their mediator, offer a prayer to the Lord. Then the leaders of the people, led by Nehemiah, signed the covenant on behalf of all (Neh. 8–11).

What was this Law that Ezra brought from Babylon, which became the standard—the "canon"—of the lives of the people? Some scholars have suggested it was Deuteronomy; some say it was the Holiness Code; still others think it was the writings of Ezekiel. There are other possibilities. But it seems most likely that it was the complete Pentateuch, the Torah. Within only a few years after the work of Ezra this writing—the first five books of our Bible, embodying the JE Document from the early monarchy, the Deuteronomic writings from the last days of Judah, and the priestly writings, which preserved very old cultic materials—was the guiding rule of Israel's faith. It is reasonable to assume that this is what Ezra disclosed that day and made the standard of faith and practice in the struggling Jewish community.

Thus he supplied what was lacking in Nehemiah's reforms, and made adherence to the Law the distinguishing mark of the Jew. Indeed, legend has identified him as a second Moses. It is true to say as one scholar does that "if Moses was Israel's founder, it was Ezra who reconstituted Israel and gave her faith a form in which it could survive through the centuries."

And thus it was that late in the fifth or early in the fourth century B.C there came into being among the Jewish people a body of writings considered authoritative for regulating the life and faith of the community. Such a writing is called a canon, that is, a "reed" or "measuring stick." The use of

the terms "canon" and "canonical" today carries the idea of an authoritative set of writings given official status by a council of religious leaders. But this understanding is late, arising in the Christian Era, and does not take account of the fact that canonical literature had an assumed status in the community long before any council conferred the title. Councils dealing with the canon have recognized and assented to established practice.

No better case in point can be found than that of the Pentateuch. It was not until the end of the first century A.D. that a council "recognized" it as canonical, yet for half a millennium previously it had functioned as the standard for Jewish life and faith. And not only Jewish: the Samaritans were one with the Jerusalem Jews in knowing and accepting the Pentateuch. When their final and complete break came, late in the fourth century, and the Samaritans withdrew entirely from the Jerusalem worship and built their own temple on Mt. Gerizim, they took with them the Pentateuch, "the Law of Moses." The Samaritan Pentateuch, still in use by the Samaritans of Nablus, Jordan, is evidence that at the time of the final schism the Torah was considered canonical by the Jews of Palestine. By the time of the Septuagint (LXX), the Greek translation of Hebrew writings made in Alexandria in the late third and early second centuries B.C., the Pentateuch, or Torah, had come to have an authoritative status among Jews throughout the world.

This was not the only body of writings the people had, of course, and we would do well at this point to remind ourselves that they also possessed a magnificent collection of historical writings: Joshua, Judges, Samuel, and Kings. In addition there was the collection of prophetic writings, the "new" history of the Chronicler, and a growing body of other material which later came to be known merely as "the Writings." The Septuagint contained them all, plus others which did not find their way into our Bible. But the Torah had a special status, which we shall see the other writings gained later.

The Sacred Library Grows

AFTER NEHEMIAH AND EZRA the history of the little Jewish community around Jerusalem goes under a cloud. The historical accounts within the Old Testament end with the work of the Chronicler, and the narrative is not resumed again until the author of I and II Maccabees picks up the account beginning with events about 175 B.C. There is thus a gap of almost two centuries in our knowledge, and contemporary records do little to fill the hiatus left in the Jewish writings. This does not mean that there are no records from Palestine of this time. There are a number, some of great importance, which illuminate aspects of the religious development. The Book of Psalms, of which more will be said later, is indispensible for understanding the worship and theology of the Second Temple; and certain "protest writings," such as Job, Jonah, and Ecclesiastes, show that there were thinkers who challenged current theological ideas and formulations.

A Samaritan priest kisses scrolls of the sacred Torah during modern Passover ceremonies on Mount Gerizim in central Palestine. The Samaritans, who limit Holy Scripture to the first five books of the Bible, built their temple on the mountain following a schism with the Jews after the Exile and have worshiped and sacrificed there almost continuously for twenty-five centuries.

Job deals with the question of the suffering of the righteous and takes issue with the ancient and ever popular notion that a man's standing before God can be measured by worldly wealth and status. Jonah, a profound treatise on the nature of God and His unsearchable mercy, makes much the same point as the Book of Ruth: No matter how much men may try to bind God by their limitations and conventions, the writer says, God will be merciful above and beyond the horizons of human prejudice. In a time of constantly narrowing outlook based upon pride of heritage, Jonah was a powerful corrective, and hardly the mere "fish story" that some today try to make of it. Ecclesiastes, on the other hand, is not so much a direct protest as it is speculation about the nature of life as represented in the theology of Israel. The mind that produced it was brilliant, nimble, and loved to toy with ideas, espousing first this one, then that, and returning to the traditional views only to play them off against still others. There is little doubt that the author remained firmly in the tradition of Hebrew thought, but his mental processes as revealed in Ecclesiastes show clearly the impact speculative thinking was beginning to have on the Jewish mind.

These writings and others from the period are important, but individually and collectively they do not provide us with anything approaching a history of the times. What we know comes from brief and unrelated glimpses and from deductions on the basis of the situation discovered when the historical cloud lifts. Politically the area appears to have been semiautonomous within the Persian Empire. The government, headed by the hereditary high-priestly family, was allowed to levy taxes, although probably only those having to do with the Temple. The common coinage was of local issue and reflected the growing incursion of Greek culture; Jewish coins modeled on the Attic standard are but one indication of the flow of western thought into the Orient prior to the coming of Alexander the Great. Since before the time of Abraham there had been commercial relations, with consequent exchange of ideas, between Greece and Palestine. In the Persian period this accelerated, and after the time of Alexander (d. 323 B.C.) the floodgates were thrown wide.

Another development of these two centuries was the gradual disappearance of the Hebrew language from anything other than religious usage. By the fourth century B.C. the combination of the Exile and existing conditions in Palestine had caused large numbers of Jews to settle in various parts of the Mediterranean world. Every major city had its Jewish quarter in which succeeding generations became less and less able to speak and read Hebrew. During this time and under these conditions the Jews of Alexandria, no longer able to read the Torah and other writings of their own heritage, had them translated into Greek, the "native" language of the Diaspora Jew. This translation, the famous Septuagint, remained influential among Jews until about A.D. 130, when Rabbi Akiba caused it to be abandoned in favor of Aquila's more literal translation of the Hebrew.

During the two centuries of relative silence it was not only in the Dispersion, however, that Hebrew was ceasing to be the everyday language of Jews. In Palestine itself Aramaic was becoming the medium of daily discourse. This ancient Semitic language of the Babylonian area had for some time been the *lingua franca* of the Near Eastern world. Under the Persians it became the common tongue of the streets. Portions of the latest books in the Old Testament were written in Aramaic, and two centuries later it was the language that Jesus spoke.

The most important development of this comparatively unknown but extremely significant time in Jewish history was the continuation of the work of Nehemiah and Ezra. Judaism grew and consolidated along the guidelines they had laid down. The Temple and its services flourished. Yet it was in the synagogue, not only in Palestine but wherever ten adult male Jews gathered for the study of their written heritage, that Judaism was evolving into the form by which it has come to be known through countless generations. "Teach me, O Lord, the way of thy statutes," sang the psalmist in praise of the Law, "and I will keep it to the end. Give me understanding, that I may keep thy law and observe it with my whole heart. Lead me in the path of thy commandments, for I delight in it" (Ps. 119:33–35).

The Law, the Torah, was not the only thing studied in the synagogues. Increasingly the writings of the prophetic tradition were finding their way into the worship and meditations of Jews. For some time the prophets had been read, studied, and treasured; already in Ezekiel's day the utterances of the preexilic prophets were considered authoritative (Ezek. 38:17). But it was not until the late Persian or early Greek period that these writings which had been circulating independently were gathered together and put into one collection that came to be known as the *Nebiim*, "Prophets."

The *Nebiim* was divided into two major parts, each filling four scrolls. The scroll, or "scribe's book," was usually made of leather joined together in a long roll. The more perishable papyrus, the traditional "paper" of Egypt, was also used in scroll form—as, for example, for the Septuagint. A papyrus sheet consisted of two layers of the native reed, first soaked in water, then laid together at right angles and pounded and polished. The dried sheets were then pasted in such a way as to form rolls usually about thirty feet long.

The first four of the scrolls of the prophetic writings were known as the "Former Prophets." These were in fact the historical writings: Joshua, Judges, Samuel, and Kings. Since the Hebrews did not make a distinction between secular and religious writings, it is understandable that they should consider books dealing with God's actions in the history of their people as prophetic writings. The second set of four scrolls, known as the "Latter Prophets," contained the writings of Isaiah, Jeremiah, Ezekiel, and the "Book of the Twelve," which consisted of the prophets from Hosea to Malachi. The "Latter Prophets" were distinguished by the terms "major" and "minor," which refer not to importance but merely to length. The major prophets are the first three; that is, those that each take up a complete scroll by themselves. The minor prophets are those found on a roll with others.

Jews and Greeks

AT THE same time the Prophets were taking their place beside the Torah in the synagogues and in the hearts of the people, great events were transpiring on the larger stage of world history. The vast Persian Empire had collapsed like an empty balloon at the first pricks of the spears of Alexander's soldiers. By the time he was thirty years old Alexander, that brash, brilliant, and bold Macedonian, was master of his known world. From Greece to India, from southern Russia to the far reaches of the Egyptian desert his banners were unchallenged and his ideas of *oikoumene* heralded the dawn of a new day in international relations. One world and one world brotherhood based upon one common culture—this was Alexander's dream. In a world where the means of understanding were common property, men would be less likely to misunderstand one another. And where they understood and respected one another their sense of unity—of brotherhood—would grow.

Alexander's vehicle for achieving his dream was to be a common culture arising from a fusion of Greek and Oriental life and thought. This blending of west and east is known today as "Hellenism." Such a blending was going on long before Alexander, but with him it became official state policy on a grand scale. He founded numberless cities and populated them with a mixture of Greek and Oriental peoples. He forced his soldiers—even his general staff!—to marry non-Greeks. Many cities had their *gymnasia*, high schools where boys learned the Greek language, customs, and mode of thought. Theatres and games were everywhere. And in religion, as elsewhere, syncretism was the order of the day. The high god of one cult was said to be the same as that of another, although called by a different name. Shrines lost their unique character. New religions, amalgamations of elements from many sources, sprang up.

The threat this posed to the Jews is obvious. For centuries their struggle had been to maintain their uniqueness. Priest, prophet, and poet had opposed syncretism whether Canaanite, Egyptian, Babylonian, or Persian, as anathema to the Hebrew way of life. Now for a century and a half after the death of Alexander they were also able to cope with Hellenism, in Palestine at any rate. For Alexander died before he could consolidate the methods for carrying out his grandiose idea. His empire was divided among his generals, of whom only Seleucus, who ruled Syria from his magnificent capital at Antioch, shared Alexander's dream. Ptolemy, who seized Egypt and with it Palestine, cared only for luxury and a bulging treasury. So long as the Jews paid their heavy taxes they were left relatively free to follow their own ways. In 198 B.C., however, the Seleucid Antiochus III, known to history as "Antiochus the Great," took advantage of the weakening of the Ptolemaic grip on Palestine to annex it to Syria. The Jews, who had up to this time not altogether escaped the effects of Hellenism, now came under the direct rule of a government devoted to its spread.

This fragment of a small Hellenistic statuette captures the quality of idealism that motivated young Alexander the Great, but fails to convey the sternness of the military genius who was master of the world by the age of thirty-three.

Even before the coming of the Syrian Greeks the Jewish community had begun to be deeply split by the Hellenist pressure and the looming power of a growing Rome, which was beginning to penetrate the east. Greek ways were popular, Greek artifacts in demand, and graceful Greek robes blended in the narrow, crowded streets with the heavy, brightly colored garments of the Oriental. For the first time sports and games enlivened and interrupted the serious ways of the Jews. To the strict Jew all this was evil. It meant self-indulgence, immorality, a weakening of the living heritage of the fathers. It was like the subtle temptations of Canaan all over again. One could almost hear Amos denouncing the luxury and the decadence of Israel; Isaiah declaiming against the daughters of Zion who "walk with outstretched necks, glancing wantonly with their eyes, mincing along as they go, tinkling with their feet." These were not the ways of God. But the worst was yet to come.

At first the Seleucids showed remarkable kindness and consideration toward the Jews, even forgiving their taxes for three years so that the city of Jerusalem could be restored to some of its former glory. However, policy of this temper was dramatically reversed in 175 B.C. when Antiochus IV ascended the Seleucid throne. Self-styled "Epiphanes" ("God manifest") but referred to by his detractors as "Epimanes" ("Mad one"), the new king decreed an active Hellenization for the recently acquired Jewish areas. This posed the gravest threat to Hebrew life since the debacle of 586.

The Seleucid policy did not, as some scholars have maintained, express a hatred of the Jews. Rather, it was motivated by the increasingly difficult situation in which the state found itself. Antiochus III had overextended himself and conquered areas which became hemorrhages in the empire of his successors. Moreover he had allowed Hannibal, the Carthaginian, to feed his ambition and urge him into an invasion of Greece, where he found himself at war with Rome. The Romans drove him from Europe and followed him into Asia, where they utterly destroyed his army and inflicted humiliating terms of peace. These included the surrender of almost all the Seleucid lands in what is present-day Turkey, payment of a huge indemnity, and the handing over of a prince, the future Antiochus IV, among other indignities. Antiochus III was dead three years later and was succeeded by a son, Seleucus IV, who during a twelve-year reign proved incapable of stopping the tailspin.

Thus when the ransomed Antiochus IV came to the throne in 175 upon the assassination of his brother, he was determined to consolidate the empire and if possible to extend it. His campaign in Palestine was a part of this process. At once he set out to break the power of the Jewish priests and thus remove the most logical center of resistance to his plans. He sold the office of high priest, considered by the Jews hereditary, to the highest bidder. He then encouraged the purchaser, Jason (note the Greek form of the Hebrew *Joshua*), to establish a *gymnasium* near the Temple, where the leading Jewish boys not only learned the language and thought of the Greeks, and to wear broad-brimmed hats (a sign of Greek culture), but also to honor certain foreign gods and engage in sports stripped naked after the Greek fashion.

The events that transpired in this crisis were complex, and the blame is not wholly on one side. The earlier decree granting Jews the right to live in accordance with their own law was abrogated. But it should be noted that this was done with the connivance of Jews who were jockeying for royal favor. Menelaus, probably not even a priest, outbid Jason for the high-priestly office when it was again offered for sale. He immediately conspired with Antiochus—an expert in such matters—to plunder the Temple and its treasury; even the façade was stripped of its precious metals.

Strong opposition was already building towards these policies when Antiochus returned from his ill-fated second adventure in Egypt, where Roman power had blocked his designs. In humiliation and a towering rage he turned north, determined that if he could not extend his empire he would at least complete the task of solidification. Jerusalem was the center of opposition to his desires. Against that city he now sent a military force which, entering the city on a friendly pretext, set upon the population with frightful massacre. The city was sacked and part of its walls pulled down. A Hellenistic settlement called Acra was built on the ruins, and for twenty-five years a Seleucid garrison was kept in the half-ruined holy capital of the Jews. With other renegade Jews, Menelaus set about to make the Temple, now the shrine of the new city, the home of a cult in which the God of Abraham, Isaac, and Jacob would be identified with Zeus. What had been Judaism was to become another of the many new cults inspired by Hellenism.

Jews who were faithful to the religion of their fathers were horrified. Antiochus, realizing at last that religion stood at the core of Jewish resistance, forbade the practice of Judaism altogether. Sacrifices ceased, and feast days—including the Sabbath—went uncelebrated. The Law was to be burned, and circumcision was forbidden. All this on pain of death. Further, Jews were to worship at pagan altars and eat the meat of swine. All pretense at the amalgamation of the Jewish God into a new cult was dropped; He was henceforth supposed to disappear entirely. In December 167 the cult of Olympian Zeus was introduced in the Temple. Pagan sacrifices were upon the altar where Abraham was said to have laid Isaac, where Solomon prayed at the dedication of his edifice, and where countless Hebrews had given thanks to the God who delivered His people from Egypt. Now the flesh of swine was burned in the most sacred precincts of Judaism. Daniel spoke of the "abomination of desolation."

Antiochus, like rulers before him and since, profoundly misunderstood the mettle of Jewish character. It was not broken; it was tempered. To be sure, a number of Jews welcomed these policies. Others, not enthusiastic but perhaps motivated by fear, meekly complied. But as Josephus was later to observe, "The whole nation is fashioned for religion." Identity cannot be destroyed as easily as Antiochus thought, nor did the Hebrew God vanish at his command. Mothers continued to circumcise their sons and were put to death with them. Groups met to celebrate the Sabbath and submitted passively to being cut

Obverse and reverse sides of a bronze coin from the reign of the Maccabean king John Hyrcanus bear the names of Jonathan, his predecessor, and Alexander, a son who succeeded on the throne.

down by the sword. Numbers refused to profane the laws of purification and were tortured to death on the spot. Men clung to their Torahs as to life itself, and ended by surrendering both.

The Book of Daniel, the youngest book of the Old Testament, was written during this persecution. It encouraged the Jews to hold fast to their faith in the sure knowledge that God would redeem them, if not in this world then in the next. Heroic martyrs would find their reward, and the godless were heirs of certain doom. Like the New Testament Book of the Revelation, also written during a time of intense persecution, this is an apocalypse, a literary form in which the writer uses weird symbolism to convey to his readers the assurance that in spite of outward appearances God holds final power in His hands. Just as Belshazzar saw the handwriting of divine judgment on the wall (Dan. 5), so those who understood the ways of God would see that His power was greater than all the godless powers on earth.

There were others who shared this view but felt that the power of God could best express itself through their strong right arms. Mattathias, an aged priest of the village of Modein, was one of these. In 168, when a king's commissioner came to his village to enforce the worship of foreign gods, Mattathias set upon him and killed him. The old priest with his five sons, known as the Maccabees ("Hammerers"), fled to the hills crying: "Let every one who is zealous for the law and supports the covenant come out with me." Many came. The incident became a revolt, and the revolt a war that lasted for twenty-six years. The outcome was wholly unexpected: Mattathias soon died, but his son Judas, "like a lion in his deeds, like a lion's whelp roaring for his prey," defeated army after army sent against him. He reverted to the old Hebrew guerilla tactics and by December 164, just three years after the desecration of the Temple, was able to reenter Jerusalem, cleanse the Temple, and restore its religious services. Rejoicing among the Jews knew no bounds, and the event has ever since been celebrated by the Feast of Hanukkah.

The rededication of the Temple was the high point of the Maccabean war. Although the Seleucids soon drove Judas from the city, they did not again seek to interfere with Jewish worship; religious freedom had been regained. But the conflict which had begun in a cry for religious freedom had become a struggle for national independence. This struggle dragged on for over twenty more years, during which the several Maccabean brothers succeeded in throwing off the Syrian yoke. But what was gained on the field of battle was lost in palace intrigue and civil conflict. Jew fell upon Jew as the Maccabeans fought one another for the throne. At the last, the Roman general Pompey was asked to settle rival claims. His solution was to annex the country to Rome. Henceforth, for half a millennium Palestine was under Roman rule.

The Jews were indeed, as Josephus said, "fashioned for religion." Misfortune, as in the days of the Exile, merely strengthened their faith. Nevertheless, since for most of them religion and nationalism were the same, they never ceased hoping for the restoration of a kingdom which would be theirs alone under God. With Judas Maccabeus this hope seemed almost realized;

but the worldly degradation of his successors brought disillusion. Pious Jews reacted in different ways. The Sadducees saw their religion as a closed system to cling to while taking the world as it came. The Pharisees, the most influential and significant of the religious groups, were dedicated to the regeneration of the people by living strictly according to the will of God as revealed in the Holy Writings. To these groups, who preserved the best of Israel's past and handed it on to the future, we are indebted for the last two parts of the canon: the Prophets and the Writings. A third group, the Essenes, described by the Roman historian Pliny as "a solitary race, and strange beyond all others in the entire world," withdrew altogether from the world into strict ascetic communities like that of Qumran, there to study the Scriptures while they awaited the coming of the Messiah. And among the common people, the "people of the land," religion was a total way of life embodied in the Scriptures.

Psalms and Scrolls

DURING the Persian and Greek periods, while the older books were being studied, edited, preserved, and venerated, pious priests and dedicated scribes had continued to produce new writings. New books were being circulated during the time that others were moving toward canonical status. Of the Jewish literature of this period, however, little got into the Hebrew canon. Most of these works—many of them of considerable literary, religious, and historical value—were consciously excluded: these have come to be known as the Old Testament Apocrypha (a collection of fifteen books so called because they were thought to contain "hidden" knowledge) and Pseudepigrapha (a collection of eighteen "false writings" known to have been incorrectly attributed to past worthies). The Apocrypha are occasionally found between the Old and New Testaments in Protestant Bibles. Catholic Bibles include them as a part of the Old Testament because St. Jerome, though not entirely convinced of their authoritative status, included them in his Vulgate, the story of which is told in Chapter Four.

These intertestamental books are important for both Judaism and Christianity. For Judaism, because they show the life, thought, and influences upon the Jews of the period that not only produced some of the greatest of the rabbis—Hillel, Gamaliel, Shammai—but also was the seedbed of the Talmud. For Christianity, because they provide the link between the Old and New Testaments and show the evolution of many themes that play an important part in the life of the early Church and in the development of Christian theology.

The two most important of the apocryphal books are Ecclesiasticus (not to be confused with the canonical Ecclesiastes) and I Maccabees. The former is a substantial and often delightful book of wisdom not unlike

*An inkstand found in the
Scriptorium at Qumran
was used by the skillful
and diligent scribes who
wrote the Dead Sea Scrolls.*

Proverbs, while the latter is one of the primary sources of information about the Maccabean war.

The Pseudepigrapha (called Apocrypha by Catholics) generally tend to follow the pattern of Daniel: cryptic language, visions, dreams, conflict between angels and demons—all designed to shadow forth in obscure language the eventual triumph of the faithful. The idea of a Messiah runs through much of this late Jewish literature. He is sometimes spoken of as "the Son of Man," as in the book of I Enoch, and is depicted in various ways: now as righteous judge, now as peaceful savior, but always as one bearing the power of the Most High God. Other themes found in the New Testament, such as the resurrection of the body, the coming Day of Judgment, and the nearness of the Kingdom of God, also occur. The Testament of the Twelve Patriarchs is especially noteworthy among this literature for its anticipation of the phraseology of the Gospels and of Paul's letters. For example, it expresses a doctrine of forgiveness similar to that found in the Sermon on the Mount: "Love one another from the heart; and if a man sin against thee, speak peaceably to him. . . ."

Until recently few ancient Jewish scrolls of any kind were known to exist. The earliest copies we had of the Old Testament, except for a few fragments, were those of the Septuagint from the second or third century A.D. and Hebrew versions from the tenth century A.D. Then in 1947 came the sensational discovery of the Dead Sea Scrolls. In the following years dozens of scrolls from Qumran were found, a few almost complete, and thousands of fragments. Many of these writings date from before the Christian Era. The story of their discovery has all the elements of a thriller—Bedouins stumbling upon the first cache of documents in a remote cave near the northwest end of the Dead Sea; excited scholars racing to beat them to other caves in the area; the haggling over possession of the scrolls, the patient piecing together, unrolling, deciphering, and studying of the finds in the midst of the Arab-Israeli war. There were heated controversies among scholars as to the date and meaning of the documents, and an immediate popular interest in the story led to the publication of a veritable library of books and articles on the subject.

The dust has begun to settle a bit now, and the following facts seem clear. What we have in this magnificent find is the remains of a large library of Jewish religious literature. It belonged to an isolated community thought to be Essenes who established themselves in the remote hills near the Dead Sea during the period of the Maccabeans. While awaiting the coming of the Messiah, these monks undertook an intensive study of the Scriptures—hence the size and importance of their library. The community was destroyed by the Romans in A.D. 68–69 as the legions pushed to besiege nearby Masada during the first Jewish rebellion.

Since the desperate community hid its precious scrolls in the caves as the Romans approached, none can be later than A.D. 68–69 (although later documents have come from other caves in the region). Of the scrolls and

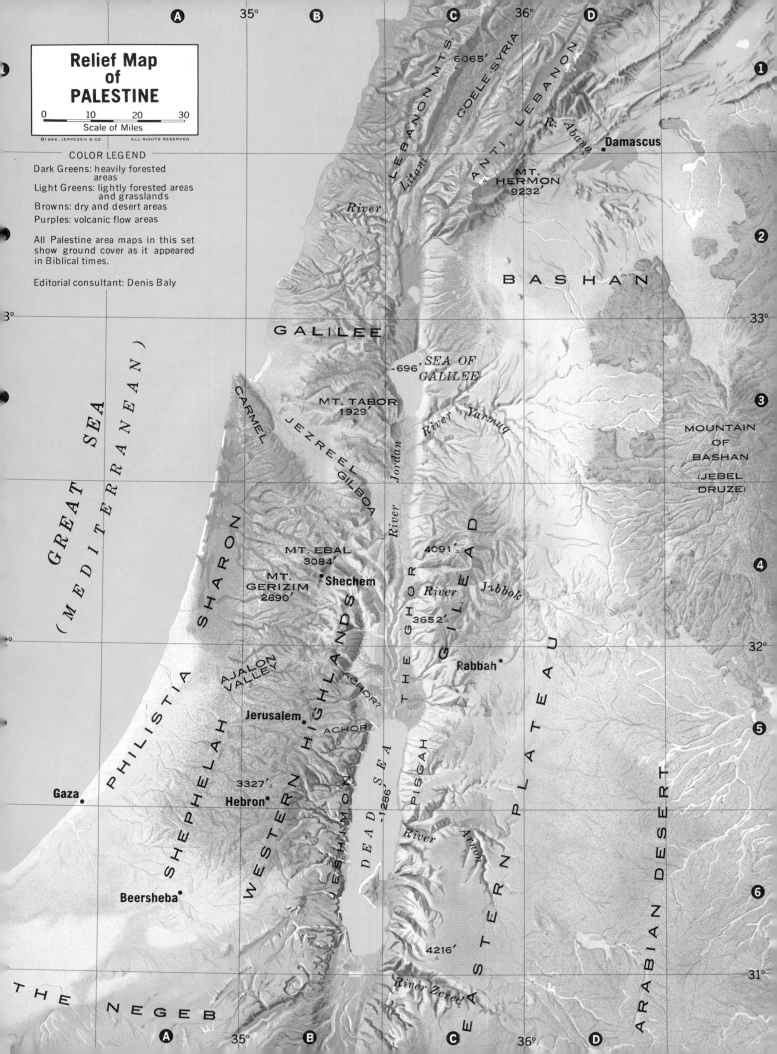

Relief Map of PALESTINE

Scale of Miles
0   10   20   30

©1966, JEPPESEN & CO.   ALL RIGHTS RESERVED

COLOR LEGEND

Dark Greens: heavily forested areas
Light Greens: lightly forested areas and grasslands
Browns: dry and desert areas
Purples: volcanic flow areas

All Palestine area maps in this set show ground cover as it appeared in Biblical times.

Editorial consultant: Denis Baly

LEBANON MTS.
6065'
COELE-SYRIA
ANTI-LEBANON
R. Abana
Damascus
Litani
River
MT. HERMON
9232'

BASHAN

GALILEE

-696' SEA OF GALILEE

MOUNTAIN OF BASHAN (JEBEL DRUZE)

CARMEL
MT. TABOR
1929'
JEZREEL
GILBOA

River Yarmuq
Jordan
River

GREAT SEA
(MEDITERRANEAN)

SHARON

MT. EBAL
3084'
MT. GERIZIM
2890'
Shechem

4091'
River Jabbok
3652'
THE GILEAD

PHILISTIA

SHEPHELAH

WESTERN HIGHLANDS

AJALON VALLEY
ACHOR?
Jerusalem
ACHOR?

JESHIMON

Rabbah

EASTERN PLATEAU

-1286' DEAD SEA

PISGAH

3327'
Hebron

River Arnon

Gaza

Beersheba

4216'

River Zered

THE NEGEB

ARABIAN DESERT

The EXODUS

→ Traditional Route of the Exodus

Many of the places mentioned in the Biblical account cannot yet be identified, and some of the sites marked here are conjectural.

Scale of Miles

0   50   100

©1962, JEPPESEN & CO. ALL RIGHTS RESERVED

GREAT SEA
(MEDITERRANEAN)

Joppa

Ai
Gibeon
Jerusalem
Hebron
Gaza
Beersheba

River Jordan

AMMON

R. Jabbok

Rabbah
Heshbon
Medeba
Dibon

Jericho
Shittim

PISGAH

R. Arnon

MOAB

DEAD SEA

Arad
Hormah

WILDERNESS OF ZIN

R. Zered

Punon

EDOM

Sela

Kadesh Barnea

Oboth

WILDERNESS OF PARAN

Ezion-Geber

GULF OF AQABA

Way of the Philistines

The Way to Shur

Succoth

WILDERNESS OF SIN?

SINAI?
(JEBEL MUSA)

(WILDERNESS OF PARAN OR SINAI?)

GULF OF SUEZ

Raamses
Pithom
Heliopolis (On)

Memphis

River Nile

JUDGES and SAMUEL

0   10   20   30
Scale of Miles

©1966, JEPPESEN & CO.   ALL RIGHTS RESERVED

A   35°   B   C   36°   D

1   1

GREAT SEA
(MEDITERRANEAN)

Sidon

Damascus

Tyre
Abel-Beth-Maacah
Laish
Kedesh
Hazor

2   2

Acco
Merom
3°   Cabal   SEA OF GALILEE   33°
R. Kishon
Bethlehem
Harosheth
Endor   MT. TABOR 1929'
MT. MOREH 1690'
Megiddo   Shunem   Ramoth Gilead
Zaananim   Jezreel
Kedesh   Bethshan

3   3

Taanach

Jabesh-Gilead
Thebez   Abel-Mehclah   Mizpah?
Tirzah
MT. EBAL 3084'   Jordan River
MT. GERIZIM 2890'   Shechem   Succoth
Pirathon   Penuel
Mahanaim?
Joppa   Aphek
Lebonah   Adam   Mizpah?
Shiloh

4   4

2°   32°

Ophrah
Bethel   Rabbah
Ekron   Gezer   Mizpah?   Michmash
Gibeon   Jericho
Eshtaol   Ramah   Geba   Gilgal?
Zorah   Gibeah   Heshbon
Ashdod   Timnah   Beth-Shemesh   Jerusalem   Madeba
Libnah   Azekah   Bethlehem
Ashkelon   Keilah   Tekoa
Gath   Hebron   DEAD SEA
Gaza   Lachish
Ziph   Engedi   Dibon
Debir   Carmel   Hachilah
Ziklag   Maon
Arad
Beersheba
Hormah
Aroer   Kir Moab (Kir Haroseth)

5   5

6   6

31°

A   35°   B   C   36°   D

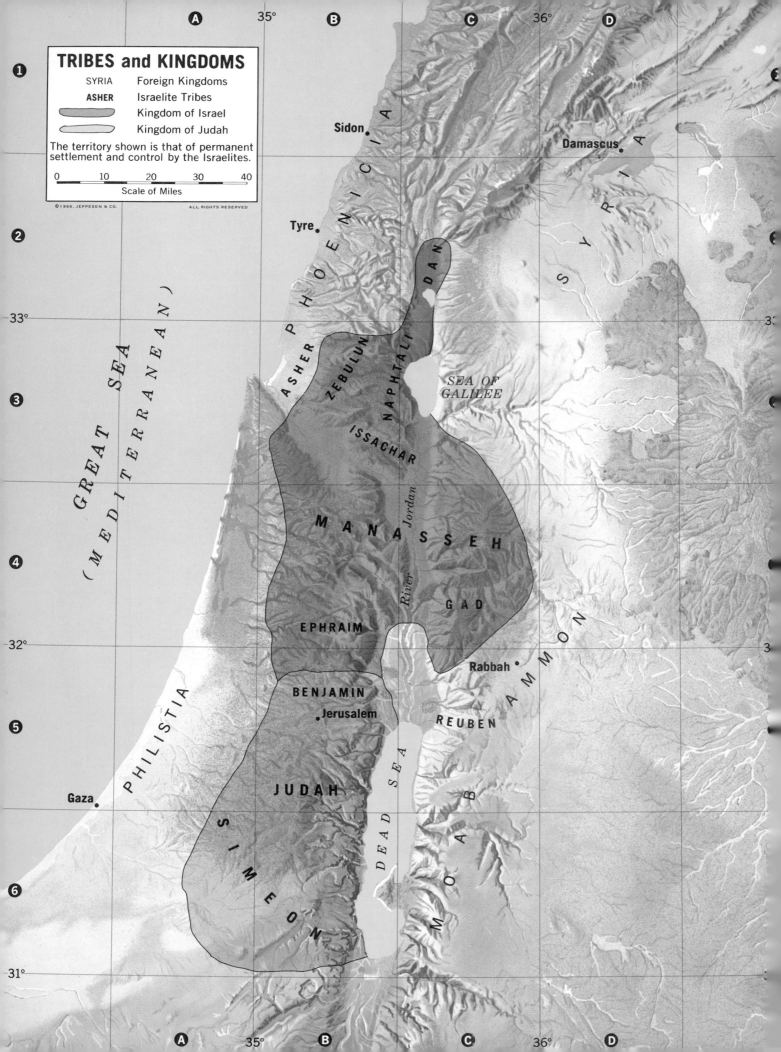

TRIBES and KINGDOMS

SYRIA   Foreign Kingdoms
ASHER   Israelite Tribes
    Kingdom of Israel
    Kingdom of Judah

The territory shown is that of permanent settlement and control by the Israelites.

0   10   20   30   40

Scale of Miles

© 1966, JEPPESEN & CO.   ALL RIGHTS RESERVED

A   35°   B   C   36°   D

Sidon

Damascus

Tyre

PHOENICIA

GREAT SEA
(MEDITERRANEAN)

SYRIA

DAN

ASHER

ZEBULUN

NAPHTALI

SEA OF GALILEE

ISSACHAR

Jordan

MANASSEH

River

GAD

EPHRAIM

AMMON

BENJAMIN

Rabbah

Jerusalem

REUBEN

PHILISTIA

JUDAH

DEAD SEA

MOAB

Gaza

SIMEON

31°

32°

33°

A 34° B 36° C 38° D

36°

SYRIAN SADDLE *River Euphrates*

Assyrian and Babylonian Invasions

CHITTIM
(CYPRUS)

1

To Anatolia
for Horses

Hamath

Arvad

Tadmor
(Palmyra)

● Kadesh
● Riblah

Desert Route
to Mari and
Assyria

34°

GREAT SEA
(MEDITERRANEAN)

P
H
O
E
N
I
C
I
A

Sidon

Damascus

S
Y
R
I
A

Tyre

2

SEA OF
GALILEE

Megiddo

Ramoth-gilead

River Jordan

Samaria

ISRAEL

Joppa

A
M
M
O
N

32°

DEAD SEA

Rabbah

Jerusalem

JUDAH

M
O
A
B

Gaza

Beersheba

Trunk Road to Egypt

Egyptian Pressure

E
D
O
M

The Way to Shur

● Sela

EGYPT

30°

Ezion-Geber

Incense Route to
Sheba and South
Arabia

Red Sea Route

GULF OF AQABA

The IMPERIAL STRUGGLE

Area of Israelite Occupation

Under Israelite Control at the
Empire's Greatest Extent

Israelite Expansion

Pressure from the Empires of
the Nile and Mesopotamia

0   50   100

Scale of Miles

©1962. JEPPESEN & CO. ALL RIGHTS RESERVED

A 34° B 36° C 38° D

NEW TESTAMENT PALESTINE

- **• Sidon**   Towns
- **JUDAEA**   Regional and Provincial Names
- ⎯⎯⎯   Main Roads
- – – –   Other Roads

Scale of Miles
0   10   20   30   40

Berytus

Sidon

Damascus

Tyre

MT. HERMON 9232'

Caesarea Philippi

ITUREA

SYRO-PHOENICIA

Ptolemais

GALILEE

Chorazin

Capernaum

Bethsaida

GAULANITIS

Cana   Magdala

SEA OF GALILEE

Sepphoris

Nazareth

Tiberias

Nain

Gadara

GREAT SEA

(MEDITERRANEAN)

Caesarea

Scythopolis

Pella

SAMARIA

Sebaste (Samaria)

Jordan

Gerasa

DECAPOLIS

Sychar

Joppa

Antipatris

Alexandrium

River

PEREA

Philadelphia

Lydda

Emmaus   Jericho

Bethany

Jamnia

Jerusalem

Qumran

Azotus

Bethlehem

Ashkelon

Madeba

JUDAEA

Herodium

N A B A T A E A

Gaza

Hebron

Machaerus

To Egypt

Engedi

DEAD SEA

Masada

Beersheba

I D U M E A

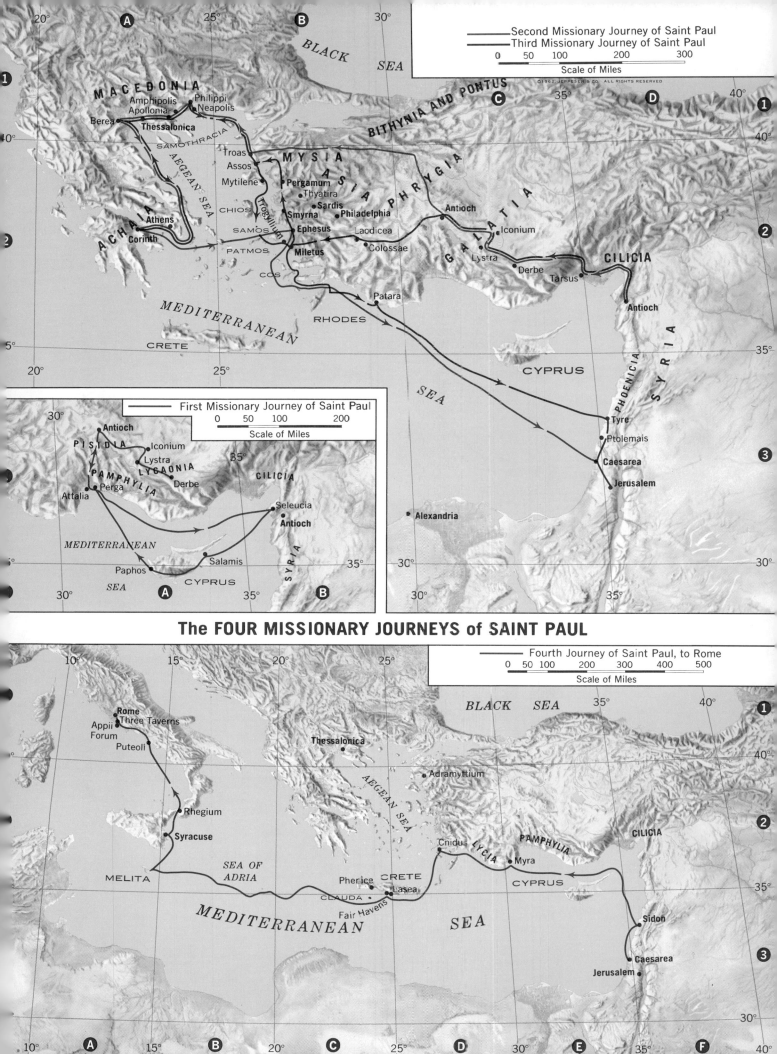

The FOUR MISSIONARY JOURNEYS of SAINT PAUL

Top map legend:

Second Missionary Journey of Saint Paul
Third Missionary Journey of Saint Paul

0 50 100 200 300
Scale of Miles

Top map labels:

BLACK SEA
MACEDONIA
Amphipolis
Apollonia
Philippi
Neapolis
Berea
Thessalonica
SAMOTHRACIA
AEGEAN SEA
Troas
Assos
Mytilene
MYSIA
ASIA
PHRYGIA
BITHYNIA AND PONTUS
Pergamum
Thyatira
Sardis
Smyrna
Philadelphia
Antioch
GALATIA
Iconium
CHIOS
Trogyllium
Ephesus
Laodicea
SAMOS
Colossae
Lystra
Derbe
Tarsus
CILICIA
PATMOS
Miletus
COS
Athens
ACHAIA
Corinth
RHODES
Patara
SEA
CYPRUS
PHOENICIA
SYRIA
Tyre
Ptolemais
Caesarea
Jerusalem
Antioch
Alexandria
MEDITERRANEAN
CRETE

First Missionary Journey legend:

First Missionary Journey of Saint Paul

0 50 100 200
Scale of Miles

First Journey map labels:

Antioch
PISIDIA
Iconium
Lystra
LYCAONIA
PAMPHYLIA
Perga
Derbe
CILICIA
Attalia
Seleucia
Antioch
SYRIA
MEDITERRANEAN
Salamis
Paphos
SEA
CYPRUS

Fourth Journey legend:

Fourth Journey of Saint Paul, to Rome

0 50 100 200 300 400 500
Scale of Miles

Fourth Journey map labels:

BLACK SEA
Rome
Three Taverns
Appii Forum
Puteoli
Rhegium
Syracuse
Thessalonica
Adramyttium
AEGEAN SEA
MELITA
SEA OF ADRIA
Cnidus
LYCIA
PAMPHYLIA
CILICIA
Myra
CYPRUS
Pherice
CRETE
Lasea
CLAUDA
Fair Havens
Sidon
Caesarea
Jerusalem
MEDITERRANEAN SEA

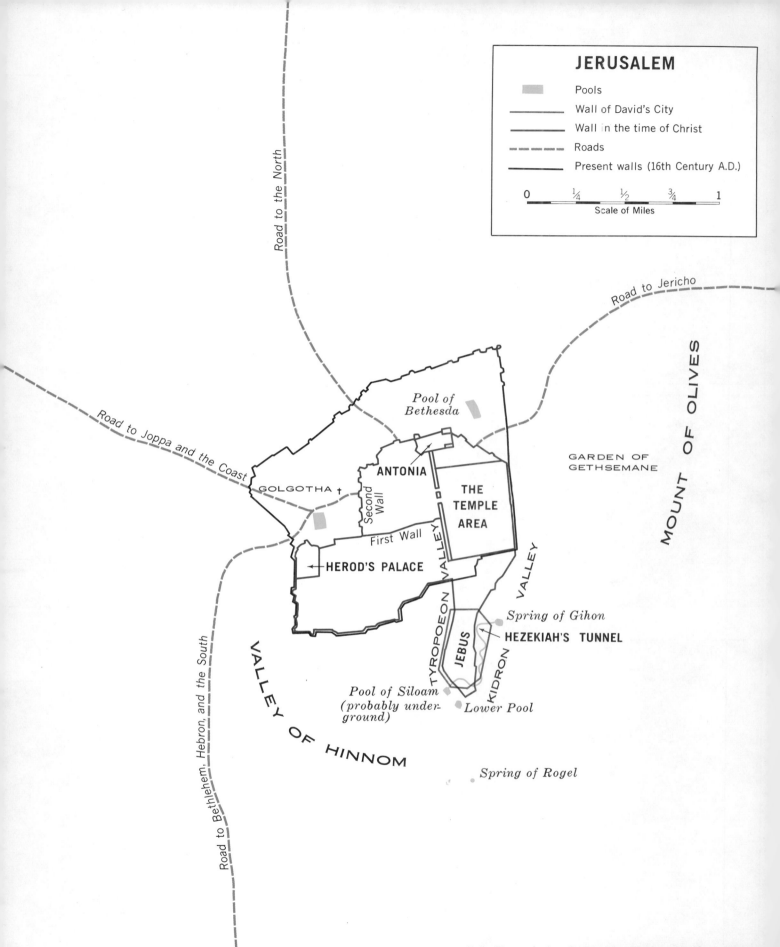

JERUSALEM

Pools

Wall of David's City

Wall in the time of Christ

Roads

Present walls (16th Century A.D.)

0   ¼   ½   ¾   1
Scale of Miles

Road to the North

Road to Jericho

Road to Joppa and the Coast

Pool of Bethesda

GARDEN OF GETHSEMANE

MOUNT OF OLIVES

ANTONIA

GOLGOTHA †

Second Wall

THE TEMPLE AREA

First Wall

HEROD'S PALACE

TYROPOEON VALLEY

KIDRON VALLEY

Spring of Gihon

HEZEKIAH'S TUNNEL

JEBUS

Pool of Siloam (probably underground)

Lower Pool

Road to Bethlehem, Hebron, and the South

VALLEY OF HINNOM

Spring of Rogel

Note: The ancient walls are not everywhere certain, but have been drawn here in what seems to be the most probable position, according to the latest excavations conducted in Jerusalem by the British School of Archaeology and the Royal Ontario Museum, under the direction of Miss Kathleen Kenyon. The evidence for this map has kindly been supplied by Dr. A. Douglas Tushingham, Chief Archaeologist of the Royal Ontario Museum, and Associate Director of the Jerusalem Excavations.

fragments recovered so far, most date from the first century B.C. and the first century A.D., though one blackened fragment may be as early as the third century B.C. The most remarkable find is a twenty-four-foot roll of Isaiah in good condition from about 100 B.C.; the most bizarre, two copper scrolls which some scholars think indicate the actual hiding places of Temple treasures. Every book of the Old Testament except Esther is present, often in many copies, as well as some of the Apocrypha and Pseudepigrapha. So vast is this find, however, that biblical books are in the minority. Most are lesser works, some previously known, many hitherto unknown, including certain local works, such as the community's own Manual of Discipline. In the ruins of the large community house at Qumran, archaeologists have discovered the writing room, or scriptorium, complete with a long plaster table, bench, and inkwells, where the scrolls were studied and copied. In the refectory the podium still remains from which the Scriptures were read aloud during the meal. There is no doubt that the life of this community revolved around the Holy Writings.

These scrolls give a rare glimpse into Jewish religious literature and thought in the crucial years just before Christ. They have shown that the texts of the Septuagint and the much later Hebrew versions faithfully represent earlier writings. Moreover, they have thrown valuable new light on the background of the New Testament. There are, for instance, remarkable

A fragment of the Manual of Discipline, which describes the Qumran community as bound by strict monastic rules and vows of obedience to superiors.

parallels between the practices and thought of this community and that of the early Church. Both emphasized baptism of the Spirit and the communal meal. Both had at the heart of their theology a Messianic doctrine, although at Qumran this took the form of two Messiahs. Both pored over the Hebrew Scriptures for an understanding of their own times and for insight into God's possible future acts. It is understandable that their writings share common themes and phrases.

The monks of Qumran, on the other hand, were an exclusive sect. It took two or three years for a novice to gain entry, whereas Jesus taught multitudes by the way and invited them to follow him. The Qumran documents contain no doctrine of incarnation, nor do they speak of redemption through the suffering of a Savior. In sum, the Dead Sea Scrolls have not revised our conception of early Christianity. They have, however, sharply illuminated the ferment of religious activity in Palestine that preceded and followed the period of Jesus' ministry.

By the time of the Dead Sea Scrolls the concept of "Scripture" was firmly established, and Jews spoke of a threefold division of the Holy Writings: Law, Prophets, and Writings. Luke 24:44 is evidence that the early Christians also recognized and accepted these three collections—not just the Law and the Prophets—as authoritative. The last major division of the canon was called simply *Ketubim,* "Writings." No closer designation was possible, since unlike the other two sections it was a miscellany of books on different themes. The *Torah* had as its central theme the Law. The *Nebiim* gathered around prophecy. The *Ketubim* included poetry (Psalms, Proverbs, Job), prophecy (Daniel), history (Ezra, Nehemiah, and Chronicles) and the "Five Rolls," a varied collection of writings used for special holy days (Song of Solomon, Ruth, Lamentations, Ecclesiastes, and Esther).

At the heart of this final collection stands the songbook of the Second Temple, the book known to us as Psalms. No other collection of poetry has entered so deeply or so pervasively into the life of western man. This book is the most familiar, most personally reverenced, and most loved of all the Hebrew Scriptures. For centuries the meter of the Psalms has resounded in worship, and as they are translated in the King James Version they are considered a standard by which to measure great English literature. In the Psalms are brought together in heightened poetical form the deepest, most moving expressions of the Hebrews' faith. Here religion and poetry are combined in sublime perfection. Who has not felt the trust and peace of the Twenty-third Psalm: "The Lord is my shepherd, I shall not want . . ."? Who cannot hear the bite and furious vengeance of the 109th Psalm:

> He loved to curse; let curses come on him!
>> He did not like blessing; may it be far from him!
> He clothed himself with cursing as his coat,
>> may it soak into his body like water,
>> like oil into his bones!

> May it be like a garment which he wraps around him,
>   like a belt with which he daily girds himself!

Who is not uplifted by the unalloyed joy of the 150th Psalm:

> Praise the Lord!
> Praise God in his sanctuary;
>   praise him in his mighty firmament!
> Praise him for his mighty deeds;
>   praise him according to his exceeding greatness!
>
> Praise him with trumpet sound;
>   praise him with lute and harp!
> Praise him with timbrel and dance;
>   praise him with strings and pipe!
> Praise him with sounding cymbals;
>   praise him with loud clashing cymbals;
> Let everything that breathes praise the Lord!
> Praise the Lord!

In stark contrast to the sonorousness of the Psalms are the pithy, worldly-wise sayings of Proverbs. Like Psalms, it is a collection of collections dating from many centuries. One is a hard-nosed, down-to-earth, "spare the rod and spoil the child" appreciation of the difficulties of everyday living. A second is a more ideal picture which understands the good life to flow from constant attention to godly matters. The third view grew out of the second and sees beyond the mere moral life to the mysteries of God and His Creation. It is perhaps because this third view of life is also the theme of the Book of Job that the latter is included among the poetry of the Hebrew Bible.

The popular process of canonizing this threefold collection of writings from Israel's heritage moved rapidly in the two centuries before the birth of Jesus. While the dimensions of the Torah had been fixed from the time of Ezra, and those of the Prophets from a somewhat later time, the question of exactly what was to be included among the Writings was not settled until late in the first century A.D. The occasion for the closing of the Hebrew canon is generally considered to have been a rabbinical council held in Jamnia, a town west of Jerusalem, about A.D. 100.

Many Writings—One Bible

By the middle of the first century of the Christian Era nationalistic groups in Palestine had worked the hope and expectation of many Jews to a fever pitch. Except for a brief interlude with Herod Agrippa, Palestine was ruled in this century by a succession of Roman governors. As a second-class imperial province, it did not have appointed to it the cream of the Roman civil service. Nonetheless, that civil service was the finest in the ancient world, and

A silver shekel from the time of the first Jewish revolt against Rome (A.D. 67) carries the inscription "Shekel of Israel" and, on the reverse side, the words "Jerusalem the Holy."

the men sent to rule the Jews were plagued by lack of understanding rather than by mismanagement or incompetence. Like most Romans, they did not comprehend Jewish ways and often wounded religious sensibilities.

On the Jewish side weariness of foreigners and foreign customs, fed by continuous mutual misunderstanding, caused the country to slide slowly but surely toward revolt. The Romans met increasing unrest with increasing severity. Uprising after uprising, incited by fanatically religious and nationalistic Zealots, was crushed with accelerating intensity. More and more the country fell into anarchy, and bitter struggles marked by treachery and bloodshed erupted between Jews, Samaritans, Greeks, and Syrians. Ruffian gangs of Zealots called *sicarii*, armed with hidden daggers, roamed the country cutting down hapless victims on both sides. False prophets arose to lure the anguished people with vain promises, while a succession of venal high priests brought the Temple into disrepute. Meanwhile the upper classes led lives of luxury and abandon that shocked the people. Torn by dissension, demoralized, the desperate Jews finally turned convulsively upon the Romans themselves, the mightiest power in the world. It was as if they were determined to destroy themselves. For their part the Romans, who loved nothing more than order, were ready to oblige.

Full-scale revolt broke out in A.D. 66 and lasted for seven years. Thanks mainly to the vivid accounts of Josephus, an eyewitness to the events, it is remembered as one of the bitterest, most titanic struggles of the ancient world. There were some early rebel successes, but the Romans, unaware of the fury of the storm, were content to leave the matter to local commanders. They were soon to regret this decision. Masada, "the Gibraltar of the Dead Sea," fell to the insurgents along with its huge cache of arms and supplies. The rebels came to Jerusalem, which had no Roman garrison, and interrupted the sacrifices to Caesar in the Temple. It was August of the year 66. War began in earnest.

The history of the struggle is long and confusing. There were plots and counterplots as Jewish groups, unable to unite against the Romans, fought each other with unspeakable ferocity. Yet at first, in spite of infighting and betrayal, things went well for the rebels. Not only Jerusalem but almost all Judea rallied to throw off foreign rule.

Two results followed. First, the conflict spread beyond the borders of Judea, and in cities like Caesarea and Alexandria Jews and their Gentile neighbors fell murderously upon one another. In the second place, Rome responded with force in Palestine. There had been only a few troops in the land, but now the Twelfth Legion, thirty thousand strong with its auxiliaries, was dispatched from Syria to put down the trouble. To the surprise of almost everyone it was defeated by a ragtag Jewish army, which sent the Roman survivors fleeing north leaving six thousand of their comrades dead upon the hills and valleys near the Jordan.

Rome had lost battles before. She did not lose wars. The full force of Roman arms fell upon the valiant but doomed Jews. In the end the land lay

Vespasian (right) led the Roman armies that marched to quell the Jewish rebellion, but in the midst of the campaign he was proclaimed emperor (A.D. 69), and it was left to his son Titus (below) to assume command and finally to capture Jerusalem. Later, Titus succeeded his father as emperor.

desolate, sown with Jewish graves instead of grain; and the Roman army, with two future emperors in command, stood before the walls of Jerusalem. The long and bitter siege was marked by a civil war that raged within the beleaguered city. Three groups sought, not control of the city, but each other's destruction. Their bloody fighting weakened defenses against the Romans and destroyed the grain supply, producing an awful starvation when Titus finally succeeded in sealing them off.

With an all-out effort the Romans breached the walls only to find the battle had barely begun. For 139 days they fought from house to house within the city itself before the sound of clashing arms ceased to resound from the ancient buildings and the flow of blood to redden the pavements. In spite of all Titus' efforts (for he meant to preserve it), the Temple was destroyed. The Zealots, who had alienated the Pharisees and other religionists and had become more gangsters than nationalists, fell back upon the citadel and the shrine. As one scholar rightly says, "It was not the pagan Caesar but the sacrilegious Jews who destroyed the Temple of the Lord." When the siege ended and quiet returned to the gentle hills around Jerusalem, the hot Judean summer sun shone through a pall of heavy smoke upon a smoldering Zion.

The Pharisees fled, leaving the Romans in possession of the treasury of the

The famous frieze from the Arch of Titus in the Roman Forum celebrates the victory over the Jews in A.D. *70. Soldiers are carrying the Menorah, sacred trumpets, and altar table out of the Temple in Jerusalem.*

Temple, but taking with them the greatest treasure the Jews possessed: their sacred Scriptures. The war that continued for three more years was no longer their affair; their eyes were fixed on the future and their concern was with the survival of Judaism. They knew it could survive without the Temple, for the synagogue had been firmly established for many years. But what steps could be taken to strengthen this central institution?

The Pharisees were the strongest surviving group in Palestinian Judaism. Under their leader, Johanan ben Zakkai, a follower of Hillel, they established themselves at Jamnia and reopened schools, reworked the ecclesiastical calendar in light of the destruction of the Temple, and devoted themselves to the question of the canon. Our story has shown that there was a canon before Jamnia. "The Law and the Prophets" were synonymous with worship in the synagogue, and latterly a third collection had found its place in popular esteem. But the recent Roman debacle and the loss of the Temple, symbol and center of Jewish unity, posed special threats to the faith. There was the danger that Jews living in the Dispersion without authoritative and well-defined Scriptures would allow the continuing spirit of Hellenism to erode their religious beliefs. There was the further danger from extreme and schismatic groups within Judaism. Apocalyptic thought and the Christians were considered a two-pronged threat. The one pushed the consummation of Israel's faith into another world; the other said that it had already taken place.

The purpose of the council at Jamnia was to counter these threats, to secure the Jewish heritage, and to adapt Judaism to its new situation. It was, in fact, a crystallization of much that had been going on in Pharisaic thought and in the wider world of the more liberal interpretations of Judaism. The most important outcome of its work was the closing of the canon, which involved a decision on what constituted inspired Scripture. As guidelines two major criteria were established. First, nothing that was not in harmony with the Torah could be included. This formulation of the superiority of the first five books led many to want to exclude Ezekiel, since in places it contradicts parts of the Torah, particularly Numbers. In the end the sheer importance of Ezekiel to Judaism, plus the fact that it was unchallenged as prophetic literature, led to its inclusion. Second, the rabbis defined the period from Moses to Ezra as the time when the authentic voice of religious authority was heard, and only books which came from that "prophetic period" could become canonical. The artificiality of this criterion is shown by the inclusion of some later books, such as Daniel, in the canon. But its success can be measured by the fact that almost all the apocalyptic writings were excluded.

There was controversy over many of the books, especially Ecclesiastes, the Song of Solomon, and Ecclesiasticus. The first two were admitted on the strength of the tradition linking them with Solomon, while the latter was excluded because it was known to have been written later than the prophetic period, in about 180 B.C. Yet it is an important part of Israel's Wisdom Literature, while the so-called Song of Solomon is a collection of Near Eastern love songs, of which many may not even be Hebraic.

All issues pertaining to the canon were not settled at this time; some questions remained. This was partly because the council did not have official status. Its members were not delegates who derived their authority from constituents, nor bishops who could impose their authority on the basis of tradition. Johanan ben Zakkai did succeed in getting many to acknowledge the decisions of the council, but the Talmud later quoted the Apocrypha as though they had canonical status, while St. Jerome, when he translated the Old Testament into Latin, was not sure of the status of the apocryphal collection. It was not until the sixteenth century that this question was finally resolved among Christians. The Protestant Reformers went in one direction and rejected the Apocrypha at the same time that the Catholic Council of Trent moved to affirm them as Holy Scripture.

On the whole the council at Jamnia did its work well. It checked the uncertainty about Jewish writings which the Septuagint and the Dead Sea Scrolls show to have existed before that time. It consolidated Judaism around its Holy Scripture so successfully that the faith was tided over the immediate crisis and was set upon a road of progress that has led to some of the notable religious achievements of western man.

3

A NEW CREATION: THE MAKING OF CHRISTIAN SCRIPTURE

A.D. 64 was a particularly grim year in Rome. The grandiose schemes of Nero for building an even greater city combined with his demented cunning to bring untold sufferings upon the populace. The fire, that awful holocaust, had spread like a prairie blaze through the slums of the city. Scores were dead or injured, many more homeless and destitute. The people were in an ugly mood, and the rumor was being spread that the Emperor himself had ordered the fire to be set. He very probably had. But with public anger mounting, a scapegoat must be found—and quickly. A particularly attractive one stood at hand. Among the many new religious groups in the city was a cult, drawn mostly from the lower, immigrant classes, which had caused trouble earlier when Claudius was on the throne and which had something in its beliefs about the world ending in a conflagration. Soon the police were everywhere, seeking out the followers of some Palestinian named "Chrestus," a man who had been put to death by a provincial governor. The soft nights were rent by the cries of Christians who were serving as torches for imperial garden parties. Before the people sickened of the spectacle, dozens of innocent men, women, and children had also fallen before the onslaught of wild beasts in the arenas of the Eternal City.

Thus did the Christian Church first come to the attention of the secular historians of the world. Note had been taken of some activity during the reign of Claudius, but it was not until Nero's time that Christians were clearly distinguished from the Jewish group out of which they had sprung.

The Christians, for their part, responded to the Neronian persecution in various ways. Undoubtedly some denied their faith and saved their lives. Many others, caring more for their Lord and their souls than for earthly life, held fast to their confession. And at about this time at least one of them produced a small book entitled *The Gospel of Jesus Christ*. His purpose was to give the Christian community's own account of the events out of which it had arisen, and of its martyred founder. He may have had in mind at the same time to show that Christianity was not subversive and ought not to be blamed for such evils as befell the Roman capital in this ill-starred year.

This little book, known to us as *The Gospel According to Mark*, was the first Gospel to be written, but it was not the first Christian literature. During sixteen or more years prior to the outbreak of Nero's madness, Paul, a Christian missionary who may have died in that same persecution of the year 64, had addressed letters to churches in widely scattered cities around the northeastern rim of the Mediterranean. But Paul was not the only, nor the first, missionary to carry the Christian gospel beyond the confines of its birthplace in Jerusalem. Of the five great cities of the Roman world—Rome, Alexandria, Antioch, Ephesus, and Athens—he founded a church in only one, Ephesus. Moreover, tradition tells us that missionaries were fanning out in all directions, not merely to the northwest. The disciple Thomas is said to have preached as far east as India, while the African Coptic Church claims Philip as its founder. Letters were being written, the teachings of Jesus were being passed by word of mouth, and tradition was being formed. As Christian communities sprang up, and visits or even letters from the apostles and disciples with personal knowledge of Jesus became rarer, more and more churches felt the need for a written account of his teaching and of the meaning of his life, death, and resurrection. So these collections of shared memories, these "Gospels," began to appear and to find use beyond the immediate communities for which they were written.

By the end of the first century A.D., when the rabbis of Jamnia had agreed upon the canon of Hebrew scripture, Chrstianity had spread to all parts of the Roman world and beyond, and a new set of sacred writings which we call the *New Testament* was well on its way to completion. The process by which these writings moved from oral tradition to canonical status was similar to that of the Old Testament, but was completed in a much shorter time, approximately three and a half centuries.

The Man of Galilee

IN THEME the two Testaments are similar in that both speak of God's redemptive action in history. There is a difference, however. The focus of the Old Testament is upon a people, while at the heart of the New is the commanding figure of a single person. Through city and town, in synagogue and home, Christian missionaries preached that God was working out the salvation of man in, through, and by this person, this Jesus Christ.

Object of faith and focal point of hope for millions—the subject of countless works of art and books beyond number—Jesus nonetheless remains practically unknown in certain respects. We do not, for example, even know what he looked like. The men who knew him, loved him, and devoted their lives to his service felt it unnecessary to record many of the kinds of biographical details that interest us today. What the biblical writers have given in the Gospels is not a "Life of Jesus," but a clear portrait of the one they believed to combine in his teaching and person the good news of God's love and mercy. Those who followed him "beheld his glory . . . glory as of the only Son from the Father" (John 1:14). This is not a subject for biography, but the glad tidings of a proclamation of faith.

Sometime toward the end of the long reign of Herod the Great (40 B.C.– 4 B.C.), Jesus was born in the Judean highlands south of Jerusalem, in Bethlehem, the birthplace of David. But Galilee, the northernmost area of Palestine, was the scene of his upbringing and the principal seat of his ministry. Apart from an appearance in the Temple at the age of twelve (Luke 2:41–50) we know nothing of his early life. It is possible to make inferences based upon known customs and conditions in the Palestine of his day, but the biblical records are silent. When Jesus appears again in the sacred narrative he is a young man, probably about thirty. And he is in the south, near the place where the Jordan River empties into the Dead Sea. Here his cousin, John the Baptist, was carrying on an extensive ministry.

Even in his lifetime John had come to be regarded as a prophet, not unlike those of old. The people eagerly if uncomfortably heard his sermons and his demands for repentance. The present order is passing away, he said, and the long-awaited Messiah is about to usher in a new age. Repent, therefore, for the kingdom of heaven is at hand.

The faithful among the Jews had long desired such an event and had earnestly prayed for it. It would be, they believed, a time of terrible judgment upon the enemies of Israel and a vindication for the Sons of Abraham. But John had given a twist to the idea and was really saying something quite different. The kingdom was coming all right, but in order to share in it character and conduct would be important, not the mere fact of being a Jew. In a radical departure from traditional thought, John insisted upon baptism—a baptism of repentance! Baptism was part of the ritual for a convert; to demand it of Jews by birth was to call into question one of the fundamental beliefs on which Judaism had been built.

Jesus accepted baptism from John—"for thus it is fitting to fulfill all righteousness," Matthew quotes him as saying (3:15). After a sojourn in the wilderness he made his way northward to his native Galilee. From village to village he went about healing the sick and preaching "the gospel of the kingdom"—the wonderful things of God. "The time is fulfilled," he said, "and the kingdom of God is at hand: repent ye and believe the gospel" (Mark 1:15).

At last he came to his home town of Nazareth, and before the assembled

OPVS GENTILIS DE FABRIANO — M·CCCC·CHEMENSIS·MAII

165

GENTILE DA FABRIANO SEC.XV
L'ADORAZIONE DEI MAGI

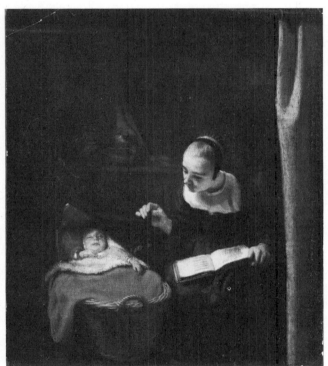

The Christmas Story, most beloved of all biblical narratives, has been a favorite subject in Christian art from the earliest days of the Church. An elaborate fifteenth-century altar piece (left) portrays not only the Holy Family, the Magi, and the traditional animals, but a vast procession thronging to celebrate the Nativity. A more intimate scene by Nicholas Maes (above) captures the tenderness of Mary with her newborn child. In a tenth-century German miniature (top), the Wise Men bring news of the birth of a Savior to King Herod, who motions to his soldiers to seek out and destroy the baby. Warned in a dream of Herod's wrath, Joseph flees with Mary and Jesus into Egypt, as shown in a carved door panel from modern Nigeria (right).

congregation, in the synagogue where he had grown up, rose and read from Isaiah: "The spirit of the Lord is upon me, because he has anointed me to preach good news to the poor. He has sent me to proclaim release to the captives and recovering of sight to the blind, to set at liberty the oppressed, to proclaim the acceptable year of the Lord" (Isa. 61:1, 2). As Jesus sat down he added, "Today this scripture has been fulfilled in your hearing." They were astonished at him and asked each other, "Is this not the carpenter, the son of Mary?" And he saw their incredulity, despite all he had been doing, and remembered aloud—referring to Scripture (I Kings 17: 8–16; II Kings 5: 1–14)—how in ancient Israel in days of distress sometimes only a Gentile had been able to receive divine help.

The people were aghast at his presumption. They had known him since childhood and would not hear such words from him; they rose up indignantly and threw him out. "A prophet," said Jesus wryly, "is not without honor, except in his own country, and among his own kin, and in his own house" (Mark 6: 1–6; Luke 4: 16–29).

He taught for a time in Capernaum and along the shores of the Sea of Galilee, and began to call others to share in his work. "Follow me," he said to simple fishermen by the lakeside, and they left their nets, their old lives, even their families, and followed him. Still others joined themselves to the company of disciples. Nearly everywhere they were preceded by Jesus' growing fame, and great crowds gathered to him from the countryside and all the neighboring towns. So great at times was the press of people that he could not find a quiet place to eat or sleep, and to be alone he often had to withdraw before dawn across the lake or into the desert hills—even there they would follow, sometimes going without food to see him. Many came in quest of healing of their diseased bodies and minds, and others to hear the message of this man who talked as no other they had heard.

For Jesus seemed to have a genius for speaking to the inmost needs of his hearers, and indeed of all men in all ages. He offered no fixed creeds, no writings, no institutions; only God and man's relation to Him. To those who longed to know God he said, "Ask, and it shall be given you; seek, and you will find; knock, and it will be opened to you" (Matt. 7:7; Luke 9:11). He cut through man's many façades and saw his fearful striving for security and frantic building of systems and adherence to them for what they were.

Trust God, Jesus said to the multitudes—and spoke of Him as Father, not as a remote almighty majesty. "Look at the birds of the air . . . your heavenly Father feeds them. . . . Consider the lilies of the field . . . even Solomon in all his glory was not arrayed like one of these. . . . O men of little faith. . . . do not be anxious. . . . But seek first his kingdom and his righteousness, and all these things shall be yours as well" (Matt. 6:26–33). This was a fundamental statement of his life and teaching: if man rightly understands his relation with God everything else will fall into place.

Always he spoke to them of the love of God and His will for men. Nothing must be allowed to come between man and God: not fears, nor riches, nor family obligations, nor the expectations of society, nor the formalities of worship. "God is not worshiped in temples made with hands," he said to a Samaritan woman, "but in spirit and in truth."

Repeatedly Jesus talked of the kingdom of God, emphasizing its goal as the spread of the love of God and the love of neighbor, and that its aims were not directed toward earthly power. He spoke of it in many ways: as a present reality, as something that was to come, as a seed growing secretly—but always as worthy of man's total devotion here and now. "The kingdom of heaven is at hand." It is the pearl of great price, it is a treasure for the sake of which a man sells all he has (Matt. 13:44–45). "It is like a net which was thrown into the sea and gathered fish of every kind" (Matt. 13:47).

The kingdom is a way of life, a pilgrimage toward fulfilling the will of God in all things—a task unending as the wind, permanent as time, and difficult as life itself. "Enter by the narrow gate; for the gate is wide and the way is easy, that leads to destruction, and those who enter by it are many. For the gate is narrow and the way is hard, that leads to life, and those who find it are few" (Matt. 7:13–14).

No one should assume by these words, however, that Jesus viewed the kingdom of God as man's work. At no point does he speak of man's building the kingdom. The ways of the kingdom are mercy, love, and service that is its own reward, but the kingdom is God's gift and God's alone. "Fear not, little flock, it is the Father's good pleasure to give you the kingdom. Sell your possessions and give alms; provide yourselves with purses that do not grow old, with a treasure in the heavens that does not fail, where no thief approaches you and no moths destroy. For where your treasure is, there will your heart be also" (Luke 12:32–34). Few things show more clearly the gulf between Jesus' view and those of the rabid nationalists among his contemporaries.

Some of Jesus' teachings were reminders of what had been taught in Judaism or at least could be found in the Law and the Prophets, though he often gave them a new impact: love of God and neighbor, care for the poor and oppressed; justice, mercy, humility.

Other teachings were new and strange, hard for people to understand or accept or even take seriously, then as now. Love your enemies, he said; do good to those who hurt or insult you; it's no great credit to you to do good only to your own friends and family. Turn the other cheek when a man hits you. If he steals your coat, give him your cloak too. Don't resist evil, but respond to evil with good. Forgive your brother not only seven times, but seventy times seven—forgive as you want to be forgiven. What you are inwardly in your heart is your real self; if you think adultery, you have already committed it; if you hate, you are the same as a murderer. Yet whatever the waste or evil of your life, God's love is always available to those who turn to Him—so he told them in the Parable of the Prodigal Son (Luke 15:11–32).

People flocked to this man who responded to their needs and knew their

IA ORANA MARIA

"*And Jesus increased in wisdom and in stature.*" The Gospels give few details of Jesus' youth, but mother and child have been portrayed by artists of every period. The formal Byzantine style of Cimabue's "Madonna Enthroned with Angels" (top, left) contrasts sharply with Gauguin's painting of the same subject in a Tahitian setting (center). An unknown Spanish painter of the fifteenth century depicts the twelve-year-old Jesus (below, left) found by Mary and Joseph among the learned doctors of the Temple and explaining, "*Did you not know I must be in my Father's house?*" Nothing more is recorded of Jesus' life until he was baptized at the age of thirty by his cousin, John, and entered the wilderness to be tempted by the devil, as shown in a panel by Duccio (above).

hearts, and talked to them in terms of familiar things such as bread, and lost sheep, and sowing and reaping, and catching fish. And his hearers remembered what he said, for he taught in pithy statements, easily recalled.

> Blessed are the poor in spirit, for theirs is the kingdom
>   of heaven.
> Blessed are those who mourn, for they shall be
>   comforted.
> Blessed are the meek, for they shall inherit the earth.
> Blessed are those who hunger and thirst for righteousness,
>   for they shall be satisfied.
> Blessed are the merciful, for they shall obtain mercy.
> Blessed are the pure in heart, for they shall see God.
> Blessed are the peacemakers, for they shall be called sons
>   of God.
> Blessed are those who are persecuted for righteousness'
>   sake, for theirs is the kingdom of heaven.
>   —Matthew 5:3–10

He taught too in parables, easily retold. Who is my neighbor, then? asked a scribe on one occasion. And Jesus told him a parable. "A certain man was going down from Jerusalem to Jericho, and he fell among thieves." Robbed and beaten, he lay by the roadside while two religious men of Israel passed him by, one after the other. But then a Samaritan, despised in Jewish society, happened along the road, stopped, and bound up his wounds and took him to an inn, where he left money for his care. "Which of these three," asked Jesus, "do you think proved neighbor to the man who fell among the robbers?" (Luke 10:29–37).

What astonished people was the authority of his words, for he spoke as if he *knew* the truth and had a right to say what it was, not like the scribes, who quoted Scripture and rabbinic interpretation in an attempt to establish their teaching. "You have heard it said of old," said Jesus, "but I say unto you. . . ."

Jesus' tone of authority was not universally endearing, however. At one time his own family apparently thought him mad. And the more educated or formally religious treated him with scorn as a man who ran around in bad company because he ministered to the outcasts of society. "Why does your teacher eat with tax collectors and sinners?" the well-educated Pharisees inquired of his followers (for this no good Jew of his day would do). And when his disciples were hungry and plucked ears of corn to eat, the Pharisees complained to him directly, "Look, your disciples are doing what is not lawful to do on the Sabbath." "Son . . . your sins are forgiven," Jesus said to a man with palsy. But the scribes whispered among themselves, He is blaspheming! Only God can forgive sins.

Again and again he said and did things that went against his critics' sense of propriety. Even John's followers asked him, Why do your disciples not fast as we and the Pharisees do? And they came to him from John in prison, asking, Are you really the one we expected, or should we look for someone else?

Still the common people came to hear; expectant throngs were everywhere. And many found in him the meaning of life, and left all and followed him. Some must have been surprised at their reception by Jesus, who asked them hard questions and told them disturbing things. Which of you, he said, "desiring to build a tower, does not first sit down and count the cost, whether he has enough to complete it. . . . Or what king, going to encounter another king in war, will not sit down first and take counsel whether he is able with ten thousand to meet him who comes against him with twenty thousand?" (Luke 14:28–32). Discipleship was not merely for the asking. There is no way, in brief pages, to cover his full teaching or the varied events of his life as recounted in the records. And we have, of course, only a very partial account of his ministry, despite the apparent profusion of detail. Thus one of the Gospels ends, quaintly, "And there are also many other things which Jesus did . . . which, if they should be written every one, I suppose even the world itself could not contain the books that should be written" (John 21:25).

His disregard for wealth and position and his seeming disrespectful talk about ritual and the Temple offended many. The professional religionists, particularly the scribes who interpreted the Law, were horrified by his attitude toward time-honored regulations and precepts. And many Pharisees, concerned for a valid application of the Law to their times, were outraged by what they considered his cavalier treatment of it. To Jesus, however, the Law and the Temple worship as carried out in his day were a barrier between man and God. Besides, he said, it does no good to cleanse the outside of the cup if the inside remains full of wickedness. What good is it to be so careful in the details of worship, if justice toward man and love of God are neglected?

When they said he healed by the power of the Devil he lashed out at them in anger. He was not afraid to speak out, and his replies could be more scathing than the attack. "You brood of vipers!" he cried at them. "How can you speak good, when you are evil?" "But woe to you, scribes and Pharisees, hypocrites! because you shut the kingdom of heaven against men. . . . Woe to you, blind guides. . . . you are like whitewashed tombs, which outwardly appear beautiful, but within they are full of dead men's bones and all uncleanness" (Matt. 12:34; 23:13, 16, 27).

Increasingly hostile faces began to appear among the crowds and threats were heard against Jesus. The Pharisees conferred as to how to deal with him. Not only was he blasphemous, presumptuous—disregarding the Law and ancient ceremonial precepts; not only did he openly show his scorn of them, the leaders of society and religion; but with his great following he might draw the attention of the Romans and perhaps get all Palestine in trouble. And like the prophets before him Jesus contended there ought to be no line of distinction between true worship and life itself—and like the prophets before him, he found no cordial hearing among the authorities. Finally he had to

Jesus taught by word and deed. A miniature in the Armenian Gospels of 1262 (top) shows Jesus talking with the woman at the well, while his disciples and townspeople register surprise at his speaking to a Samaritan. Another illumination from the same century (near right) illustrates the famous parable of the Widow's Mite. "The Calling of Matthew" (above), by the Dutch artist von Hemessen, depicts the rigorous demand that a disciple be prepared to forsake family and friends to serve the Kingdom of God. Two illustrations from the tenth-century Reichenau Gospels (below, opposite) portray Jesus being awakened by his frightened disciples to still a storm on the Sea of Galilee, and casting demons out of a possessed man into pigs, which plunge headlong into the lake. In his painting of the Sermon on the Mount (upper right), French artist Claude Lorrain emphasizes the pastoral imagery of Jesus' words.

leave Galilee, yet in Judea and Jerusalem he was to meet with even greater hostility.

Opposition with all its risks was to be expected. Misunderstanding, however, was as great a danger, and there were clear signs that it underlay some of his popularity. Many, in thinking of him as the Messiah, the Anointed One of the house of David, supposed he came to deliver the Jews from their bondage. Jewish tradition envisaged the Messiah in a number of ways: sometimes he was understood as a spiritual savior, sometimes as an apocalyptic judge at the end of days. But more often in restless Palestine of the first century he was seen as a political deliverer. With the country close to rebellion, the tormented Jews longed more than ever for a leader, a king, who would throw out the hated Romans. Too frequently those who followed Jesus showed their misapprehension by hailing him as that sort of leader. Why should he not be? He was clearly full of strength. The reports of his miracles, his talk about the coming kingdom, and the strange quality of power that attracted so many, all increased their expectations. Several times he himself eluded the crowd, knowing that they "meant to come and seize him and proclaim him king" (John 6:15).

He consistently refused the nationalistic role in which many had cast him, and seems to have avoided use of the term "Messiah," preferring instead the phrase "Son of Man." This was an honored Old Testament title designating one who stood in a special relationship with God; it did not have nationalistic overtones. The crowds began to thin as many disappointed zealots drifted away to seek other ways of fulfilling their hopes.

The disciples, men of their time, were not immune to such longings either. As he sensed a growing perplexity among his closest followers Jesus apparently felt the need to withdraw temporarily from the popular gaze and take stock of his mission. In the northeastern desert near the Hellenistic city of Caesarea-Philippi he questioned his disciples as to what the masses thought about him. As might be expected, they told him that men called him many different things, and compared him with various figures from the history of Israel. When Jesus asked who they, his disciples, thought he was, Peter—impetuous always—blurted out: "You are the Christ, the Son of the living God." Which is to say: "You are the Messiah who will fulfill in our midst the ancient promises of God."

Jesus began to tell his disciples what the role of the Messiah really was (Matt. 16:17 ff.). He would not be what they or the multitudes thought. There would be no victorious armies, no glory as the world understands it; instead there would be suffering and death. The Son of Man himself "must go to Jerusalem and suffer many things from the elders and chief priests and scribes, and be killed, and on the third day be raised."

"God forbid, Lord!" said Peter, voicing their consternation. "This shall never happen to you." But Jesus rebuked him and spoke again of his coming death, adding that any man who wanted to be his disciple must likewise "take up his cross and follow me."

From that time forward he devoted himself more and more to the instruction of this small band of faithful companions who, though often perplexed by the direction of his ministry and the meaning of his words, clung tenaciously to the leader they were convinced had the "words of life."

With the awareness that it would not be fitting for a prophet to die outside of Jerusalem, he was more and more drawn toward the holy city, there to grapple with the darkness and overcome it so that the full light of God's glory might shine upon men. So he went up gradually toward Jericho and then up to Jerusalem, with his disciples and a train of followers, teaching and healing still.

Finally, when the great crowds that came for the Passover Festival were milling about the streets as holiday crowds do, Jesus entered the city riding on an ass, surrounded by excited people who spread their garments and fresh-cut branches in the way and cried, "Hosanna to the Son of David! Blessed is he who comes in the name of the Lord."

Years earlier the prophet Zechariah had written of the coming Messiah:

> Rejoice greatly, O daughter of Zion!
>> Shout aloud, O daughter of Jerusalem!
> Lo, your king comes to you;
>> triumphant and victorious is he,
> humble and riding on an ass,
>> on a colt the foal of an ass.

Jesus' followers, and no doubt others as well, knew the prophet's words and would clearly see the implications. So would the priestly authorities.

Soon there was another incident which showed the boldness and sense of fulfillment that marked Jesus' actions. The massive Temple of Herod, by almost any comparison an impressive structure, was the symbol for Judaism of God's presence and a visible reminder of past days of national greatness and of the future hope of Israel. On this spot Abraham was said to have offered to sacrifice Isaac. Here, except for brief periods, the sacrificial fires of the Hebrew people had burned continually for over a thousand years. Here King David himself planned to build the Temple which his son Solomon did actually erect and dedicate. Here the exiles wept for joy upon their return. To this holiest of places the pious among the Jews were now drawn to offer their prayers and sacrifices as countless ancestors had done before them.

Jesus had been there many times before. We do not know when he first expressed his indignation at the sight that met his eyes in the Court of the Gentiles: pilgrims from everywhere trying to buy offerings at the tables of the usurious money-changers and then going to the place of sacrifice. The money-changers themselves, with their devices for converting various currencies into special Temple money—with their animals, their sacks of grain, doves, and other items offered for sale at outrageous prices—they filled the air with their hucksters' chatter and cluttered up the court meant for worship and prayer.

Deep compassion and bold conviction marked Jesus' ministry. Rembrandt's renowned "Hundred Guilder Print" (opposite) shows him welcoming the sick, the outcast, and the young; the same artist's moving "Head of Christ" reveals a face etched by the suffering of men. Shortly after his triumphal entry into Jerusalem, depicted below in a relief from a fourth-century sarcophagus, Jesus indignantly threw the money-changers out of the Temple court, a scene dramatically recorded by El Greco (bottom). The authority of Christ is emphasized in a sixth-century diptych (left) of the enthroned Lord with Peter and Paul.

Jesus fell upon them, whip in hand. "It is written," he said, overturning tables and scattering animals, " 'My house shall be a house of prayer; but you have made it a den of robbers' " (Matt. 21:12–13; Luke 19:45–46; see also Isa. 56:7 and Jer. 7:11).

For reasons not entirely clear—perhaps because of his popularity with the people—the authorities took no immediate steps against him. Jesus taught each day in the Temple, and his enemies sought by flattery and cunning to induce him to betray himself in the eyes of either Jewish or Roman authorities or both. "Tell us," they said, "by what authority you do these things." His reply was not without dry humor. I'll answer you, he replied, if you will tell me by whose authority John baptized. But they could not, for any answer would have embarrassed them. Then neither will I tell you, he retorted (Matt. 20:1–8).

With an air of honest confusion as to their duties under Jewish and Roman law, "Teacher," they said to him, "we know that you speak and teach rightly, and show no partiality, but truly teach the way of God. Is it lawful for us to give tribute to Caesar or not?" Jesus called for a coin and asked whose head was on it. "Caesar's," they said. "Then," he advised them, "render to Caesar the things that are Caesar's, and to God the things that are God's."

Yet for all his insight into the motives of his disputants, and for all his ability to deal with them, he did not delude himself as to the lengthening shadows that were overtaking his career. He had taken a public stand, and his claim to the lordship of the Temple was enough to galvanize the bitter enmity of priests and leaders into action. Now they took counsel "how they might put him to death." It must be both cautious and swift; a badly managed arrest or a lengthy trial might stir up the populace and make the Romans declare martial law. How could it be done in just the right way? The answer came in the person of Judas Iscariot.

Jesus could hardly have been unaware of the intentions of his enemies. The records say he knew what was to come—had long predicted it, and probably suspected who might turn traitor. But his sense of impending crisis did not lead him to withdraw or to protect himself. He continued to appear among the people, teaching and disputing with his opponents. In the evenings, as was his habit, he went out from the city and sought a quiet place where he could pray. On Thursday evening, before the Passover began on Friday night, he ate with his disciples in an upper room near Herod's palace. There he talked with them of many things. As he blessed the bread and broke it he said to them, "This is my body, which is given for you: this do in remembrance of me." And so with the wine, when he had given thanks, "This is my blood of the new testament, which is shed for many."

During supper Jesus washed his disciples' feet, saying, "What I am doing you do not know now, but afterward you will understand" (John 13:7). When they had finished they sang a hymn, and then left Jerusalem and went out to their customary place, on a hill, among olive trees. There Judas came with his new companions and identified Jesus with a kiss and the greeting, "Hail, Master."

Events now moved swiftly. Jesus was taken to be questioned by the former high priest, the corrupt Annas, who sent him to his son-in-law Caiaphas, then holder of the office. He in turn, with others in authority, brought him to Pilate, the Roman governor. The charges they put forward to Pilate included blasphemy against God and sedition against the Roman state. The first was of no concern to the governor, but the second touched his vital interests.

The exact role of Pilate in the condemnation and death of Jesus is not known. The Gospel writers, perhaps wanting to show that Christianity was not a subversive element in the Empire, later emphasized that Pilate thought Jesus innocent of the charges brought against him, but was forced by expediency to put him to death. It is quite possible that this represents solid historical fact. There is abundant evidence that Roman governors were notoriously uninterested in adjudicating religious quarrels brought to them by provincials. Still, there is no question that Jesus' death was by crucifixion, and this could not have occurred without a judgment and a specific order from the governor. At the very least, it seems likely that Pilate collaborated with a small group of men whose vested interests were threatened.

Five days after Jesus' "triumphal entry" many of those who had shouted "Hosanna to the Son of David!" stood near a cross and read the title over the dying man's head: "Jesus of Nazareth, King of the Jews." In a surprisingly short time—altogether six hours—Jesus cried out with a loud voice, "Father, into thy hands I commit my spirit!" and his body slumped, lifeless. Because of the Passover, the Jewish authorities wanted all three of the crucified men buried at once. The Romans, who normally left bodies to rot on their crosses, agreed so as not to offend Jewish religious sensibilities. Joseph of Arimathea came forward to claim Jesus' body. He was a rich and influential man, interested in Jesus and his teachings, who had dissented from the action taken against him. Thrusting a spear into Jesus' side to make sure he was dead, the Romans handed the body over to Joseph. Quite near the place of execution was a garden, with a new rock-hewn tomb which Joseph had intended for himself. Here Jesus was laid, and the tomb sealed and a guard set to prevent disorder.

Had that been the end of the matter, as anyone might reasonably have expected, Jesus would perhaps have been remembered by history only as a minor figure in the prophetic line, a briefly popular leader swiftly disposed of by the authorities in the turmoil of restless Judea. But the story of the Bible, indeed the entire history of the western world, was transformed by the spread of news first reported by some women who visited Jesus' tomb the Sunday after he was buried. They were so stunned by what they found they "fled from the tomb; for trembling and astonishment had come upon them." They hurried to the disciples with a startling account of an empty tomb and of an angel who told them not to seek Jesus among the dead, but among the living. Jesus had risen! The Lord was alive!

This news must have electrified the small band who had seen their master humiliated and destroyed like a criminal. Could the report possibly be true? Or were the women merely telling idle tales? But any shock or doubt was

The Crucifixion and Resurrection of Christ are the central events of the New Testament. An ivory casket lid shows moments during Jesus' last days (below, from left): Jesus in the garden of Gethsemane; Judas arriving with Roman soldiers; Peter denying Christ; Jesus on trial before Pilate; Judas being paid as Jesus is led away. A fragment from a building in Caesarea dedicated to the Emperor Tiberius (left) is the only archaeological find bearing the name of governor "PILATUS" (second line of inscription). The Crucifixion is portrayed along with the suicide of Judas on an ivory panel from the fifth century (below). The angel and women at the empty tomb are shown in a golden panel from Lüneborg (near right) and in an ivory panel (far right) which also portrays Christ ascending into heaven.

soon replaced by a spirit of confident joy and assurance. For they were soon testifying to all who would listen that Jesus was alive and had appeared to them, not once, but many times. To the disciples and all who accepted their testimony this meant that the long quest for the eternal God had ended. The spiritual pilgrimage of Abraham, Isaac, Jacob, the prophets, Israel herself, had been fulfilled in this Jesus of Nazareth, who was the Christ, the Messiah. "God," Paul was later to say, "was in Christ reconciling the world to himself" (II Cor. 5:19). And more—through the death and resurrection of this lowly Galilean, salvation is offered to all men who will repent and believe.

This was the heart of the message the disciples began proclaiming some fifty days after the first report of the Resurrection. There were scoffers then as now who called the affair a trick, a plot, an illusion, saying the disciples had stolen and hidden the body. But Jesus' followers were unshakably confident, united and mobilized by a new spirit of joy and peace, boldly preaching their "good news" in the face of skepticism, ridicule, and opposition.

Soon the message had spread beyond Jerusalem. Within weeks it was heard outside Palestine. And within a few years it was being proclaimed in every part of the known world. By 381 the religion based upon this gospel was the official religion of that Empire whose representative in Judea had put Jesus to death.

The Young Church

THE FIRST TASK the earliest Christians undertook was to testify to the living Christ himself—to this great event which had brought with it hope and new possibilities for man. They were thus not primarily teachers nor churchmen, but witnesses. Everywhere Christians were attesting to their belief that God had spoken decisively in Jesus, that He had raised him from the dead and designated him both Lord and Christ. The eternal life Jesus had taught them about was real. In him they were in touch with it.

These "first proclaimers of the fact" had no special writings. Like other Jews they continued to regard the Old Testament as Holy Scripture, the authoritative written revelation of God to man. But believing that God now revealed Himself in Jesus, they saw those Scriptures in a new and distinctive light, with the strong emphasis upon *fulfillment* that is found throughout early Christian preaching. Jesus was the fulfillment of the ageless promises of God enshrined in the sacred writings. Passages formerly dark and vague became at once brilliant and precise in their reference to Christ: "The stone which the builders rejected," said Psalm 118:22, "the same has become the head of the corner." Who, viewing the rejection and exaltation of the Church's Lord, could doubt this was a description of him?

Many prophetic passages dealing with the triumph of the sufferer and the vindication of God's Word and ancient pledge were now brought together by Christians and circulated as "testimonies" to show that He had fulfilled His promises in Jesus. Prominent in such collections was Isaiah's description of the "Suffering Servant." This use of Scripture underlined the Christian emphasis upon the continuity between historic Jewish beliefs and the new faith, proving that the "good news" about Jesus was no haphazard occurrence but part of God's design, clear in authoritative writings. Small wonder that Christians have always resisted attempts from inside and outside the Church to diminish the importance of or to do away with the Old Testament!

Important as they were, however, the Old Testament and the testimonies drawn from it did not stand at the heart of Christian preaching. The core of that preaching was the gospel, the message of salvation centering in belief in the Resurrection. Today the term "gospel" is almost exclusively associated with a certain body of writings. But it was at first oral, and only later came to be used for the writings because they contain the original spoken word. There was, then, a gospel—a message—before the Gospels. It was urgent and authoritative in the early Church, its authority guaranteed by the evidence of eyewitnesses and by the new life that sprang from it.

The form of this gospel, this "good news" of the early preaching, is thought to have been rather consistent, always including at least the following points: (1) The plan of God seen in the Jewish Scriptures has reached its climax and the promises made through the prophets have been fulfilled. (2) This has been done in Jesus of Nazareth, who carried on a healing and teaching ministry among men. (3) The enemies of God through ignorance and hostility conspired against His anointed, treated him cruelly, and finally hung him upon a cross to die. (4) But God raised him from the dead, exalted him to the right hand of Power, and through him offers salvation to all men. (5) Repent, therefore, and be baptized in the name of Jesus Christ.

The substance of this message, particularly prominent in Acts 2—10, may be found throughout the New Testament. Scholars call it the *kerygma*, a Greek word referring to the content of something proclaimed. Around the kerygma began to gather other recollections of Jesus, not yet written but passed on by oral tradition.

The most important parts of the Christian tradition, and the first to be written down, were of course those that met the needs of the emerging Church. Accounts of the Last Supper, the central rite of the worshiping community, and of Passion Week, so necessary for the instruction of converts, were probably first to be committed to writing. Here at the very beginning of the reduction of the oral tradition to written form we see the principles that were to operate throughout: the writings of the Church grew out of the needs of the Church, as well as the natural desire to have a true record of the Messiah's life and teaching, especially as eyewitnesses to them became fewer. At first there must have been rather simple requirements for worship and instruction. But almost immediately problems of discipline and the need to preserve the tradition and protect it against heresy from within and threats from without made clear the necessity for authoritative written Scriptures.

These problems and needs grew as Christian preachers went north, east, south, and west proclaiming their gospel—everywhere telling the story of Jesus. The message of salvation for *all* men was readily received by those who had little or no status; by the disenfranchised, the poor, and by women. Many, too, increasingly found the old state religions meaningless and turned to this new religion that spoke to the individual on a personal level. But Christianity did not sweep all before it. More often than not Gentiles saw the preaching of the cross as "foolishness," and opposition from Jewish communities which rejected the Messianic claims made for Jesus was increasingly intense. In Jerusalem itself, the home of apostolic activity, the eventual ferocity of this antagonism caused many to flee the city. Together with the command to "go into all the world," this was one cause of the explosion of missionary effort in every direction.

The Jewish Christians of Jerusalem sought to be good Jews. They participated in synagogue worship and went faithfully to the Temple to offer prayers. At the same time, they did not merely lead their own individual lives but lived in an *ecclesia*, a "congregation"—a close fellowship of believers in the Resurrection, sharing their worldly goods (Acts 1:12–26; 4:32–5:11). They wrote little or nothing during this time. As Jews they reverenced and studied the Scriptures, while as Christians they discussed and meditated upon the words and doings of Jesus, still fresh in their memories. Since they were part of the religious structure of Judaism they would see little need or purpose in organizing their fellowship.

But this unstructured community living in the dazzling light of what had so recently taken place, soon found that not only organization but some clear idea of accepted tradition was necessary. From the very first, converts streamed into it (Acts 1:15; 2:41, 47; 6:7). The stream became a river and the river a flood. To meet this rapid expansion a division of labor was made: men called deacons were elected to serve the internal needs of the fellowship so that the apostles would be free to preach (Acts 6:1–6). The evidence in Acts shows that this was not a hard and fast division; deacons, too, were out proclaiming the Messiah. One of them, Stephen, was killed by a "lynch mob" for doing so (Acts 6:8–7:60).

The murder of Stephen was spontaneous. But organized opposition, especially in Jerusalem, became a serious threat to the Christian fellowship and took the form of outright violence aimed at the leaders of the young Church. Most of them left the city and continued their missionary activity wherever the chance presented itself. A few chose not to leave or could not get away, and some of these were imprisoned or put to death.

As the gospel spread far beyond Palestine and increasing numbers of non-Jews confessed Jesus as their Lord, the question of the relation of Judaism to the new faith became a burning issue. Would converts submit to Jewish demands? Judaism itself, whose ethics had attracted many Gentiles to the synagogues during the early Roman Empire, solved the practical question by a sort of half-membership: a Gentile who did not wish to satisfy all requirements of the Jewish Law would become a "godfearer," that is, a man attached to the synagogue but not a full member. But this presented serious theological problems to Christians. If salvation lay in Christ, then what possible role could the Jewish Law play? Must one become a Jew in order to enter the Christian community and share in salvation? Already at Antioch a vigorous missionary Church had tacitly assumed that the answer was No, while the Church in Jerusalem was taking it to be Yes indeed!

Antioch—where followers of Jesus were first given the name Christians—was the former imperial capital of the Seleucids. In apostolic times this splendid city was third to Rome and Alexandria in its importance in the Roman Empire. A thriving cosmopolitan center halfway between Palestine and Asia Minor, it was a perfect setting for the expanding mission to the Gentiles. In the ensuing struggle, the issue for the Jerusalem group was the continuity of God's action in the history of His people. For the Antiochenes —including many who had fled persecution in Jerusalem—it was the sufficiency of Jesus' death and resurrection for salvation. Among the more eloquent spokesmen for Antioch's position was the brilliant, rabbinically trained convert named Paul, who at one time had been a rabid anti-Christian. To him the sacrifice of Christ was completely and uniquely sufficient. Quite apart from practical arguments, he felt the Judaic demands should be rejected on theological grounds, and in the end his position prevailed. Leaders in Jerusalem eventually agreed that the Antioch missionaries could accept Gentiles into their fellowship without requiring them first to become Jews (Acts 15:1–35). But for itself, the Jerusalem Church laid emphasis upon the requirements of the Law—and later the inheritors of this outlook, considering themselves the truly pious, moved into oblivion, while the preachers of universality instead of separatism went from victory to victory among the pagans of the eastern Mediterranean.

Letters from Paul

MOST OF THE CREDIT for these victories is commonly assigned to St. Paul, whose towering figure dominates our knowledge of early Christianity. Yet he came onto the stage relatively late; missionaries were on the roads before him, and many of the trends he followed had been set in motion already. But this is not to deny his genius or his immeasurable contribution to Christianity. A good deal is known about Paul: he was a Jew from Tarsus in Asia Minor. Apparently he inherited Roman citizenship. Like other promising rabbinical Pharisees of his day, he had gone to Jerusalem for study and sat at the feet of the godly Gamaliel, one of the greatest rabbis. As a Jew of Asia Minor trained in the Holy City, Paul was singularly well equipped to interpret to

Gentiles the new faith, which owed so much to Judaism. The energy of his earlier persecution of Christians—even in "consenting" to the stoning of Stephen—is now remembered as background to the almost incredible endurance and unflagging enterprise of his Christian life and preaching. It is a quirk of history that this man, who had a hand in the death of the first Christian martyr, should himself be one of the most famous to die for the gospel.

His complete reversal of dedication came about, by his own testimony, through a soul-shaking vision of Christ on the road to Damascus (Gal. 1:11–17; Acts 26:4–23). On a mission against the Christians of that city, Paul was suddenly struck down by an overpowering awareness of the One whose people he sought to destroy. The experience convinced him that Jesus lived, as the Christians claimed, and that the risen Lord called him to become a witness instead of a persecutor. Henceforth, his sole aim in life was to be faithful to Christ.

Paul's movements in the years immediately following are not entirely clear to us today. He did go on to Damascus, where he astounded everyone by preaching that Jesus was alive and was the Son of God, offering salvation to all men. The fury of the surprised Jews, who had expected him to be their right arm against the Christians, forced him to flee over the wall of the city at night. There was a time of withdrawal into the desert, and then a short visit with the leaders of the Jerusalem Church. He made his way back to his home city of Tarsus, there apparently intending to live out his life as a witness to Christ, who had called him, as Paul said in recounting the vision that altered his life, "in order that I might preach him among the Gentiles."

But events were afoot that were to draw him to the very center of Christian missionary activity. About ten years after Paul's vision on the Damascus road, Barnabas, a Jew from Cyprus but a member of the Jerusalem Church, was sent to Antioch to investigate the practices of that rapidly developing Christian center. He became persuaded of the rightness of the Antiochene mission to the Gentiles and determined to undertake a similar effort on his home island. In preparation he sought out Paul in Tarsus, who agreed to go with him, and in the forties of the first century they were sent officially from Antioch on a missionary journey through Cyprus and southern Asia Minor.

Although the Antioch Church accepted Gentile converts without requiring that they first become Jews, the question still hung fire everywhere. Various answers had been given in practice. Peter himself, a stalwart of the Jerusalem Church, had baptized the Roman centurion Cornelius without any demands beyond a confession of faith (Acts 10:1–11:18). Called to task for this, he satisfied the Church that he was obeying a vision which commanded him to join this uncircumcised Gentile to the community. The example, however, did not set a precedent or embody any general principle which that Church followed. When uncircumcised Gentiles began to increase the membership at Antioch, the Christians at Jerusalem determined to force the issue.

Today we can see that nothing less than the future of Christianity was at

stake. Would it remain a sect of Judaism, forever tied to separatist requirements—or become an independent, universal religion? In Paul's mind, of
course, these questions took a different form. He was not concerned for a
new religion, since he did not think of Christianity in those terms. Rather, he
opposed man's attempt to justify by his own efforts a hold upon God's grace,
something that could only be freely given. To impose Judaic practices upon
Christian converts was to question the sufficiency of God's act in Jesus
Christ. For Paul, man's role in salvation was to have faith—that is, to respond
to divine grace as revealed in Christ; it was not the carrying out of regulations, as if he could do something to merit his salvation. Paul was thus
unalterably opposed to any requirements other than faith in Jesus as Lord for
entrance into the Christian fellowship. "For there is no distinction between
Jew and Greek; the same Lord is Lord of all and bestows his riches upon all
who call upon him. For every one who calls upon the name of the Lord will
be saved" (Rom. 10:12–13). "We hold," he said bluntly, "that a man is
justified by faith apart from the works of law. Or is God the God of Jews
only? Is he not the God of Gentiles also? Yes, of Gentiles also, since God is
one. . . ." (Rom. 3:28–30a). "There is no distinction," he insisted time and
time again, "since all have sinned and fall short of the glory of God, they are
justified by his grace as a gift, through the redemption which is in Christ
Jesus, whom God put forward as an expiation by his blood, to be received by
faith" (Rom. 3:23–25).

When Paul accompanied Barnabas to Jerusalem to represent the Antioch
Church, he did not budge from his position. "For in Jesus Christ neither
circumcision nor uncircumcision is of any avail, but faith working through
love" (Gal. 5:6). This he stoutly maintained in the face of all arguments the
Jerusalem brethren could bring to bear. As the conference was about to
break up without resolution of the issue, James, head of the Jerusalem
Church, suggested a compromise. He saw validity on both sides and asked all
to agree that Gentiles might be admitted without first converting to Judaism,
but these new Christians should observe various dietary regulations and
refrain from unchastity (Acts 15:13–21).

This compromise seems to have carried the day, and Paul and Barnabas left
Jerusalem in what appeared as a measure of harmony with the Church there.
But ingrained attitudes and habits die hard. In actuality the compromise seems
never to have been implemented. The Jerusalem Church continued to stress
Judaic practices, and Peter, on a visit to Antioch, refused to share in communal meals with Gentiles because he "feared them that were of the circumcision"—which produced an ugly scene with Paul, who accused him of
duplicity and cowardice (Gal. 2:11–21). To Paul's mind it was a betrayal of
the Gentile Christians by a leading member of the Church and in direct
contradiction of their agreement.

But worse was yet to come, for to the end of his days Paul's missionary
activities were plagued by the counterefforts of the "Judaizers," the Jewish
Christians in various places who sought to undermine his work and intrigued

ScS PAVLVS   TYMOTHEVS

The Apostles Peter and Paul guided the early church through the perils of heresy and of the persecution begun under the Emperor Nero (above, left) in A.D. 64. A fourth-century bronze lamp (top, right) shows them in a ship symbolizing the Church, "the Ark of Salvation." A mosaic from the Palatine Chapel at Palermo (below) represents the Apostles appearing before Nero to dispute with Simon Magus, a strange and apparently powerful figure who was often viewed by early Christians as a threat to the faith. In an illuminated page from the eleventh-century Bible of St. Cecilia (below, left), Paul, whose visits and letters encouraged young churches in many cities, is shown handing Timothy the manuscript of his Letter to the Romans.

to alienate his congregations from him, especially in Galatia. Not until the fall of Jerusalem in A.D. 70, some years after his death, did conflict cease, Christian and Jew going their separate ways.

A few years ago some scholars mistakenly came to view Paul as the "founder" of Christianity, and even today uninformed people sometimes speak of him as having perverted the simple teachings of Jesus into a highly complex theology. This is not true. His teachings are in harmony with those of his Lord, and his view of God and man are in accord. There was, of course, a new factor in Paul's thinking: the Resurrection faith. But this was not uniquely Pauline; he shared it with the early Church. What fundamentally created Christianity was overwhelming belief in the resurrection of Jesus. Early Christians were a fellowship of the Resurrection; all they thought, did, said, and wrote centered on this. It cannot be emphasized too often that the earliest Christians did not think of themselves as moral teachers, but as witnesses to a unique and epoch-shattering act of God in history. Paul joined himself to this company of witnesses, he did not create it. And the message he proclaimed was the common apostolic tradition, established before his conversion, which he sought to pass on.

"For I delivered to you as of first importance," he wrote to the Corinthians, "what I also received, that Christ died for our sins in accordance with the scriptures, that he was buried, that he was raised on the third day in accordance with the scriptures, and that he appeared to Cephas [Peter], then to the twelve" (I Cor. 15:3–5). This embodies the heart of the "good news" announced by the early Church. Paul elaborated it with his own variations, as did every preacher, but he set forth the same gospel as Peter, Stephen, Philip, and the other evangelists. Paul did carry the implications of this position to their logical conclusion, asserting the all-pervading sufficiency of faith in Christ. But it must be remembered that he was a brilliant spokesman for this view—not its originator.

We have said that he did not think of his faith as a new religion. On the contrary, he saw himself and the movement to which he devoted his entire energies as a continuation of the ancient story of God's action in the history of his people. The Christ-event, the complete and final revelation of God, is the outcome of the history of the Hebrews. And while it "makes all things new," it is not strictly speaking a new thing. This conception of continuity and uniqueness Paul summed up in his use of the phrase "the new Israel" for the post-Resurrection community.

In his missionary activities Paul gave active form to his theology concerning Israel, the Gentiles, and the new Israel. When he came to a new place, he went first to the Jews. Only if he was rejected by his Hebrew brethren would he turn to the Gentiles. This pattern was repeated over and over again in city after city. Not all Jews rejected his message, of course; some left the synagogues and became a part of the new churches, while many, perhaps most of the first Gentile converts, came from the synagogues too. These were the "godfearers." Thus in a sense the Jewish communities of the Dispersion were stepping stones for the spread of Christianity, and the widely known Bible of the Dispersion, the Greek Septuagint translation of the Hebrew Scriptures, now interpreted by Christians with their own emphases, provided an ancient and authoritative foundation for the new faith. Not only did the missionaries use the Septuagint in the Jewish communities, but as they addressed their gospel to Gentiles, for whom the *lingua franca* was Greek. So much did the Christians use this Bible that within two centuries this fact among others caused the Jews to abandon it and seek a new translation for themselves. The Alexandrian Greek version of the Hebrew Scriptures had been literally taken over by the Christians.

There were other factors that facilitated the expansion of Christianity. *Pax Romana* ruled. At the beginning of the Christian Era the ancient world saw more than three centuries of peace, constructed on a basis of political unity. The same law and to some extent the same culture were to be found in all parts of the Empire. Roads were good and relatively safe; mail traveled rapidly. A hundred years before Paul, Cicero marveled that a letter could go from Tarsus to Rome in only two weeks. Travel by sea was safe from piracy and swift: The freebooters who had swarmed on the waters after the demise of Athenian naval power had been swept away by the Romans. The Mediterranean was a Roman lake.

Paul traveled by land and by sea. In all he made three missionary journeys, not counting his final sea voyage by way of Malta to Rome and imprisonment. His companions at different times were Barnabas, John Mark, Luke, Silas, and Timothy. His first journey with Barnabas to Cyprus and southern Asia Minor was followed by a second that penetrated deeper into Asia Minor and crossed into Europe, founding churches at Philippi, Thessalonica, and Corinth, and passing through Athens on the way. In the course of his third journey he spent over two years at Ephesus, chief city of western Asia Minor. Here, as was his custom, he established missionary headquarters where he trained others who went into the countryside and evangelized the neighboring cities, towns, and villages. From Ephesus he sent preachers down the Lycus Valley to Colossae, Laodicea, and other cities of this famous valley which formed the trade route between east and west. Paul did not visit them personally, but made use of letters to extend his missionary influence. He wrote to these churches and also to those he had founded, confirming the gospel that had been preached among them and elaborating upon it, strengthening the often struggling infant congregations, answering various questions that had been raised, countering what he considered wrong understanding of the gospel, rebuking behavior not in keeping with a Christian confession, and giving instructions for worship.

We possess ten—possibly thirteen, if we accept I and II Timothy and Titus as Pauline—of these letters in our New Testament (hardly anyone today agrees with the earlier belief that Paul was the author of Hebrews). But these are by no means all the letters Paul wrote. He himself mentions two others to Corinth (I Cor. 5:6, II Cor. 2:4) and one to Laodicea (Col. 4:16), and we

Chester Beatty Papyrus P46 from about A.D. *200 is the most important manuscript containing the letters of the Apostle Paul.*

may be sure that this inveterate letter-writer was the author of numerous communications since lost.

Paul would be amazed to learn that many men of faith now regard his letter to the Romans more highly than they do the Book of Deuteronomy, or that every day his instructions to the Corinthians regarding the Lord's Supper are read aloud as men prepare to celebrate that holy meal. It would have doubtless bewildered him to know that these letters, often written in the heat of the moment, would constitute the oldest and one of the greatest treasures of Christianity, and that after nineteen centuries men would still be probing for their full meaning. For Paul, who is now regarded with reverence as the author of almost half the New Testament, these letters were nothing more than tools, missionary tools. They were vigorous, thoughtful, but often hastily composed responses to specific situations. Only one—Romans—is carefully worked out, yet even here Paul's effusive spirit and excitement about Christ combine to render some passages almost incomprehensible.

Mostly he wrote to deal with growing pains and other troubles in the churches he and his deputies had founded. And there were troubles and trials almost beyond bearing. The frequent misunderstanding through quite honest motives could be dealt with, though not without much effort. More difficult to handle were the many enemies who were drawn into the swirling Pauline dynamism. Now the Judaizers were almost always present, seeking to undermine his work. There were personal attacks upon him and his authority. And there were questions about his understanding of the gospel. To the Corinthians he wrote, having to justify himself as against his rivals, "Are they servants of Christ? I am a better one—I am talking like a madman—with far greater labors, far more imprisonments, with countless beatings, and often near death. Five times I have received at the hands of the Jews forty lashes less one. Three times I have been beaten with rods; once I was stoned. Three times I have been shipwrecked; a night and a day I have been adrift at sea. . . ." (II Cor. 11:23–25).

Paul counted suffering for Christ's sake as nothing, for his gaze was beyond the mundane and his devotion to Christ kept him going "in toil and hardship, through many a sleepless night, in hunger and thirst." This man who had given so much for the sake of the kingdom of God could not understand why those who claimed to be serving Christ should try to bend to their own ends churches they had neither founded nor nurtured. Why were they not off blazing new trails? His method had always been to go where others had not been, to preach the gospel in the face of privation or active hostility, to found a church if possible, and to support himself with the work of his own hands. He expected no less from others.

The modern reader of the New Testament will hardly be aware of the splendor and variety of the Greco-Roman setting in which the early missionaries worked. Paul, for example, preached by design in the larger cities, using them, as we have seen, as a base of missionary operations for the surrounding area. Most of these cities were masterpieces of Hellenistic architecture and city planning, with broad colonnaded streets, theaters, temples, forums, and amphitheaters. Archaeology has shown that Ephesus, for example, was entered by way of the *Arkadiane*, a wide avenue with colonnades and shops that led from the Harbor Gate all the way to a mammoth theater, the ruins of which suggest a seating capacity of about 24,000. Even this magnificence was not its crowning glory. In the northeast section of the city stood the dazzling Temple of Diana, one of the seven wonders of the ancient world. Excavations begun in 1877 have not yet determined the exact size of this structure, but it is now thought to have been approximately 180 by 360 feet, with a hundred columns over fifty feet high. A profitable silversmithing industry centered upon this building, and when Paul left Ephesus it was because of a riot instigated by the makers of silver images of Diana, whose trade had been seriously damaged by the success of his preaching.

All about him were the marble and silver of the Hellenistic cities, a tribute to the mind and hand of man. But Paul's gaze was steadily upon "a temple not made with hands," and his purpose in life was to call attention to God's mind as revealed in Christ. God, he told people again and again, had been working out His plan through the ages, as the history of Israel shows. Then "in the fulness of time, God sent forth his Son" to offer salvation to all men and break down "the dividing wall of hostility" that man in his alienation had erected between himself and his fellow man, and between himself and God. But God did this great thing out of His infinite love—not because man had in any way put Him in his debt. Indeed, according to Paul, the depth and quality of that love may be seen in that "while we were yet sinners Christ died for us." Thus unequivocally Paul sets forth the basis of his theology in God's unmerited action on man's behalf, and from this touchstone flows the thought that has inspired and baffled man ever since.

The fact that Paul's letters were usually responses to need gives them their freshness and immediacy. It also gives the reader of the New Testament a somewhat one-sided picture of Paul. There was theological trouble in the Colossian Church, a return to Jewish practices in the Galatian Church, trouble with pagans at Philippi and Ephesus, and factionalism, quarrels, wild orgies of prophesying "with tongues," and even sexual immorality in the Corinthian Church. The impression is that Paul lived his whole life in controversy and combat. And indeed, much of it was so. But it should be remembered that for most of those who responded to Paul's preaching his trumpet call to salvation was the breath of freedom.

Of Paul's death we know nothing. The Book of Acts ends with him in prison awaiting trial. Traditionally he is said to have perished in the Neronian persecution, but in fact he disappears mysteriously into the mists of history. His work and his influence do not. In Roman Catholic piety he stands next to Peter in esteem, and his thought has been more important to Catholic theology than Peter's. For the Protestant, Paul is the primary example of the man of faith, and his thought is the fount from which the Reformation sprang. This "man in Christ" was the first of the great theologians of the

Christian heritage. If it is in some sense true to say that "subsequent philosophy is but a footnote to Plato," it is true to say that "subsequent Christian theology is but a footnote to Paul."

And Paul did not merely contribute to the Christian heritage. He drew upon it. His letters, the oldest Christian documents we have, embody the thoughts and practices of some of the earliest Christian people. Their preservation, as we have seen, we owe to the needs of an expanding Church. In the absence of other writings dealing with matters of faith and order the churches circulated the letters and gradually came to look upon them as authoritative. Later, sometime toward the end of the first century, they were collected and passed on, copied, and treasured as a group.

The Gospel and the Gospels

At almost the same time that Paul's personal activity came to an end—very likely in that terrible year in Rome, A.D. 64—the needs that were preserving some of his letters were producing a new form of literature: the Gospels. Christianity was spreading rapidly. New congregations were forming in areas remote from Palestine. At first the rule of faith and order was contained exclusively in the preaching of those who had been "eyewitnesses and ministers of the Word." Now missionaries as well as churches were multiplying; and eyewitnesses were beginning to die. If there was an early, intense expectation of the Second Coming, it was dying with them. Outside enemies were growing in proportion to the success of the new faith. Congregation after congregation grew, willy-nilly, without any authoritative guide for its life. The need for a written form of the tradition became increasingly acute.

It is, of course, inexact to speak of "the tradition" as though there had been only one during these years. Many traditions were circulating about Jesus, and these had regional variations. Yet there is a sense in which one may validly speak of *the* tradition. There came a time when the Church, pressed by needs on every hand, isolated a common understanding of that tradition which began with the earliest followers of Jesus—the apostles—and enshrined it in what have come to be the canonical books of the New Testament. This tradition continued in certain of the noncanonical books, notably the collection called the "Apostolic Fathers," which we shall note later. It is in this direct stream that Paul stands, and this is the tradition the four Gospels embody.

The apostolic tradition placed much emphasis upon the death and resurrection of Jesus and upon the authority of his words. It also has much to say about the necessity for Christians to give a good witness to those outside the Church, and on the need for strong but loving discipline within it. The Gospels are most clearly concerned with the first two of these points, although the perceptive reader will be aware that the churchly concerns of the Gospel writers are much in evidence.

Today the Gospels are popularly viewed as biographies of Jesus. They certainly do give various details of his life and thinking. Yet they are not by any stretch of imagination correctly understood as biographies. They are exactly what their name indicates: *Gospels*, the written form of the oral gospel—in short, a continuation of apostolic preaching. This existed from the beginning of Christianity and had a more or less set form, which means that the Gospels—the written kerygma—have a certain nature or character different from other kinds of historical documents. The earliest Christian preaching set forth the belief that God acted in Christ in a way that continued and fulfilled His past acts in the history of Israel. Now, however, His action had a finality and a decisiveness about it which it had never had before. This, said the preachers, might be seen in the ministry of Jesus and his words, and preeminently in his death and resurrection, to which they were witnesses.

Christians probed these themes for their deeper meanings. The Gospels come at the end of a generation of such reflection. They are not mere hodgepodge collections of facts which the authors have scrupulously refrained from interpreting—no historical writings worth reading ever are. Few today would hold that there is such a thing as purely objective history in the sense that the historian does not interpret what he records. Even his selection of items worthy of recording, and his omission of others, involve value judgments which are in themselves an interpretation. This does not mean falsifying, of course; but it does imply that the writer presents his understanding of the facts as the key to their true meaning.

The Gospels represent a selection and compilation of materials from the rich tradition of the Church. They convey what their writers understand as the real meaning of the Christ-event. There is no reason to object to them as historical documents, once their nature is recognized and it is clear that the writers did not view themselves as writing objective history. What they wrote about was for them—literally—the central happening of all time, which previous history foreshadowed and from which later history takes its point of reference. They are religious writings: statements of faith about man and his world and God's relation to them.

The first three Gospels are called the *Synoptics* because they look at things from essentially the same perspective. They have an organic relation to one another, report many of the same happenings and sayings, and share a similar interpretation of the meaning of Jesus's life, death, and resurrection. This is not to say that there are not significant differences in content and form. But Matthew, Mark, and Luke stand much closer to each other in every particular than any one of them does to John. In form, style, and theological interpretation, John seems to represent a quite different body of material.

For a long time it was assumed that there were no differences or contradictions among the four Gospels, or at most that they were more apparent than real and could be harmonized. While such a view is important because of the high value it places upon the Scriptures, it is in fact a position imposed on the Gospels and not arising from them. Moreover, it prevents appreciation of

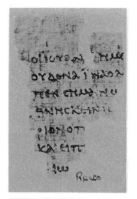

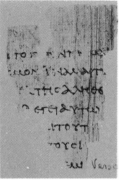

The oldest known manuscript of any of the Gospels is the John Rylands Fragment of John written in Egypt early in the second century.

the positive gains that can be made by working with the differences as well as the similarities in these writings.

One such positive gain is the awareness that Mark was the first Gospel to be written. We know this because almost all of it (all but thirty verses) is repeated in either Matthew or Luke, in the same sequence and often verbatim. Obviously Mark is not only the principal source for the other two Synoptics, but provided much of the framework they followed.

Further inquiry into the written sources of the Gospels shows that a great deal of the material in Matthew and Luke which does not come from Mark appears in both those Gospels, though often with variations. This suggests that there was another source common to both, and this presumed source, which scholars have reconstructed from passages common to Matthew and Luke apart from Marcan passages, is designated "Q" from the German *Quelle*, or "source." "Q" seems to have been an early compilation of Jesus' teachings. Whether it once contained parts of the Passion narrative is not certain. At any rate, Matthew and Luke apparently used it to augment what they have from Mark, an account containing relatively little of Jesus' teaching. If the Mark and "Q" sources are now put aside, Matthew and Luke each still retain material of their own, which shows that each was acquainted with oral or written traditions not included in any of the other Gospels.

This unraveling of literary sources makes it clear that behind all the Gospels—John as well as the Synoptics—and behind "Q" and Paul too, lay a rich lode of tradition available to all. Now, what were these sources of our own sources? Where did they come from and what did they consist of? Research has discovered that it is possible to isolate and classify various parts of this tradition, and on the basis of such work reasonable assumptions can be made about the "life situation" that produced and preserved a saying or the report of an incident. Immediately after Jesus' death a wealth of memories existed about his life and teaching. In the glow of the Resurrection the disciples came to understand what these words and actions meant as they never had before. In time these blended memories and interpretations were shaped into collections of stories and sayings: separate little groups without narrative connection, preserved because they were valuable to the community. In the process, as happens with oral tradition, the forms these memories took became fewer in number, and some material was lost. Some dropped away when it was all put in written form. Paul reports things Jesus said that do not occur in the Gospels, and it is certain that much else has disappeared. (Students of the New Testament who have tried to estimate the actual daily living-time accounted for in the Gospels have come up with the rough approximation of two or three weeks, by contrast with the year—possibly even three years—of Jesus' total known ministry.) Yet a great deal was kept; given this long process of preservation, we have more than we have any right to expect.

This remarkable preservation we owe mainly to the community's careful passing on of material that seemed to it to have most meaning. This accounts for the apparent early date of the written form of the Passion narrative, which was so vital to the first preaching. It also explains why there is less variation in reports of it than about anything else in the Gospels. But other things also had meaning for the Church. The tradition met the needs of Christians who worshiped and lived in a common fellowship; it supported their faith, illumined their practices, and answered questions about Jesus and about such matters as sin, salvation, a right way of life as regarded all sorts of things—including the Sabbath, the Temple, fasting, divorce, taxation, and many others—and finally, the meaning of the kingdom of God.

This is not to say, as some have maintained, that the community preserved only what made it appear in the best light. A number of unexplained elements remain, such as the baptism of Jesus at the hands of John the Baptist, whose followers may have been rivals of Jesus' disciples; and the fact that Jesus was put to death by order of a Roman governor. This latter circumstance was not only embarrassing to the early Christians but a source of danger, when they were later accused of being subversive to the Empire. It is not surprising that Pilate is portrayed as relatively innocent of the whole proceeding.

The theme of early preaching was God's action in and through Jesus of Nazareth, and the Church's tradition—whatever the thrust of individual units—continued to proclaim this gospel. When the four evangelists set it forth in orderly fashion, each wrote—as John says—"that you may believe that Jesus is the Christ, the Son of God, and that believing you may have life in his name" (John 20:31). Yet in the over-all unity of the four Gospels, each has a unique interpretation of the gospel, and each author his own motives for writing. Mark, for example, was probably written in Rome during the Neronian persecution (ca. 64) and it seems that one of his purposes is to show that Christians are not politically subversive and Christianity not ideologically anti-Roman. He also holds up the example of the faithful, unflinching Jesus before a Church trying to hold fast under persecution, and this may account for the focus on the life, death, and resurrection of Jesus and the relative absence of the teachings. Traditionally, it has been thought that Mark's Gospel is closely associated with Peter, and was written after Peter's death to record first-hand memories that died with him. It is partly through this understanding that it came to be included in the canon.

Like Mark, Luke's Gospel is addressed to Gentiles. Indeed, together with the Acts of the Apostles, its companion volume, it was written by a Gentile— probably in Asia Minor during the mid-eighties of the first century. There is little reason to doubt that the author of both was the Luke who traveled with Paul. In compiling this Gospel he used Mark as his basic source, but reworked much of the material, refining some of the crudely written Greek into the sonorous phrases of his own polished style. He also added much, including a collection of beautiful stories about Jesus' birth which have a strongly Semitic flavor and may have come to him in some Aramaic form. Luke says in his preface (Luke 1:1–4) that he carefully surveyed the body of Christian writings and traditions and from them compiled his own account of the coming of the gospel among men. He begins in his first book with its initial appearance at a stable in Bethlehem and ends, in the Acts, with its proclamation in Rome.

Matthew's Gospel, of about the same date as Luke's, was not written by nor primarily for Gentiles. While it may have been compiled at Antioch, as many scholars believe, it is the most Jewish of the Gospels and draws heavily upon the Old Testament prophecies to show that Jesus is the promised Messiah. Very likely Matthew had at hand one of the collections of prophecies, known as "Testimonies," that circulated in the early Church. As the Dead Sea Scrolls reveal, such collections were used by the Qumran community in much the same way as Matthew uses Old Testament quotations. In keeping with his orientation toward the Hebrew Scriptures, he shows Jesus as a second Moses called to deliver his people from bondage. The Sermon on the Mount is set forth in such a way as to show Jesus as the Mosaic prophet foretold in Deuteronomy 18:15. He has come and has given a new Law. At every point Matthew rejoices in the fulfillment of the ancient promises and prophecies held dear in the hearts of his people.

The Gospel of John is at once the most profound and most enigmatic book of the New Testament. Scholars are in sharp disagreement about almost every question concerning it. For example, a tradition dating from the second century says it was written in Ephesus by the Apostle John, the son of Zebedee. But an equally ancient source attributes it to a John the Elder who lived in Ephesus. Nor is Ephesus by any means unanimously accepted as its place of origin; Antioch and Alexandria also have their proponents. On the question of date, some consensus is beginning to emerge. It used to be fashionable to assign the Gospel to the end of the second century, and to say that it was the outcome of a long process of theological thought. Now, in light of archaeological finds such as the Dead Sea Scrolls and certain papyrus fragments, and on the basis of greater knowledge of Hellenistic thought, it is dated much earlier. It probably comes from the last decade of the first century.

John has similarities with the Synoptics in that it reports many of the same incidents and alludes to others which they narrate. But the differences are more striking than the similarities. The style is such that none of his sources can be identified with certainty. His long dialogues and highly developed monologues are in marked contrast to the pithy statements and parable forms found in the other Gospels. And perhaps more important, John's chronology of the life of Jesus is somewhat different. The Synoptics record only one visit of Jesus to Jerusalem during his adult life, which suggests a ministry lasting only a year. John reports a number of visits and indicates a ministry lasting three years. The Synoptics contain no reference to an extended ministry of Jesus in Judea and Jerusalem immediately prior to his crucifixion, while John says he was in Judea from October until April.

The Fourth Gospel's understanding of Christ is not the same as that of the first three. They are guarded in their statements of his Messiahship and view it as a secret of the kingdom, but John's Gospel opens with a most eloquently profound statement that the long-desired Savior has appeared in the midst of men. This theme is pursued to the very moment of the crucifixion. "And I, if I be lifted up from the earth," says Jesus, "will draw all men unto myself" (John 12:32). To be "lifted up" has a double and symbolic meaning, as do so many of John's words and phrases: it betokens not only crucifixion but enthronement. The crucified Jesus is the regnant king who takes possession of his realm by conquering death. This is a different, but not inharmonious, emphasis from Mark's faithful Jesus, Matthew's Mosaic prophet, and Luke's praying Messiah.

Many Writings—One Word

THE WRITING of the Gospels was only one sign of the rapid expansion of Christianity. "We are but of yesterday," proudly wrote Tertullian to Roman authorities at the end of the second century, "yet we overspread your empire; your cities, islands, forts, assemblies, camps, palace, senate, forum, all swarm with Christians." Many years before Tertullian's boast, the new faith had spread east beyond Mesopotamia and west to Spain, Gaul, and across North Africa. It probably had adherents even in Britain and in Germany. But the great centers of Christianity were Antioch, first home of Gentile Christianity; Alexandria, a seedbed of Christian intellectual activity; Carthage-Hippo, later to produce St. Augustine; Ephesus, which served the area most densely populated by Christians; and Rome, not yet on a par with the others but growing in stature.

And the body of Christian literature was growing. There were gospels, letters of various sorts, manuals of teaching and discipline, apocalypses, apologies, and other writings as well. Some have been attributed to pillars of the Jerusalem Church: Peter, James, and John. They are said to have written six letters—I and II Peter, James, and I, II, and III John—which, together with a letter reportedly from the hand of the apostle Jude, are today referred to as the "Catholic (i.e., general or universal) Epistles."

I Peter, James, and I John were known and treasured quite early. But the others are late and not referred to before the end of the second century; their apostolic authenticity has always been in doubt, and it was not until the sixth century that they gained universal acceptance as canonical in all parts of Christendom. Of these pseudo-apostolic writings II Peter is the latest, and from our point of view in this volume the most interesting. This letter from the last half of the second century shows the growing authority of certain Christian writings. "And count the forbearance of our Lord as salvation," says the author. "So also our beloved brother Paul wrote to you according to the wisdom given to him, speaking of this as he does in all his letters" (II Pet. 3:15-16). This writer also speaks of the Letter of Jude, which for him has become a source of correct doctrine. This indicates that some Christian writings were beginning to be thought of as equal in stature to the Hebrew Scriptures. The canon of the New Testament was thus gradually forming, by the same process we have seen with the Old Testament. A major factor in the process was the popular use of the documents as authoritative guides.

The Catholic Epistles also reflect the tendencies and problems of developing Christianity. Theologically their main thrust is in understanding the person and work of Christ. As Christians began to think through the implications of their beliefs about Jesus they were forced to develop a comprehensive view of the Christ-event. This reached definite formulation in the Apostles' and Nicene creeds of the fourth century but is already visible in the writings attributed to the apostles. It is also the central concern of the Epistle to the Hebrews, a first-century work of unknown authorship.

The Church continued to have internal difficulties with discipline and organization, and felt increasingly the pressure of the Roman state. These concerns, too, are evident in the Catholic Epistles, but receive their clearest focus in other writings of the New Testament. The Revelation to St. John the Divine, which stands last in the order of biblical books, is believed to have been written during the nineties of the first century. The Emperor Domitian (A.D. 81–96) had launched a persecution designed to eradicate the Christians. John, author of the Revelation, writes from his lonely exile on the island of Patmos to comfort and encourage his fellow believers under the constant threat of disaster. With poetic imagery and apocalyptic vision he reminds his readers that, although the kingdoms of this world have conspired to destroy them, they can find courage to face what the morrow brings by fixing their gaze firmly upon Christ, the slain Lamb, whose kingdom endures forever. A key to interpretation of this enigmatic book—an apocalypse akin to Daniel in the Old Testament—may be found in the passage made famous by Handel in his *Messiah:* "Hallelujah! The Lord God omnipotent reigneth" (Rev. 19:6).

The internal problems of the Church are also mirrored in the Pastoral Epistles (I and II Timothy and Titus), so titled because they deal with pastoral concerns. The letters contain instructions in the duties of church officers, the respect due them, and the personal responsibilities of these men. Particular attention, says I Timothy, should be given to the preservation of the apostolic "deposit"—the tradition by which false teachings are to be distinguished from true.

We have already seen to some extent how the preservation of apostolic tradition was guaranteed, not merely by admonition, but by the collecting and circulating of certain writings that embodied this "deposit." Before the turn of the century a collection of Paul's letters had become a standard of belief and practice in the churches. Even the Church at Rome, which seems to have rejected his personal pleas for support in a missionary endeavor to Spain, now accepted his writings as a criterion.

Not only Paul's letters but a collection of Gospels was circulating in the Church. The Gospel of Luke, detached from the Acts, was joined to Mark,

Christians decorated the walls of their burial caves (catacombs) with scenes and heroes from the Bible. These third- and fourth-century frescoes from the Catacomb of Calixtus in Rome show the Good Shepherd, probably David (left), and Moses striking water from the rock (below). Moses and David were particular favorites in the early Church because they were understood to "prefigure" Christ.

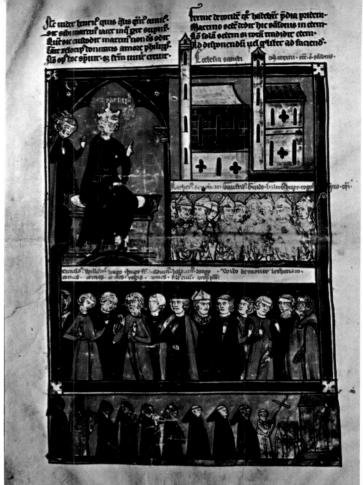

A miniature from the ninth-century "Bible of Charles the Bald" (below left) portrays St. Jerome handing out copies of his Bible translation, the Vulgate, which became the standard Latin text copied by monastic scribes. The miniature at left shows King Philip I of France presiding at the founding of a monastery as noblemen, prelates, and monks assemble. Preserving and adorning the Bible text was a demanding task: initial letters (far left) and title pages (lower right) were often elaborately designed in brilliant colors. Two very important Bible manuscripts are a tenth-century Torah Codex (top right), which follows the Masoretic Text, a system of vowel markings that became the foundation of modern Hebrew Bibles; and the Codex Vaticanus (center right), a fourth-century Greek Bible. The eighth-century Lindisfarne Gospels (bottom right) is one of the most beautiful of all Bible manuscripts.

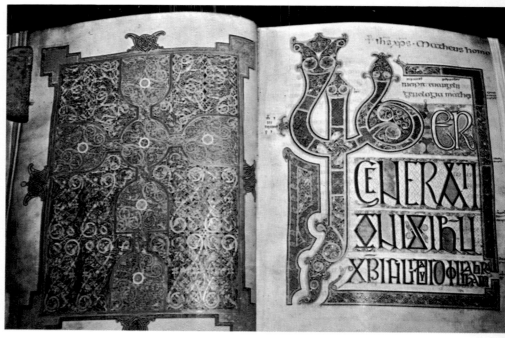

Christic was understood by the Church to be the fulfillment of Old Testament prophecy. Miniatures from a sixth-century codex (right) portray Jesus bringing to pass the predictions of four prophets by washing the disciples' feet and breaking bread at the Last Supper.

Miniatures in the Four Gospels of 1480 from Germany (below) were the work of the Master of the Hausbuch. This gilded illumination pictures St. John writing his Gospel at a desk resembling those of medieval scribes.

Matthew, and John in a "Four-Gospel Manuscript" in the form of a scroll; Matthew, being the most popular, was placed first since it was thus more easily accessible. Matthew never lost this place of prominence even after the Christians developed the codex, or leaf-book, to hold their precious Gospels. Soon Gospel codices became popular, and this new form of book permitted bringing larger collections of authoritative writings together. Whereas formerly at least two scrolls would have been needed to contain the Gospels, Acts, and Paul's letters, all these were now included in one codex which could be opened and read at any point. These particular documents, in this form, are known to have been in use in Rome about A.D. 170. The Muratorian Canon, our earliest list of New Testament books, shows that Paul's letters and the Acts had become attached to the Four-Gospel Codex, forming the nucleus of the New Testament as we know it. It remained to be seen what other writings would be joined to this core. The pressures for a decision were mounting as the Church grew, new writings appeared, and diverse interpretations sprang up.

The decision was not easily nor hurriedly made. There was already a vast body of literature, and before the canon of the New Testament was agreed upon through *de facto* general acceptance by the end of the fourth century, Christianity had become even more of a literary religion. The generation immediately following the apostles is noted for its productivity, and a collection mentioned earlier, called the "Apostolic Fathers," has come down to us. The title is honorific, bestowed because these writers preserved and continued in their writings the thought of the apostles. Some authors of the documents are identified. There is Clement, the somewhat colorless bishop of Rome whose letter to the Corinthians moved in and out of authoritative lists of books for years. There is the aged martyr Polycarp, whose confession of faith as he met death in the arena served as inspiration for many Christians facing the same fate. Perhaps the most sharply defined figure among them is Ignatius, the prolific bishop of Antioch. Arrested and taken to Rome, he was allowed to write to various churches before being martyred during the reign of Trajan (A.D. 98–117). These seven hurried, spontaneous outpourings of a doomed but joyful man give a unique insight into the life of Christians in the early second century.

"The Doctrine of the Apostles," or *Didache* as it is more popularly known, was written about the same time as Ignatius' letters; this anonymous work also adds to our knowledge of the religious life of the times. Of the three remaining writings of the Apostolic Fathers, the piece labeled II Clement (bearing no relation to I Clement) is a sermon, possibly from Corinth in the middle of the second century. The Letter of Barnabas, whose author and place of origin are unknown, highlights the intense conflict between church and synagogue. According to Barnabas Judaism has misinterpreted the Hebrew Scriptures, and by its failure to acknowledge Jesus as the Messiah has forfeited its rights to God's promises, which now rest in the Christian Church, the New Israel. The last of the writings of the Apostolic

Fathers is an unpretentious apocalyptic treatise by Hermas, brother of the Roman bishop, probably written about A.D. 150. This document is called *The Shepherd* after its central figure. Hermas was interested in a moral reform of the Church based upon the beliefs and practices laid down by the apostles.

But not everyone was as careful as the Apostolic Fathers in keeping and passing on the "deposit." There were many heretical sectarian groups who adopted and adapted Christian literature to their own purposes, and provided a large number of new works embodying their own points of view. The Ebionites, Jewish Christians who rejected the redemptive death of Jesus and demanded strict observance of the Mosaic Law, were particularly attracted to the Gospel of Matthew. They found its Jewish emphases appealing and edited, rewrote, and circulated it to justify their theological position. The Gospel of John was likewise later adopted by a heretical branch of Christianity: the Christian Gnostics, who with their interest in symbolism and their dualistic doctrines so identified themselves with the Fourth Gospel that many Christians thought it should be removed altogether from the list of authoritative writings. In addition the Gnostics wrote a vast number of works embodying their views. In 1945–46, near the Egyptian town of Nag Hammadi, thirteen papyrus manuscripts were discovered containing more than forty previously unknown Gnostic writings, among them the apocryphal Gospels of Thomas and Philip, a "Gospel of the Egyptians," and a "Gospel of Truth." In addition there were Acts attributed to the apostles Peter and Matthias, and apocalypses said to have come from the hands of Peter, James, John, and Paul. Some of these may be as early as the second century, although most of them are somewhat later.

It should be pointed out that writers of the period commonly attached the name of an ancient worthy to works not written by him. Our ancestors did not share our view of this sort of practice. It was all the more important, therefore, to have a separate standard for judging the worth of any document that came to hand.

While the Ebionites and Gnostics adapted certain Christian writings to their own uses and added others under apostolic names to augment their literature, Marcion—the fascinating leader of a large movement in the second century—thoroughly altered the Christian works. In A.D. 144 he left the Church at Rome, of which he had been a member for four years, having come there from Sinope in Asia Minor where he had become wealthy in the shipping business. He was a strait-laced man whose theology was tinged with Gnosticism; but more important, it was based upon a radical view that denied any connection between the God of the Hebrew Scriptures and God as revealed in Christ. This led him to reject not only the demands of the Mosaic Law but the entire Old Testament—the very Bible of the early Church! Paul, Marcion claimed, held the same position. Thus the Pauline letters were to be given priority as a standard; but not their entire content. Marcion expunged them. Parts not in keeping with his views were removed. He also expurgated the Gospel of Luke, and commended the abridgement to his followers. This emasculated but clearly defined canon of Scripture played a powerful role in the growth of the widespread Marcionite sect during the following centuries.

In addition to the schismatic new cults, the Church was confronted by two major external problems. The unprecedented growth of Christianity coupled with the Christian refusal to participate in certain religious and civic formalities within the Roman culture made the churches objects of hostility everywhere. All over the Empire—in North Africa, in Gaul, in Asia Minor—local persecutions broke out, and many died. Soon the flames of this hatred were fanned by a new attack on Christianity: a literary polemic.

The new front for the conflict was intellectual. Tracts, books, and even popular speeches (many of them written down and circulated) were thrown into the struggle against the onrushing new religion. Christians were accused of immorality, atheism, sedition, and antisocial tendencies, or as Tacitus put it much earlier, "hating the whole human race." The most famous of these literary attacks was the *True Doctrine* of the philosopher Celsus. The major significance of this polemic was the literary response it elicited from the Christians. They counterattacked with literature which in scope was different from any previous Christian writings. These were "apologetic" writings; that is, *apologias*—speeches (or documents) in defense. The Christians drew upon almost every form of apologia known to the ancient world, and varied their method and theme according to the station and thrust of their adversary.

The first of these works was apparently addressed to the emperor himself and set a pattern which many of the apologists followed. One Quadratus, an Athenian, wrote a defense of Christianity intended for Hadrian, but so little of this now exists that it is impossible to reconstruct its contents. Aristides, another Greek, addressed another to the same emperor. But the greatest of the imperial apologias were those of Athenagoras, another Athenian. This noble, skillful, and generous author wrote both to Marcus Aurelius and to his son Commodus, refuting point by point the charges brought against Christians. His method was to compare the Christian faith with various philosophies, not in an attempt to discredit the latter, but to show that his religion was as respectable and as deserving of rights as any philosophical system. The apologist Justin is famous for his refutation of the charges made by a certain Trypho, who was pursuing the Jewish line of attack upon the Church. Justin was a philosopher from the upper class and he reasons with all the skill of a trained mind. Tatian—a student of Justin but hardly his intellectual equal—wrote seeking to show the superiority of the Christian faith to Greek philosophy, which he considered barbaric, arrogant, and deceptive. His apologia was hardly calculated to win friends among the intellectual classes.

But Christianity did win friends and strong adherents among them. By the third century "learned theology" was beginning to flow from the minds of mental giants such as Clement of Alexandria, Lucian of Antioch, Origen, Cyprian, and Tertullian. Theological schools of unequalled brilliance were developed at Alexandria and Antioch. In the west the majority of Christians now spoke Latin, not Greek, and it is not without significance that the first major Christian document in Latin, the *Octavius Dialogues* of Minucius Felix, defends Christianity with the close reasoning and graceful ease of a distinguished and skilled rhetorician.

Yet neither rhetoric nor intellectual skill could give the new faith the consolidation and strength it needed to withstand the constant buffeting by internal and external storms. During the turbulent second century vast strides were made toward securing twin safeguards of authority: discipline and tradition.

"In These Alone"

THE HERESIES within and persecutions without forced the Church to tighten its structure. Prior to this time organization had taken various forms, and these differed widely from one geographical area to another. As a part of the same freedom, anyone who felt himself moved by the Spirit could have a voice in the affairs of the Church, whether theological, organizational, or otherwise. But now it became necessary to have more discipline. Chief consideration was given to the words of authorized men, to clergy and teachers duly chosen, ordained, and regarded as official spokesmen. The Pastoral Epistles show a concern for the proper training of such leaders for the young Church. In the Apostolic Fathers, however, this tightening-up may be even more clearly seen. Already at the end of the first century, Clement of Rome emphasizes the need to obey the bishop. And Ignatius, writing shortly after, has the same emphasis and much the same tone: "Obey the bishop, the elders, and the deacons. . . . Do nothing without the bishop."

Even more important was tradition. At the heart of this sturdy oak now overspreading the Empire was the gospel, embedded in a solid core of apostolic teachings. We have seen that a collection of Pauline materials had become associated with the four Gospels and Acts to form an emerging canon. This Pauline collection was expanded by the Pastoral Epistles to include thirteen letters, while the overall canon was soon further enlarged by the addition of I Peter and I John. James, Hebrews, II Peter, II and III John, Jude, and Revelation had uncertain status for one reason or another, and at various times I Clement, *The Shepherd*, and the Letter of Barnabas were included among the sacred writings.

The third century saw a sifting of these disputed books. Use and authoritative status had regional variations. There was never any doubt anywhere about the core documents, but others moved in and out of the collection. Tertullian in North Africa apparently did not know James and II Peter; Hebrews he attributed to Barnabas and would not allow it a place among the Scriptures. Clement of Alexandria recognized as authoritative for the Church in Egypt all books now included in the New Testament plus four to six others. Serapion, Bishop of Antioch (A.D. 190–212), once commended the use of the Gospel of Peter in his Church. Upon closer examination, however, he decided it was heretical and no longer permitted it to be read aloud in the services.

Thus the writings under discussion were being judged by their apostolic connections and their intrinsic soundness. We have seen that an apostle's name attached to a document was no guarantee against heresy. Use in worship was also a major factor in determining the books of the New Testament, as it had been in defining the Old Testament canon. And finally, persecution—particularly that of Diocletian—played its part in forming our Bible.

Roman persecution of Christians was not, as most people think, a consistent and ruthlessly pursued policy. The Romans did not know what to do about Christianity; they tried first one thing and then another—they cajoled, they seduced, they ignored, they accommodated, they persecuted. Eradication was an often-tried method of the military Caesars. Diocletian is the parade example. For years this emperor had followed a deliberate policy of toleration. But in February 303 he issued an edict ordering the destruction of all Christian churches, forbidding assemblies for the purpose of Christian worship, and demanding the surrender and burning of all their sacred books. What books were sacred? Which could the bishop surrender? Which were not to be surrendered at any cost? The Gospels must be kept safe, and also Paul's letters, and Acts, and—what else? I Peter? I John? I Clement?

The edict of toleration issued by Galerius in 311 did not end the quest for the canon, although it relieved some of the urgency. In 320 Eusebius, the first Church historian, reports intense controversy over canonical lists. The persecution was over, but heretical schisms—the luxuries of peace—were gaining in strength and number. In the Latin West, Hilary, Ambrosiaster, and Ambrose drew up lists which were notable because of questions raised about James, II Peter, and Hebrews. But the authority of these books was gradually recognized, following the pattern of the Greek east, until by the time of Augustine (397) Hebrews was included in the Pauline corpus.

The Greek East was less conservative. Hebrews early found a place, and the doubts about II Peter and II and III John were soon removed. The Revelation, however, had a more difficult time. Cyril of Jerusalem, Gregory Nazianzen, and Amphilochius did not include it, while Basil, Gregory of Nyssa, and Epiphanius did.

The thirty-ninth Pascal Letter of Athanasius, read in Alexandrian churches on Easter 367, is considered to be the watershed in the development of the canon. He listed the twenty-seven books now included in the New Testament, and in the same order as we have them (this has, of course, no relation to order of composition). For him they are all apostolic and canonical, and no distinction is to be made among them. The *Didache* and *The Shepherd*, although not authoritative, are to be used for the instruction of converts; they have the same status as the Wisdom of Solomon, Ecclesiasticus, Judith, and Esther (note the question about the place of Esther!).

Athanasius' letter did not end all controversy. Christian authors occasionally cited noncanonical writings in the same manner as canonical ones. It was not until the sixteenth century, during the Reformation and at the Council of Trent, that Christians, both Catholic and Protestant, made absolute declarations concerning the contents of the Bible. However, from the middle of the fourth century twenty-seven books embodying the apostolic tradition about Jesus Christ had been joined to the Hebrew Scriptures to form the Christian Bible. "In these alone," Athanasius said, "is proclaimed the good news of the teaching of true religion."

4

PRESERVING THE PRICELESS TREASURE: THE MIDDLE AGES

The Vulgate

AT ALMOST the same time Athanasius was instructing the faithful concerning Holy Scripture, there appeared in a province of the Roman Empire one of the most intriguing figures in Christian history: Eusebius Hieronymus, whom we know today as St. Jerome. A Roman of Romans, he belongs to the classical world. Yet he faced forward, too, toward the Middle Ages. In the growing dimness of the Roman Empire he lit a torch and, as it were, hurled it far ahead—out of the Empire and beyond, even as far as our own day. For Jerome was the architect of that famous Latin Bible known as the Vulgate, which today is still the official Latin text of the Roman Catholic Church. The Christian west owes its Bible largely to the work of this remarkable man, who devoted his life to bringing order out of the mass of manuscripts in possession of the ancient Catholic Church. By the third century there were already differing versions of the Christian Scriptures in Greek, Syriac, Coptic, and Latin, to name only the major ones. To stem this growing tide and give the Church a uniformly acceptable text of Holy Writ: this was the challenge that focused and absorbed Jerome's abundant talents. More than any other single person, he is responsible for making the Bible *a* book.

Born about A.D. 342 in Stridon, on the northeastern flank of the Dinaric Alps, now part of Yugoslavia, Jerome was reared by his wealthy parents in the Christian faith. At the same time he was given the classical Roman education available to youngsters of his time and social class: primary schooling with a private tutor, then grammar and the Latin classics at a local *grammaticus;* next on to Rome at about the age of fifteen for the standard "university" program—learning the art of rhetoric. This meant studying how to build a written or spoken argument. "Even now that my head is gray and bald," he later wrote, "I often seem in my dreams to be standing, a curly-haired youth, dressed in my toga, to declaim a controversial thesis before the master of rhetoric." The finished rhetorician might become a civil servant, or he might write philosophy or poetry; but for a man like Jerome, whose nature was intense and creative, the civil service of the weakening Empire would have been simply time-serving, and as for philosophy and writing, in Jerome's day these bore the stamp of weariness, disenchantment, and despair. There was little incentive here for a man of his spirit.

This monk's cave just east of Bethlehem was occupied during the time of St. Jerome and has been used almost continuously since then by hermits seeking solitude and salvation in the desolate wilderness.

So he continued to study, storing up knowledge for the future while waiting, it seems, to see what life might offer. He began to create a personal library, laboriously copying manuscripts that interested him. At the same time his insatiable curiosity took him to little-known corners of the world. All the while—studying, copying, learning, writing, traveling—he sought a cause to which he could devote himself. At last, about the year 370, he was back in Italy and seemed to have found his calling. His need for a cause and his Christian upbringing had drawn his attention to a strange new breed of Christians, men who renounced the pleasures of the flesh and exiled themselves to deserts and other remote places to live harsh lives of penitence, contemplation, and study. In his mid-twenties Jerome became a Christian monk, a "spiritual athlete" dedicated to the service of God alone, denying himself and the world. Thus began the pilgrimage which was destined to shape decisively the experience of western Christianity.

In Jerome's seeking spirit a flame burned. With some friends he formed an ascetic society in Aquileia, a town leveled by Attila's army not twenty years earlier. For three years they prayed together and studied the Scriptures. Then some conflict or calamity broke up the group. Jerome calls it "a monstrous rending asunder" but gives no other details. Whatever it was, it scattered the members but did not dampen Jerome's spirit. With a few friends from Aquileia he decided to go to the Holy Land. Traveling the post road to the northern end of the Levant, he reached Antioch and found himself exhausted. While recuperating at the home of a friend he once more took up copying manuscripts for his library, and then, in an epidemic that swept the city, fell seriously ill. One feverish night he heard in a dream a voice that reproached him for his interest in secular writings. "You are a Ciceronian," it said, "—not a Christian."

This incident changed the young man's life. With renewed dedication he threw himself into a career of Christian commitment. In the desert of Chalcis, east of Antioch, he lived for five years the solitary life of a hermit-monk. He ate raw food, his hair grew long. His body, clothed in sackcloth, turned black from the sun and from rolling in ashes. In his cave he prayed constantly, fought torturous fantasies of the flesh, wrote innumerable letters, and devoted himself to mastering biblical Hebrew and Greek. The Christian won out not only over the classicist but over any other worldly allurement.

Finally he was ready to reenter the world. In 379 he returned to Antioch and then made his way to Constantinople to study under the leading theologians. He soon gained reputation as a biblical scholar and in 382, with the official patronage of Pope Damasus, began to produce his Latin translation of the sacred writings of the Church. Twenty-two years later, in Bethlehem of Judea, his task was finally completed. In the tradition-hallowed birthplace of Jesus, the Christian Holy Scriptures had been given to the world as a single, unified book.

Consider the situation Jerome faced. Various versions of the Scriptures had proliferated in the first centuries of the Christian era, until there was a regular

Medieval scribes often em-bellished initial letters with scenes from biblical or monastic life: the "A" shows a scribe at work.

flood of texts. The rapid missionary expansion of Christianity had been producing vernacular translations of one or both Testaments into Georgian, Coptic (Egyptian), Ethiopic, and Gothic in addition to several Old Latin versions, and the pressing needs of missionary work had resulted in hurried editions by men only minimally prepared for such demanding labor. In some cases, the faith was established in cultural settings where the Scriptures were made available only after local people became able to take up the translating task. In a few cases, as has happened many times since, a whole new written language was created expressly for the purpose of translating the Christian Scriptures. These many versions, each with its own idiomatic character, each the center of a diverging manuscript tradition, contributed to the strong likelihood of corruption of the text. "There are almost as many forms of the text," Jerome lamented, "as there are copies."

In the prefatory letter to his version of the Gospels he reminded Damasus of the burden the Pope had laid upon him and of the method by which he sought to discharge his obligation.

> You urge me to revise the Old Latin version, and, as it were, to sit in judgment on the copies of the Scriptures which are now scattered throughout the whole world; and, inasmuch as they differ from one another, you would have me decide which of them agree with the Greek original. The labor is one of love, but at the same time both perilous and presumptuous. . . . Is there a man, learned or unlearned, who will not, when he . . . perceives that what he reads does not suit his settled tastes, break out immediately into violent language, and call me a forger and a profane person for having the audacity to add anything to the ancient books, or to make any changes or corrections therein?

He knew that some churchmen would have preferred him to select his text by a kind of majority rule, by simply comparing the different Latin texts and choosing the one most commonly used. But, argued Jerome, "if . . . we are to glean the truth from a comparison of *many*, why not go back to the original Greek and correct the mistakes introduced by inaccurate translators, and the blundering alterations of confident but ignorant critics, and, further, all that has been inserted or changed by copyists more asleep than awake?"

Jerome's basically simple procedure had some radical implications, particularly in the case of the Old Testament. For the Old Testament of the Church had been based on the Greek translation of the Jewish Scriptures, the Septuagint, and the older Latin versions had also followed this source. At first he continued the practice and made moderate revisions based upon the Septuagint and certain writings of the Church Fathers, particularly Origen's *Hexapla* (see page 154). But progressively he abandoned this method. This may be seen in his work on the Psalms. Here he produced three versions. The first was the Roman Psalter, a slight revision of the Old Latin which Damasus accepted as official. Later, there was a more complete revision based upon the secondary Greek texts, first adopted by the churches of Gaul and thus now called the Gallican Psalter. Still later, he went back to the Hebrew Psalter and made a thorough revision of the existing Latin text.

But when Jerome did decide to make a genuinely new translation of the Old Testament based on the best existing Hebrew and Aramaic manuscripts, he discovered a new problem: these manuscripts did not contain certain books (and parts of books) found in the existing Latin versions. These writings, which he named Apocrypha, became a central concern for Jerome. The name means "hidden" and seems to have been used to designate esoteric works; Jerome used the term to distinguish "ecclesiastical" from "canonical" books. If he had had his way the entire Apocrypha would have been omitted from the Roman Bible. But the pressure of Christian tradition weighed heavily; in the end it was all retained. He himself grudgingly agreed to translate Judith and Tobit, as well as the additions to Daniel and Esther found in the Septuagint but not in the Hebrew. These, he rationalized, were to be found "everywhere" in the Old Latin versions and therefore he personally did not want to "seem to the uninformed to have cut off a large portion of the volume." They were thus included. But he flatly refused to translate some of the books, such as Esdras, I and II Maccabees, and the Wisdom of Solomon, and instead adopted older Latin versions. It seems fairly clear that he did not think these books should be considered canonical, even though they were accepted by most of the Church. By his separation of the Apocrypha from the other writings, Jerome bequeathed to Christians a problem that has never been solved; it is still a difference between Catholic and Protestant Bibles. During the Reformation of the sixteenth century Luther put the Apocrypha into a separate section of his German translation of the Bible—not as Scripture, but as books "useful and good to be read." This practice of grouping them into a separate section between the Old and New Testaments was followed among Protestants until the nineteenth century, when British and American Bible societies, refusing to recognize the Apocrypha as Scripture, dropped them altogether from their publications. Other publishers followed suit, and until recently the Protestant Bible was rare that contained them.

When the Vulgate was completed it appeared as another competitor in the field. Jerome had introduced sweeping changes, primarily because of his decision to translate the Old Testament from the Hebrew. Many were suspicious of his judgments, in some cases because he had consulted Jewish scholars whenever he needed help with the Hebrew text. And too, some of his critics apparently felt that the older Latin texts Jerome had altered were themselves divinely inspired, and his work therefore cast aspersions on God's truth. Under heavy attack, he became bitter: "Let those who will keep their old books with their gold and silver letters on purple skins . . . if only they

An initial letter "I" shows a cleric preaching.

will leave for me and mine our poor copies which are less remarkable for beauty than for accuracy." He once blasted his critics in a letter to a friend as "two-legged asses."

Some parts of Jerome's translation were immediately accepted, but it was not until 580 under Gregory the Great—when Jerome had been dead for more than a century and a half—that the Vulgate began seriously to challenge the hegemony of the older Latin versions. Its accuracy and excellence became more and more widely recognized by Church authorities. In liturgical usage, however, the older Latin remained popular for centuries. German Christians still quoted from these versions in the ninth century; the English and Spaniards in the tenth; and in the French province of Languedoc the Old Latin Psalter was still in use in the twelfth century. Indeed, Jerome's Latin Bible was not given its familiar label "Vulgate" (implying common use) until the thirteenth century. And, as we shall see, the Vulgate was not made the official Bible of the Roman Catholic Church until the Council of Trent in the sixteenth century.

Jerome probably did not labor alone on his translation. The most reliable manuscripts of the version suggest that more than one hand was at work. It is not uniformly accurate in its rendering of the Greek and Hebrew, and is often uneven in style. But the Vulgate can be confidently attributed primarily to Jerome's vision, talents, and labor. On the whole it is a magnificent product of its age, remarkably accurate, and impressive in its style and quality as a translation. Notably, the sensitiveness with which Jerome captured the spirit of some of the poetry of the Old Testament, in particular that of the Psalms, has shaped and informed the piety of the Church from his day to our own. There is strength and grace in the Latin, as in his rendering of Psalm 46.

Initial "I" portrays the Apostle John.

> Fluminis divisiones laetificant civitatem Dei
>   sanctam tabernaculum Altissimi.
> Dominus in medio eius, non commovebitur.
>
> *There is a river whose streams make glad the city of God,*
>   *the holy dwelling place of the Most High.*
> *God is in her midst, she shall not be moved.*

Jerome's translation of the Beatitudes also moves with simple dignity.

> Beati pauperes spiritu, quoniam ipsorum est regnum caelorum;
> Beati mites, quoniam ipsi possidebunt terram.
>
> *Blessed are the poor in spirit, for theirs is the*
>   *kingdom of heaven;*
> *Blessed are the meek, for they shall inherit the earth.*

Until the time of the Renaissance, when scholars had once again mastered the skills required for the labor of a Bible translator and critic, Jerome's work was the only adequate standard by which the Church could test its tradition and spiritual life against the norm of Holy Scripture.

The Cloister Copyists

THE MAJOR DIFFICULTY in transmitting the Bible of the Christian Church from the early Middle Ages to later generations was quite simply the preservation of an accurate text. Textual corruption was the inevitable result of medieval publishing techniques, which were all based on hand copying. Even Jerome's new translation did not solve this problem, for copies of it soon began to reflect other, more familiar versions. Unfortunately, this was most evident precisely in places where he had changed the earlier wording in the interest of accuracy. Wherever he substantially altered the popular tradition, the chances increased that some later scribe, more familiar with that tradition than with the translation under his hand, would (often perhaps unconsciously) restore the text to its earlier, less accurate form.

By the time of Jerome in the fourth century, the transmission of Church traditions, including Holy Scripture, was beginning to be centered in the monasteries. Christian monasticism became a bulwark against the social turmoil that was reducing human life to its lowest common denominator: a simple struggle for survival and security amid overwhelming changes.

Monastic Christianity had begun in the deserts of the Eastern Empire. The role it came to play in the Middle Ages would have seemed inconceivable to its pioneers, lonely desert ascetics like Jerome himself or the famous St. Anthony, who lived in self-imposed exile from all human society for almost thirty years. From the east and from the deserts of Egypt, monasticism spread and grew until eventually bands of hermits began to appear and cloistered communities arose throughout Christian Europe.

The father of this communal form of monasticism is believed to have been one Pachomius, who had founded ten monasteries and a convent by the time of his death in the middle of the fourth century. St. Athanasius, the biographer of St. Anthony, introduced the ascetic ideal into the Western Empire. The first major monasteries there were founded in Gaul by St. Martin of Tours, and from Gaul western monasticism spread to Ireland, where it found fertile soil. Here the faith became a potent cultural force with the appearance of St. Patrick in the fifth century, and monastic Christianity proved so attractive to the Celtic spirit that thousands of men and women renounced the worldly life to enter the cloister. By the early sixth century, monasteries and convents were flourishing in a country that had been virtually illiterate only a short while before. Ireland, which had remained outside the Roman

Empire, was thus drawn into the European community; its cloisters became centers of learning and culture. Students came to them from all over Europe, and returned to their homelands to found churches and monasteries on the Irish models. Within a century Ireland became an influential force in western cultural history. It is no wonder St. Patrick is honored as a national hero.

About this time the Rule of St. Benedict, which became the guiding light of western monasticism, had risen in the south of Europe and was moving north. Benedict of Nursia established the first major regularization of monastic life; his Rule allowed about equal time to the active and the contemplative, providing for daily periods of meditation, cultural activity (such as manuscript copying), reading, prayer, and common worship, as well as the farming and physical labor upon which the continuing life of the community depended. The secure if somewhat sober regulations of these self-supporting communities must have seemed an attractive alternative to the precarious secular life of the seventh and eighth centuries.

Christian monasticism was saturated with the sense of man's eternal destiny. Events of the troubled history of this period gave support to traditional beliefs about the impending last days of judgment before the end of time. In the teaching of the Church lay the means of salvation from the coming doom. In a time of uncertainty and turmoil, many men were willing to sacrifice their personal fortunes and also their lives to preserve the traditions and institutions of the Christian religion. A real urgency was felt in the task of maintaining the continuity of Christian teaching. The training of priests, the teaching of Scripture to the devout, and the instruction of initiates were tasks of such importance that the monasteries became educational centers as well as spiritual havens of refuge.

The education offered by the Church could not, at first, compare with the classical training upon which it was modeled. Reading and writing were taught, of course, based on the Bible and later Christian writers. Students learned largely by rote, memorizing parts of Scripture, especially the Psalms, whose devotional temper often fitted quite well the spirit of the times: "How long, O Lord, how long shall the wicked triumph?" While there was great variation from place to place, the medieval curriculum was rudimentary at best. Minimal literacy in the Christian tradition was the goal, with the possible addition of a little grammar and rhetoric. But for centuries the Bible remained the cornerstone of learning, often the "last reader" as well as the first.

The demand for Bibles, Psalters, and Gospels in Latin grew ever more insistent as the medieval system of education became more complex, first with the founding of cathedral schools beginning about the late sixth century, then with the growth of universities from about the twelfth century on. Editions of the four Gospels and the Psalms were often published separately; these materials soon became more popular and familiar than the other books of the Bible. The work of producing these much-needed texts was carried on largely in the monasteries. Some of the most beautiful surviving art treasures

A medieval initial letter "A" shows St. Benedict reading his monastic Rule to monks. The Benedictine requirement of stabilitas loci, binding each monk to one cloister for life, helped to preserve monasteries as stable centers of learning and of faith in a period when political and cultural institutions were breaking down in western Europe. The Benedictine Rule was strictly observed at the great French monastery of Cluny, a powerful center of reform from its founding in the tenth century. Only a tower and part of the sanctuary remain from the abbey church (opposite), at one time the largest in Europe.

Around his self-portrait in the twelfth-century Eadwine Psalter a proud scribe wrote: "Scribe, nay Prince of Scribes, am I. Neither my praises nor my fame shall ever die. Let the letters traced by my pen declare the man I am."

of the Middle Ages are handwritten manuscripts, sometimes richly inscribed upon purple parchment. At least one has come down to us written in ink made partly of gold dust! The initial letters of chapters and paragraphs were brightly illuminated with elaborate symbolic decorations, or sometimes ornate miniatures of biblical scenes (see pp. 136–38 and 144). Often these books were turned into treasures by the setting of gold and jewels in their hand-wrought bindings.

One of the most beautiful and famous products of this art is the *Book of Kells* from the seventh or eighth century. This is a manuscript of the Gospels filled with bright, lavish decorations, considered by many the finest hand-written book in the world. It is in the "half-uncial" script that came into use in fifth-century Ireland. The earlier book hand of the west was blunt and angular, evolved from Roman capital letters with the addition of informal "cursive" devices to produce a faster, more graceful hand; that script is called "uncial," from the Latin word for inch. The half-uncial script was produced when scribes sought an even faster, handsomer style; the gifted Irish monks developed it into an art form.

For sheer beauty, the *Book of Kells* is closely rivaled by the *Lindisfarne Gospels*, created at the end of the seventh century on the island sanctuary of Lindisfarne off England's northeast coast. Tradition has it that in the ninth century, long after the Gospels were finished and bound between jewel-studded covers, a Danish raid on the island sent the monks scurrying to their boats. The priceless book was taken along—perhaps in a leather bag, for although the boat capsized, the book is said to have washed up on the beach later, only slightly water-stained.

In the Middle Ages, good scribes were highly prized members of their society; there was always copying that needed to be done. Some orders conferred special status by excusing scribes from regular chores connected with farming or maintenance. In Ireland, we are told, scribes were so highly thought of that the punishment for killing one "was as great as that for killing a bishop or an abbot."

The methods used to produce books were similar all across Europe. Monasteries under the Rule of St. Benedict made copying an important part of the daily routine. Each monastery usually had one large room, or a series of smaller rooms, arranged to afford the scribes the best possible light. If they worked in individual cells, for example, one wall would be open to daylight. Lamps or candles could not be used because of the danger of fire. Scribes worked in relative isolation, since noise and distraction could cause copying errors; as a rule only working scribes and certain monastery officials were allowed to enter the scriptorium.

The scribe sat at a slanted desk. In front of him was a *quaternion* of parchment or vellum—eight leaves so arranged that both facing pages were either the "hair side" of the animal skin or the "flesh side." The page surfaces had been prepared by rubbing them smooth with a pumice stone. A rotary awl (a wheel with tiny metal spikes) was used to make holes as guides down

The climactic events of the New Testament took place in Jerusalem, the Holy City. The Dome of the Rock (opposite), a Moslem mosque, rises above the temple area where Jesus came to teach during his last days. His execution on a hill outside the city is shown in an illumination, "The Descent from the Cross" (right), from an elaborately decorated fifteenth-century manuscript, "The Hours of Charles the Noble." The appearance of the Resurrected Christ, illustrated below in a thirteenth-century Greek New Testament, marked the rebirth of hope among his followers.

Archaeological discoveries have cast new light on first-century times and places. The Dead Sea Scrolls represent the most important find of manuscripts bearing on the Bible and the beginnings of Christianity. Writing desks, benches, and inkstands were found in the Scriptorium (above, foreground) of the Essene monastery at Qumran. The scrolls themselves were placed in jars (top left) and hidden in nearby caves. One copper scroll (left) was found among the papyrus scrolls.

The Apostle Paul passed often along the Arkadiana at Ephesus (below), a splendid street once lined with columns, statues, and altars.

In a twelfth-century illumination from German Saxony, the birth of Christ is portrayed beneath symbolic figures proclaiming the Savior's dominion over heaven and earth. Early in his adult ministry, Jesus gathered followers who left all to serve him. A tempera-on-wood painting by Duccio di Buoninsegna re-creates the calling of the fishermen Peter and Andrew.

either side of the page to be worked on, and between opposite holes lines were drawn with a dry, pointed instrument; margins were marked out, and the page was ready for the text to be copied. In classical times, scribes in Roman publishing houses often copied from dictation, a method which may have been used in the monasteries when multiple copies of a work were desired quickly—a dozen or more monks could write down the text as it was slowly read aloud by a superior. But normally the scribe would set up the book to be copied at his elbow, or rest it in a frame above his desk, working directly from the text itself. His pen was made from a reed or quill, its tip cut in such a way as to allow him to vary the width of his line by changing his grip on the pen. Colored inks were sometimes used, but most texts were copied in a standard black ink made from soot, gum, and water, or sometimes from plant galls, gum, and iron sulphate.

Scribes usually worked by natural light in unheated rooms. Each finished manuscript page was checked for accuracy and legibility by another monk.

COPYRIGHT 1896 BY JOHN W. ALEXANDER

A scribe at work on a text might copy for as long as six hours a day. It was not easy work, especially in unheated buildings during the winter months, when the fingers grew numb. "A blessing on the soul of Fergus," wrote one monk on a manuscript he was copying, and then added, "I am very cold." Another noted that "while the fingers write, the back is bent, the ribs sink into the stomach, and the whole body suffers."

If he was working in a large scriptorium among his fellow monks and needed to check a point in some other book, he asked for it silently by making a conventional sign. If he wanted the Psalter, for example, he would make motions of turning the pages of a book, then put his hands to his head to show David's crown. Of course the rule of silence had to be rigorously observed. When the scribe had finished with his quaternion he passed it on to a proofreader, who checked for errors. Then it was sent to the illuminator, who added the colored initial letters, made ornate page borders if these were

A thirteenth-century Latin Bible from France, here opened to the Book of Job, is typical of the handsome, laboriously produced Bibles of the Middle Ages. The illuminated initial letter depicts Job with one of his comforters.

called for, and perhaps provided miniature paintings to illustrate the text. The finished manuscript was taken to the binder, who sewed the quaternions together and then bound them, usually between leather-covered wooden boards, the preferred simple cover which would not tempt thieves to steal the book.

Madonna and Child are shown within an initial "O."

There were special manuscripts, however, which seemed to demand covers with a beauty to match the texts themselves. Gold, silver, gold-tooled leather, even hard-carved ivory were used in bindings. In the sixth century a Lombard queen presented a Bible to the Basilica of St. John the Baptist in Monza that was "bound in two plates of gold bearing a cross set with precious stones and cameos. . . ." Mellissenda, a twelfth-century countess of Anjou, owned a Psalter bound in ivory boards and dotted with turquoises.

Finished books, at least the large ones placed in churches, were often chained to within about six feet of their proper place, in much the same way as telephone books are fastened nowadays, to permit public access while discouraging theft. The labor expended to produce these Bibles in the Middle Ages seems almost incredible; but it was a labor of love, and thousands of Bibles, Gospels, Psalters, and other devotional books were made available in this way.

As the Bible came into greater general use, more and more copying was done outside the monasteries, and the emphasis began to shift from the splendid to the practical. The newly founded universities became centers of Bible production. At the University of Paris, for example, thousands of Bibles were turned out by teams of scribes who worked in professional guilds. These were largely without ornamentation and were copied in a compressed script, two columns to a page, which made them smaller and easier for scholars and students to use. Still, Bibles remained relatively expensive. According to thirteenth-century records, a copy of the Bible cost more to produce than did the building of two arches for London Bridge. A folio of parchment pages numbering two hundred probably required the skins of about twenty-five sheep, and even cheaper materials were expensive to produce in quantity. Demand kept the price high. Bibles could be rented, but owning a Bible remained the privilege of the well-to-do. Not many persons outside the Church and its monasteries and the universities, of course, could read Latin, and the demand for Bibles began to be universal only as vernacular versions or selections became available. We shall turn in a moment to these translations. But in any case, not until the middle of the fifteenth century, with the adoption of movable-type printing in Europe, did it become possible to produce both Bibles and other books so cheaply that almost anyone could own one.

The universities were not centers of Bible production, merely; great energy was also expended in biblical scholarship, especially in revising and standardizing the text of the Vulgate. It had become the practice by this time to divide it into clauses, sentences, and paragraphs, as was done with all Latin texts to make them more manageable. These divisions became the familiar "verses" of our Bible. In the early thirteenth century Stephen Langton, an eminent theologian of the University of Paris and later Archbishop of Canterbury, began the practice of dividing the books into chapters as well.

Into the Common Tongue

THROUGHOUT the Middle Ages vernacular translations of the Bible were being produced. In the early years the chief spur for such translating was missionary work. Christianity spread to areas beyond the limits of the old Roman Empire, where Latin was to all intents and purposes an unknown tongue. England was reached with the gospel by the fourth century, and experienced a "second conversion" in the sixth century. By the tenth century eastern Europe was Christianized, as was Norway. By the end of the thirteenth century the gospel had reached lands half the globe apart. Inroads were made into the Orient; there were Christians in India by the third or fourth century and in China by the ninth.

Where Latin was not a commonly spoken language, translations became very important. Thus, according to tradition one Caedmon, a poor Northumbrian peasant, made the first "translation" of biblical materials into the English vernacular in the seventh century, composing songs which were rough paraphrases of biblical stories told to him by monks. Another bard of the time, Aldhelm, Abbot of Malmesbury, used to take his harp to the highroad, where he would sing popular melodies, introducing Christian themes into his performance when possible. He was also responsible for the first written translation of biblical literature into Anglo-Saxon. He rendered the Psalms into his native tongue, and persuaded his bishop that the same should be done for the Gospels. Within a very few years the most learned man in England, the Venerable Bede, finished a translation of the Gospel of John—almost with his dying breath, it is said. Urging his scribe to write quickly, he dictated the final sentence on the eve of Holy Thursday, A.D. 735, and then died, whispering a prayer. In the next century King Alfred issued his Book of Laws, which began with the Ten Commandments and ended with the Golden Rule. He was also patron of a vernacular translation of the Psalms.

This sketch of the history of English vernacular translations could be paralleled in other lands. For example, Sahak, the Patriarch over Armenia, commissioned a translation of the Bible into the vernacular national language as a reaction against the use of Syriac in worship. He called upon one Mesrop, whom tradition holds to be the founder of the Armenian alphabet, to produce this translation along with an accompanying liturgy in the Armenian tongue. The result was a beautiful rendering of the Bible which survived to undergo many revisions during the Middle Ages. Some scholars feel that this is the most accurate of all the ancient translations.

Even when missionary zeal cooled, there remained a need for understanding the Holy Scriptures of the Church. During the tenth century in England, translations or paraphrases began to be written between the lines of some Latin manuscripts. These interlinear glosses set a pattern for later independent vernacular versions. The Anglo-Saxon *Wessex Gospels* appeared about the year 1000 as a vernacular translation without the accompanying text in Latin. The tendency to produce such translations seems to have paralleled the development of a vernacular literature in the various countries of Europe. But Church authorities grew increasingly suspicious of any unauthorized translation after some particularly unpleasant experiences with heretical sects in southern France. So attention was focused on standardizing and editing the Latin Vulgate.

It is a common opinion that ignorance of the Bible prevailed throughout the Middle Ages. This idea can be very misleading. Of course ignorance was widespread in medieval times, if that period is to be judged by our standards, and ignorance of the Bible is a necessary corollary of general illiteracy and

A tenth-century manuscript illumination of the famous Irish bishop St. Killian, preaching to Germans. Missionary efforts and preaching in the vernacular increased the demand for Bibles translated into the everyday language of the people.

lack of education. But the Bible remained at the center of intellectual life and also continued to occupy a central place in the piety of the Church. Christian thought was shaped and guided by the development of biblical interpretation from its beginnings in New Testament times.

Keys to Meaning

THE STORY of the Bible through the ages is not merely that of the transmission of the biblical text. Indeed, however fascinating its details, the story of the text is not nearly so important in understanding the influence of the Bible on western religion and culture as is some grasp of the way in which it has been understood and interpreted. Many feel that the meaning of biblical texts—"what the Bible says"—is self-evident, that there could be no serious disagreement about interpreting the Bible except in minor subtleties of doctrine. But a look at the ways in which it has been understood shows that thinkers have disagreed, not only about its teachings, but even about the proper approach to finding its central meaning. Particularly in the Middle Ages, Christian interpreters were faced with the problem of determining what should be the authoritatively *Christian* interpretation of Holy Scripture. The main lines of Christian exegesis were laid down in a long process of study, commentary, and consolidation involving both the methods by which to approach Holy Scripture and certain accepted conclusions about its teaching.

For the first century of its life, at least, the Bible of the Christian Church was the Old Testament. The earliest Christian thought focused on two major concerns: first, to grasp the significance of Jesus Christ; and second, to find a way of reading the Old Testament in the light of the new faith. These two concerns were inextricably interwoven. "Christ died for our sins," writes the apostle Paul, "*according to the Scriptures.*" For Paul—and he is typical of the first Christians—the meaning of Christ was part of the total plan of God, which began with the history of the old Israel and reached its climax in the new Israel: the Church. Paul's way of reading the Old Testament consists largely in finding key events in the history of the old Israel that foreshadow the final culminating events of the life, death, and resurrection of Jesus and the community of the new Israel. Adam, Abraham, the giving of the Law to Moses, the near-sacrifice of Isaac—these and other events are all examples of such foreshadowing; or to use the technical term, they are "types" (*typos* is the Greek word for "shadow") of Christ. Thus Paul can write: ". . . our fathers were all under the cloud, and all passed through the sea, and all were baptized into Moses in the cloud and in the sea, and all ate the same supernatural food and all drank the same supernatural drink" (I Cor. 10: 1 ff.), and affirm a few verses later that "these things happened to them as a warning, but *they were written down for our instruction*, upon whom the end of the ages has come" (I Cor. 10: 11—emphasis supplied).

Paul's "reading back" of the Christian celebrations of baptism and the Lord's Supper into the experience of Israel startles us; we are not so startled when he applies patterns from the old Israel to speak of the new. Thus he makes use of the imagery of sacrifice, drawing upon the Temple worship of Israel, to interpret the meaning of the death of Jesus for Christian faith. Jesus Christ is our Passover Lamb, our "sin offering" (a technical term from the Temple worship), our "mercy seat" (a technical term referring to the Ark of the Covenant in the Temple).

Paul's way of interpreting the Old Testament was passed on to the second century as an authoritative tradition, although it was apparently as baffling to some churchmen in that age as it is in some aspects to us. The author of II Peter, one of the latest books to be included in the New Testament, commented, "So also our beloved brother Paul wrote to you according to the wisdom given to him, speaking of this as he does in all his letters. There are some things in them hard to understand, which the ignorant twist to their own destruction, as they do the other scriptures" (II Pet. 3:15–16).

The opening verses of Mark in the Wessex Gospels, the first known Anglo-Saxon translation and forerunner of all later English versions.

Allegorical interpretation of the Old Testament is reflected in this illuminated initial: Joshua's Conquest of Canaan represents Christ's continuing war against the forces of evil.

As the Church moved out into the Roman Empire, its understanding of the Bible was enriched and broadened by "schools" of interpretation which arose in the major urban centers, such as Antioch, Alexandria, and Rome. Most prominent in its own day and most influential through the medieval period was the Christian school of Alexandria, which flourished in that center of culture from the late second century well into the early Middle Ages. Alexandria had long been famous for the brilliance of its intellectual life. Philo Judaeus, one of the most important representatives of Hellenized Jewish religious thought, lived, wrote, and taught there. Great Gnostic teachers such as Basilides had been heard in the streets and in the centers of learning, and wandering teachers of the various schools of Hellenistic philosophy had exhorted their listeners to take up the search for true wisdom and peace of mind.

The Christian school of Alexandria emerges into the light of history through the writings of its two greatest representatives, Clement of Alexandria (d. 215) and Origen, who died a martyr around 250 in the Decian persecution. The Alexandrian school taught that God is the source of all true wisdom, or as Clement put it, that "the divine instructor is Jesus, the Word [*Logos*], who is the guide of all humanity." This implied that the Alexandrian teachers were willing to listen to the voice of wisdom whatever its source—whether Greek philosophy or the sacred books of the Jewish people. Clement, especially, emphasized that God had intended philosophy among the Greeks to be the same sort of preparation for the gospel of Jesus Christ that the Law of Moses had been for the Jews.

Thus devoted to the pursuit of wisdom, the Alexandrian teachers also refused to become preoccupied with the "earthly" significance of a philosophical teaching or biblical passage; rather they concerned themselves with the "heavenly" meaning intended by the divine *Logos* who is the source of all wisdom. In this way the Alexandrians developed the principles of a "spiritual" interpretation of the Bible which became the mainstream of biblical exegesis in the early Church and through the Middle Ages.

Origen, Clement's successor as head of the Alexandrian school, was perhaps the most brilliant thinker of the patristic Church. Today he is remembered for his speculative thought (which got him into trouble with Church authorities), but the bulk of his labor as a scholar and teacher was devoted to interpreting the Bible. He produced the first critical text of the Old Testament, setting forth in parallel columns the Hebrew and five separate Greek translations, including the Septuagint—the entire edition being called the *Hexapla*. He also produced an impressive series of commentaries and interpretive notes covering virtually the entire Bible.

Origen's method of interpretation was both subtle and simple. He strove to uncover *layers of meaning*, which he called "senses." First was obviously the plain, literal meaning—what the text states and intends. But beyond this surface layer Origen probed the text for the meaning that God, the divine source of all wisdom, intended to convey—its *spiritual* meaning. Thus when the Old Testament attributes actions to God which are irrational or perhaps even immoral by human standards, Origen believed the interpreter was entitled to look deeper to find the true message beneath the surface. Or when Jesus speaks of coins, mustard seeds, or wineskins, the exegete must be willing to go beyond the bare words to find the hidden spiritual significance. The distinction between the literal and the spiritual meaning of a text became the basis of what we know as *allegorical* interpretation.

This kind of interpretation is obviously a powerful tool in the hands of a sensitive reader. It frees interpretation from the pitfalls of wooden literalism and from the moral dilemmas that arise when the Old Testament is read in a Christian setting. (Did God really command the Israelites to kill all those women and children? Did He really command that bear to eat those boys?) Allegorical interpretation can also be used to make sense of obscure biblical passages, providing the interpreter is ingenious enough to discover a spiritual meaning on which the text can shed light. Origen and the later Church Fathers of the patristic period became masters of this style of

Medieval engineering and construction methods are graphically revealed in an eleventh-century miniature portraying the story of the building of the Tower of Babel.

interpretation, and it dominated both preaching and theology from the third century until the high Middle Ages.

The Alexandrian school did not have the field of biblical interpretation to itself, however. Its great rival was the Christian school of Antioch, which emphasized the literal and historical meaning of the biblical texts. The Antiochenes were suspicious of Alexandrian methods, which they felt could erode the *reality* of the biblical story of man's redemption. After all, if Adam was not really *a* man, if there was really no tree, no fruit, and no serpent, then how did sin enter the world and why did Christ die that we might be saved? The school of Antioch furnished a healthy balance to the more creative but sometimes erratic allegorizing of the Alexandrians. The views of the school of Antioch were preserved in the work of the great preacher of the early Church John Chrysostom and in the writings of St. Jerome, creator of the Latin Vulgate. Although Antiochene methods of interpretation remained somewhat submerged during the Middle Ages, interest in the literal and historical meaning of the biblical texts was always present. At the time of the Protestant Reformation in the sixteenth century, this concern for the plain meaning of the Bible became the key to interpretation, and has remained the most prominent method of interpreting the Bible ever since.

As the long and complicated enterprise of biblical interpretation continued, it became more and more necessary to reconcile the varied and divergent views represented in Church tradition. St. Augustine, the famous Bishop of Hippo, a monumental figure in the genesis of medieval theology, also made significant progress toward the standardizing of biblical interpretation in his treatise *On Christian Teaching*, intended to prepare the Christian for explaining the Scriptures. Augustine commends careful study of the original languages of the Bible, and emphasizes the importance of the literal meaning of the text and the author's intention. At the same time, he insists, the language of the Bible is necessarily symbolic, since it deals with spiritual realities in this-worldly language. The sensitive interpreter must never forget that "God is the Author of Holy Scripture" and that He may have intended the *interpreter* to find in the text a meaning which not even the human *author* could have foreseen or intended. Thus Augustine tried to preserve both the literal and allegorical approaches of interpretation.

He is also important because his massive body of writings gave a distinctive structure to developing Catholic theology, which came to focus on the major themes of Augustine's thought. Thus a series of "topics" came to the center of Catholic religious thinking: the nature and attributes of God, grace, election and free will, the nature and destiny of man, the Church and the sacraments, and the purpose disclosed in human history. Biblical studies, as a branch of Church theology, tended to revolve around these themes also.

A further step in solving the difficult problem of an authoritative Christian interpretation of the Bible may be seen in the work of a fifth-century monk, Vincent of Lérins, whose name is taken from the island of Lerinum on which his monastery was located. In A.D. 434, a brief three years after the death of

Augustine, he wrote a tract called *Commonitorium* in which he tried to establish a rule by which true Catholic teaching could be measured. "The rule of a right understanding of the prophets and apostles," he wrote, "should be framed in accordance with a standard of ecclesiastical and Catholic interpretations." And then he continues with the famous "Vincentian rule":

A magnificently decorated thirteenth-century Psalter illustrates the personal piety of a French noblewoman, shown praying to the Virgin and Child.

"In the Catholic Church . . . we hold that faith *which has been believed always, everywhere, and by all.*" Thus the Latin phrase *semper, ubique et ab omnibus* became a medieval watchword of orthodoxy. Vincent also included in his treatise a list of sacred books which were to be authoritative in the Catholic Church. He considered the truth of Christianity to be complete in an authoritative *source*, the canonical Scriptures, and authoritative *tradition* that furnished the rule for interpreting these writings. The Catholic teacher was to interpret the Bible according to the tradition of the Church expressed in creed, dogma, and the consensus of the Fathers and theologians of the Church.

Vincent's rule of universality, antiquity, and consensus determined the course of biblical interpretation in the Middle Ages. Bible study was carried on through a process of consolidation. The opinions of the Fathers were collected on various passages and sometimes written into the margins of biblical manuscripts or even between the lines of the text. Collections of patristic comment on various passages are called *catenas;* when written into biblical manuscripts they are called *glosses.* This process of collecting and consolidating biblical interpretation is the direct forerunner of our modern commentaries on the Bible.

By the twelfth century, Bible study was being carried on in a formal, laborious, and painstaking fashion, especially in academic settings. The teacher slowly read out the glosses, comments, and questions on disputed topics, which the student either copied into his own biblical text or wrote out separately. The student's copy was then checked and approved by the teacher. Finally the teacher gave his formal lectures on the material he had provided for his pupils.

Interpretation of the Bible during the Middle Ages was thus very complex, as the interpretation of the word "Jerusalem" serves to illustrate. According to the scholars, its *literal* meaning was obviously the city of the Jews; in its *allegorical* meaning it could represent the Church, as in the Book of Revelation in the New Testament. Medieval scholars also found a *moral* meaning for the term, in which it stood for the soul; and finally, Jerusalem could also stand for the heavenly kingdom of God! Such complicated symbolism may be found in biblical commentaries throughout the Middle Ages and even as late as the sixteenth century. Even the Reformers occasionally made use of this style of biblical interpretation, and it is sometimes found today among very conservative scholars.

The Bible in Culture

THE INFLUENCE of the Bible on medieval culture was by no means limited to intellectuals who concerned themselves with studying and interpreting the text itself. From earliest times the Bible had its effect on other aspects of culture. The earliest examples of specifically Christian art, found in the

frescoes of the Roman catacombs, of course prominently display biblical themes. The main theme of such art was the Christian hope of eternal life; but the imagery of these early frescoes is drawn from the Old Testament, the earliest recognizable figures being Noah and Daniel.

The liturgy of the early Church also furnishes ample evidence for the influence of the Old Testament on Christian practices. In fact, we may have a clue to the presence of Noah and Daniel in those early burial frescoes when we note the ancient prayer for committing a soul to its eternal rest:

> Deliver, O Lord, the soul of thy servant as thou didst·
> deliver Noah from the deluge,
> As thou didst deliver Daniel from the lion's den. . . .

The prophet Daniel became a favorite subject in Christian art because he, like Christ, had been delivered from death.

The miracles of Christ also appear in early Christian art, as do the familiar figures from his parables: the Good Shepherd, the Prodigal Son, or the Vine and the Branches. Episodes from the Gospel stories are depicted, such as the raising of Lazarus and the miracle of the loaves and fishes. Gradually Christian art came to be dominated by the central mystery of the drama of redemption: the life and destiny of Jesus, whose birth, Passion, death, resurrection, and ascension became the classic cycle of this great body of art.

When, under Constantine, Christianity became the official religion of the Roman Empire, art came out of the catacombs and into the churches and monuments of the Empire. By the fourth century, as we have seen, the practice of illustrating biblical manuscripts had begun as well; some rich examples of this art have been preserved, such as the so-called "Vienna Genesis," a fifth-century manuscript of the Purple Codex, perhaps the most lavish surviving monument of the piety of the Justinian era. These fifth-century illustrations show the tendency to spiritualize the characters and symbols of the biblical stories which we have already noticed in the history of interpretation. The figures are abstracted from their setting in earthly time and space and made transparent to their eternal significance. The Old Testament story of Melchizedek, for example (Gen. 14:18–20), is clearly intended to reflect its fulfillment in the Christian celebration of the Lord's Supper, as the mythical priest blesses Abraham and his clan by bringing forth bread and wine from an altar and cup like those used in the Church. Through the Middle Ages, art gradually drew free from strict ties to the text of the Bible, as in the beautiful stained-glass windows and sculpture of the great cathedrals, but the emphasis on biblical themes was never lost.

The liturgical chanting of the Bible in Jewish and Christian worship also gave rise to western music—at least in the view of many historians of music. The early Church kept the Jewish cantor as its *psalmista;* it preserved the Jewish "thrice-holy blessing" in its *Sanctus,* and even some of the melodies of synagogue worship were carried over into the liturgy. All ancient Christian music was vocal; its setting was the drama of the Mass, its substance the celebration of salvation in Christ. Gregorian and Byzantine chants formed the first integral heritage of western polyphony, and that only after a long period of development. Instrumental music was viewed by some with suspicion. Although organs were used in churches as early as the ninth century, as late as the *mid-eighteenth* century Pope Benedict XIV warned, in his encyclical *Annus qui hunc*, against the worldliness of "musical" chant and noted that "the use of organs and other instruments is not yet admitted throughout the Christian world." Full musical settings of the Mass were in use from the eleventh century, however, and the period of the *Ars Antiqua* in the history of music coincides with the period of Gothic art and scholasticism in philosophy and theology—the high Middle Ages. The high point of church

A fourth-century ivory reliquary from Bresca is decorated with thirty-four scenes from the Bible, in addition to medallions of Christ and the Apostles and numerous Christian symbols.

music in the Middle Ages comes in the fourteenth century and may be represented by the brilliant Guillaume de Machault, whose career and talents marked clearly the transition from sacred to secular art which we have seen in other areas.

Out of the drama of the Christian worship service, dramatic representations of other Bible stories were elaborated which eventually became cycles of "mystery plays." These were often mixtures of religious themes with secular folk tales—sometimes in a fashion which seems to us irreverent. From performances in the nave of the church during festival seasons such as Christmas and Easter, these plays eventually moved out into the marketplace in a pattern similar to that of other art forms.

What is true of the art and music of the Middle Ages is true of the culture as a whole. Christendom gradually evolved a style of life which attempted to apply the faith in politics, economics, and social and family life as well as within the narrower circle of devotion. The ideals of medieval society were well exemplified in its saints, in the great thinkers of the Church, and in the "perfect society" of the Church itself. Just as the mundane events of the biblical stories were seen as bearers of the truth of the Gospel, so did the circumstances of everyday life become a vehicle of the Christian's spiritual pilgrimage. In the thought of the Church, the style of life that characterized medieval Christendom was magnificently worked out in a rational structure, although how far these ideals sifted down to its lower levels may be debated. The social order was viewed as a well-balanced hierarchy in which the lower levels existed to serve the needs of the higher. The serf toiled to feed the king or feudal lord; the king or lord represented the earthly authority of God; and the Church and its hierarchy symbolized the spiritual kingdom of God, Creator, Sustainer, and Redeemer of "this world."

Winds of Change

THE MEDIEVAL idea of a Christian society was under great pressure, however, from rapidly changing political and social conditions in the late Middle Ages. Most significant was the rise of a middle class of merchants, artisans, and townsmen who were economically established and politically self-conscious. By the beginning of the thirteenth century, European Christendom was witnessing the birth pangs of national states. The old understanding of the social order as a "cosmos of callings" was rapidly becoming irrelevant; paradoxically, this happened just as the ideal of a Christian society was being given its finest intellectual expression within the Church. Thus the thirteenth century witnessed both the apex and the decline of the Middle Ages so far as the cultural ideals of Christianity were concerned. It was a golden age for theology, liturgy, canon law, philosophy, art, and architecture. Its history is emblazoned with the names of Thomas Aquinas, Bonaventure, Albert the

Great, Francis of Assisi, and a succession of influential popes from the magnificent Innocent III to the pitiful Boniface VIII. Augustine's historic vision of the founding of an earthly "city of God" seemed to these men almost a reality. And while they could not stem the historical currents that were eroding the foundations of their society, they nevertheless bequeathed to subsequent generations a matchless intellectual and cultural heritage.

By the fourteenth century, new conditions of life were producing new religious stirrings, both inside and outside the Church. For a time it seemed that the mass of religious seekers might be satisfied with "entering the Church"—taking monastic vows or pursuing a religious vocation. Earlier currents of religious revival had been drained off in the Crusades, the last of which left Europe for the east in the thirteenth century. But the net result of the Crusades was to stimulate even more radical changes in Europe. The commerce they engendered enriched the towns of northern Italy; the sacrifice of feudal property which they demanded fostered the rise of medieval cities and the "third estate"; the mental horizons of the west were broadened and deepened by contact with the ancient and splendid civilizations of the east, both Christian and Muslim.

The religious revivals that swept over Europe in the late Middle Ages were popular in character even when controlled by the Church, and they have a direct bearing on the story of the Bible. Within the Church they resulted in the reform of the monastic orders and a close scrutiny of clerical morals generally. Even more significant, a new form of Christian piety arose, grounded in devotion to and affection for the human Jesus rather than the exalted heavenly Christ whom the medieval Church had pictured as the ruler and judge of the universe. This *devotio moderna* has been most attractively preserved in the still popular hymn whose lyrics are attributed to St. Bernard of Clairvaux:

> Jesus, the very thought of Thee
>   With sweetness fills the breast.
> But sweeter still thy face to see;
>   And in thy bosom rest.

The new piety meditated on the lowliness and meekness of Jesus, his poverty and suffering. It saw in him a living witness to the love of God which has always kindled the Christian heart.

The most perfect expression of this new kind of devout life may be seen in St. Francis of Assisi (1186–1226), born Giovanni Bernadone, son of a cloth merchant. It is significant that his background lay among the common people, indeed among the "third estate" mentioned above. His early life was gay and carefree. He and his companions enjoyed youthful mischief and revelry to the full. But his heart was eventually captured by the ideal of Christlike compassion and love. During a service in February of 1209, in a small church on the outskirts of Assisi, he heard the words of Christ to the Apostles as though addressed to him personally:

The earliest known portrait of St. Francis of Assisi is a fresco in the Chapel of St. Gregory in Subiaco. The motto in his hand is "The Lord's Peace Be with You."

And preach as you go, saying, "The kingdom of heaven is at hand." Heal the sick, raise the dead, cleanse lepers, cast out demons. You received without pay, give without pay. Take no gold, nor silver, nor copper in your belts, no bag for your journey, nor two tunics, nor sandals, nor a staff; for the laborer deserves his food.

—Matthew 10:7–10

"The Most High Himself," he later said, "revealed to me that I ought to live according to the model of the Holy Gospel."

From that day until his death in October 1226 he devoted himself to works of love, meekness of spirit, and Lady Poverty. The witness of his life attracted followers, eventually leading to the founding of a monastic order in his name. His life was a concrete expression of the devotion that turned man's attention once more to the humble Jesus of the Gospels.

Outside the Church the religious revivals of the late Middle Ages brought to the fore those anti-Church sects which had lived a precarious underground existence since the early centuries of the Christian era. There were also groups such as the Waldenses of southern France, stern critics of worldliness, who began on the fringes of Christendom but were driven out by opposition from within the Church. Eventually military force was used to eliminate the Waldenses—devastating much of southern France in the process—but the ideal of a new Christian perfection which these sects projected survived. For like St. Francis, the Waldenses and another group, the Cathari, had called men's minds back to the ideals of New Testament Christianity. All over Europe people were captured by this vision and troubled by the gap between the ideals of sacrifice and self-denial and the actual preoccupation of the Church with its own security and internal problems. The crisis of medieval Christendom was near at hand.

In response to the Cathari and Waldenses, Church authorities had forbidden the laity to possess the Scriptures (except in the Breviary or Psalter used in worship), and vernacular translations were especially denounced. Authorities were also extremely sensitive to any criticism of the Church, even when directed toward reforming admitted abuses. The Synod of Toulouse, held in 1229, saw the beginning of a systematic "inquisition" to discover and extirpate heresy and opposition before it could break out in open schism and rebellion. In this the Church reacted rigidly and defensively rather than creatively; Christianity had produced a civilization aptly named Christendom, but times were changing and the Church itself seemed somehow cut off from the society it had engendered and nurtured. Cries for reform were heard everywhere.

From the beginning this call to reform was linked with the Bible. The influence of the New Testament on the new ideal of personal dedication and the widespread popularity of the preaching friars, themselves often disenchanted with Rome, called attention to the bad times on which the Church had fallen.

Oxford University in England had been the scene of the last great flowering of medieval scholasticism in the person of William of Ockham, a brilliant and original thinker. Ockham was a Franciscan, and aside from his creative work in philosophy, theology, and politics he lent the power of his mind and pen to the cause of reform by protesting abuses of papal power during the period when the popes were being drawn into the sphere of influence of the French kings. Ockham defended the radical thesis that the pope possessed no temporal power and no right to confer it—that it comes to secular rulers directly from God. This view undercut the foundations of medieval Christendom and of course brought Ockham into disfavor with the papacy. But his voice was a powerful addition to the cry for reform.

This detail from a mural by Andrea da Firenze shows the Dominican monks St. Peter Martyr (left) and St. Thomas Aquinas refuting Albigensian heretics. The Dominicans were known as "dogs of the Lord"—"Domini Canes"—and are represented below destroying the wolves that have attacked the flocks of the faithful.

Ockham was followed at Oxford by another brilliant scholar, writer, and teacher, John Wyclif, who in the 1320's poured out a flood of tracts and treatises in Latin and English advocating radical reform of the Church on the basis of the New Testament. He declared that only Christ is the sure head of the Church, not the pope, and that a pope who grasps at worldly power and interposes his position in the Church between the Christian and Christ is certainly no fit governor of the Church on earth. Wyclif argued that God had given the earthly Church into the governance of its rulers as a fief, and he insisted that an evil tenant in office forfeits his stewardship. "Ye curates," he thundered, "see these heresies and blasphemies which follow from your wicked life and wayward teachings. Forsake them for the dread of hell and turn to the good life and true teaching of the gospel and ordinances of God." Wyclif placed the full authority of true Christianity in the Bible, which he viewed as the constitution of the Church.

Wyclif also took on a more constructive task. Convinced of the absolute claim of the Bible as the Word of God, he determined to give the Scriptures to the common people in their own language. Between 1382 and 1384 he and his colleagues at Oxford translated the Latin Vulgate into English. His vivid and powerful translation had a noteworthy effect on the development of the language as well as on deepening religious awareness in England. Eager Englishmen flocked to buy it. Some who could not afford a whole manuscript "gyvve a lode of hay for few chapters of S. James or S. Paule." Many, many copies must have been produced, for despite widespread confiscation and suppression more than 150 manuscripts of the translation survive today.

Coupled with the vernacular Bible translation, Wyclif sent out "poor priests," who came to be called Lollards, to preach the gospel in the countryside. His conception of reform, as we shall see, had a permanent effect on the character of the Church of England. In the words of Milton, Wyclif "sounded forth the first . . . trumpet of Reformation." His profound insight into the Bible, his own deep piety, his intellectual prowess and fervent patriotism, all combined with great personal magnetism to make his career a landmark in the waning of medieval Christendom and the coming of the Protestant Reformation.

Wyclif's ideas were carried to the Continent by a curious chain of circumstances. First a marriage alliance was concluded between Richard II and Anne of Bohemia. Her country proved open to ideas of reform in the wake of a cultural revival there during the fourteenth century. There followed a student-exchange program which brought Bohemian students to Oxford, and the resulting interchange of ideas increased pressures that reached a climax in the career of a great Czech patriot and reformer, Jan Hus.

At the turn of the fifteenth century, Hus was promoted to the post of preacher at Bethlehem Chapel in Prague, where he gained an immense popular following by his fiery sermons. However, he alienated the hierarchy of the Bohemian Church through his strident criticisms of the worldly clergy. It became obvious that he was publicly and insistently advocating

The Dominican Inquisition, begun as a preaching mission to the Albigensian heretics, developed into a judicial tribunal. Berruguete's panel portrays St. Dominic as the Inquisitor condemning two heretics to be burned at the stake.

Wyclif's ideas of reform. An open rebellion threatened, and Hus was summoned to the great Council of Constance (1414–1416), called by the Emperor Sigismund to heal the breach in Christian Europe caused by rival claims to the papal throne and by widespread heresy. Hus was promised safe-conduct, but upon his arrival at Constance was imprisoned. Sigismund reneged on his promise on the grounds (pressed upon him by the Council Fathers) that an "accused heretic" like Hus forfeited all civil rights and privileges. With Hus safely in prison, the Council condemned Wyclif and ordered his grave opened and his bodily remains publicly burned. With this grisly edict the fate of Hus was sealed. Although he steadfastly maintained his innocence of the formal charges of heresy brought against him, he resolutely

Woodcuts from the Nuremberg Chronicle show the city of Constance at the time of the famous Council, which ordered Jan Hus burned at the stake and his ashes cast into the Rhine (left).

refused to save his life by submitting to the authority of the Council. In July of 1415 he was burned at the stake, an early martyr to the cause of reform.

The movement Hus had spearheaded in Bohemia did not die with him; it exploded into revolt after his execution. In the bloody aftermath the work of reform moved forward in Bohemia, when the Church grudgingly permitted Bohemian Catholics to remain in communion with the Bishop of Rome while enjoying certain technically forbidden privileges, such as distributing to the congregation both bread and wine in celebration of the Mass. The civil and ecclesiastical upheavals attending the careers of early reformers like Wyclif and Hus, however, served to harden the opposition of the Church to radical reform, which was viewed as threatening her very existence.

Thus the Middle Ages drew to a close. New stirrings in southern Europe were producing the intellectual and cultural revival we know as the Renaissance. The earlier heritage of the Bible had produced and nurtured a Christian culture in the Middle Ages. As that form of Christendom disintegrated, new light shone forth from the Bible into the future.

NEW LIGHT BREAKS FORTH: RENAISSANCE AND REFORMATION

MANY FACTORS contributed to the decline of the Middle Ages, by no means all of them religious. The rise of medieval cities, along with a politically conscious middle class, gradually undermined the economic base of medieval Christendom—a process which can be traced back into the twelfth century. The power-seeking kings of France, England, Spain, and the German countries fostered strong national feelings all across Europe, thus setting up increasing tensions within the political structure of a theoretically united Christian Europe. While the Church remained a vital institution, it was beset by dissension from within and growing pressure from without, and its influence on society at large was apparently declining. The basic assumptions of the Catholic vision of a Christian society, resting on the biblical witness to God's redemptive concern for man, seemed to be called in question.

The fortunes of the papacy furnish striking evidence of the decay of the prestige and influence of the Church. The medieval papacy reached its zenith and its nadir in the same century. Innocent III (1198–1216) raised pontifical power and prestige to their high point. As a successor to Peter he believed himself to be king above all kings and was actually able to control the kings of France and England, and even dictate the succession to the throne of the

Holy Roman Empire. Boniface VIII (1294–1303), whose ambitions and claims were just as far-reaching, was reduced to angry, ineffectual scolding in a running battle with Philip of France, for Philip's troops invaded Italy in 1303 and Boniface was made a virtual prisoner in the fortress of Anagni. After being humiliated and manhandled, he was eventually set free and died shortly after, shattered by his downfall. Soon the papacy was drawn into the sphere of influence of the French kings, and the papal court moved from Rome to Avignon, where it remained for three-quarters of a century.

Along with these economic, political, and social changes, the climate of opinion was also changing throughout Christendom. This was partly because of the recovery of the literary remains of Greco-Roman civilization, and partly because of increasing contact with the Christian and Muslim east. Men were able to cast their eyes over the riches of Byzantine culture and view the glories of ancient Greece and Rome. They decided that the noble Greeks and Romans, although pagans, and even the hated infidel Turks, did not compare unfavorably with noble Europeans of the late Middle Ages. By the end of the fourteenth century thinkers like Ockham, Roger Bacon, John of Salisbury, and the great Dante had shown clearly the tendency of the age to criticize the prevailing norms of thought in philosophy, theology, politics, science, and literature. It was a time of testing and intellectual ferment.

The fifteenth century in Europe has become known among scholars as the period of the "Renaissance"—as indeed it was viewed by its intellectuals in their own day. Interest in art and letters heightened; culture was seemingly reborn before the eyes of the cultured. However, the term renaissance can be misleading, since there were cultural flowerings in the ninth, tenth, twelfth, and thirteenth centuries. That of the fifteenth century was more far-reaching than the others: changing conditions of life were joined with rapidly expanding mental horizons to produce striking new achievements. The arts prospered under the patronage of kings and in free cities such as Florence and Venice. The Church too played the role of patron to artists and artisans; high rewards followed upon recognition of artistic excellence and permitted artists and entrepreneurs to pursue even more intently their goal of reviving the glories of classical antiquity.

Printing and Cultural Change

THE MOVEMENT of cultural rebirth was accelerated by the European development of a revolutionary invention: printing by means of movable type. Of course printing itself was not invented in fifteenth-century Europe. There are wood-block prints from China that go back at least to the ninth century. Movable type was in use in the Orient from the thirteenth century on—separate wooden blocks, combined to produce a given text, could be stored until needed again. In Korea, by the fourteenth century such type was being

cast in metal. It is not certain, but probable, that the art of printing from movable type reached Europe from the east. Travelers such as Marco Polo ventured far into Asia and may have brought back examples of it: playing cards, money, or even scrolls. In the thirteenth and fourteenth centuries the dreaded Mongol armies hovered on the eastern borders of Christendom; block-printed items may have found their way into Europe during this prolonged confrontation. Whatever the explanation, block-printed playing cards and other objects appear in France by 1250, and wood-block illustrations are found in fourteenth-century manuscripts.

One interesting result of the wood-block technique was the printed "picture Bible"—the comic book of its era. These "poor man's Bibles" (*biblia pauperum*), each with its illustrations and few lines of text, might show a scene from the life of Jesus together with scenes from the Old Testament that taught the same lesson. Since manuscript books were so expensive, and most householders would have been unable to read a Bible had they owned one, the picture Bible met a genuine need. A complete Bible was as rare in the medieval household as a diamond tiara; one can imagine that these modest pamphlets of only a few pages would have been passed from hand to hand until worn out.

By the middle of the fifteenth century, the making of playing cards and religious pictures had become a thriving industry in Germany and to a lesser extent in other parts of Europe. Some printers were beginning to mold individual pieces of type in metal. Presses had long been in use in manufacturing paper and for printing on textiles; painters had developed an oily ink which would stick to metal type; metal workers had devised improvements in casting techniques. All these achievements combined to make possible the movable-type printing of entire volumes. We do not know who actually was first in Europe to use this process. Some claim that Laurens Coster of the Netherlands was the pioneer, while others think it was Johannes Gutenberg. Still others give credit to Johann Fust. Gutenberg will probably always be given pride of place in the story of European printing because of the Gutenberg Bible, published at Mainz in 1456. This was a beautiful monument to the new art, set two columns to a page, forty-two lines to the column, in an impressive Gothic type. Ironically, scholars now believe that by the time it was finished Johannes Gutenberg was no longer associated with the publishing house that produced this famous book. Johann Fust and his son-in-law apparently financed Gutenberg's work and then drove him into bankruptcy after becoming his partners in the Mainz firm.

Once the art had been mastered by the German printers, they carried it into other European countries. By the late fifteenth century there were presses in Italy, France, and Spain, and the turn of the century witnessed the printing of some eight million volumes in twelve different countries. More books appeared in the last half of the fifteenth century than in all previous human history! Nearly half dealt with religious themes: more than a hundred and fifty editions of the Bible were represented, mostly Latin Vulgates.

Printing methods of the sixteenth century are shown in a detail from the title page of a book printed in 1536 (above) and in a photograph of the reconstructed press on which Gutenberg produced the first Bible printed with movable type.

The baptism of Christ and related scenes and prophecies from the Old Testament are portrayed in a page from one of the medieval biblia pauperum, the *"poor man's Bibles" heavily illustrated with woodcuts.*

The spread of printing coincided with the rise of national feeling; thus one result was a flood of native-language Bibles or parts of Bibles along with the other literature in national tongues. Competition was fierce. Publishers were known to excuse the careless printing of a text with the apology that they were frantically trying to beat other publishers to the marketplace.

A host of mystics, writers, philosophers, theologians, musicians, artists, and artisans had drawn inspiration from the Bible throughout the Middle Ages. Now it took on an important new function. Bible translations were helping to fix the form, style, and vocabulary of the vernacular languages of emerging national literatures, and this was made possible through the powerful force of printing.

The Renaissance brought a crescendo in this movement. Writers, painters, and sculptors who shared the spirit of the new age were drawn as if by some elemental force to devote their creative energies to the foundations of Christian civilization. At first they had been attracted to the newly recovered classical culture, but a shift from classical to Christian themes became more marked as the Renaissance moved northward across Europe. This trend was perhaps abetted by increasing patronage from the Church. While the Italian Renaissance had been almost completely classical in tone, even in treating Christian subjects, the northern phase of it is more intense and perhaps less eloquent. To grasp the difference, one has only to compare Michelangelo's "David"—essentially a Greek god—or his "Pieta"—a model of classical understatement and restraint—with the more pious work of Dürer.

The northern Renaissance was destined to be highly important from the point of view of our story. While the increasingly worldly popes celebrated a regeneration of culture in the south, scholars and artists in the north raised their voices in a battle cry which was to shake Christendom to its foundations: Reform! For the Christian Renaissance of northern Europe has its beginnings in the fine schools established and maintained by the Brethren of the Common Life, a pious churchly group dedicated to simple Christian discipleship. It arose out of the religious revivals that swept across Europe in the late Middle Ages. Through their schools the Brethren trained able men in the new learning of the Renaissance as a part of the discipline of Christian living.

In England this northern ideal found an able exponent in John Colet (d. 1519), dean of St. Paul's cathedral in London. Colet was more a man of letters than a theologian, but he became famous for his penetrating studies of the literal meaning of biblical texts. In this he was applying the tools of Renaissance philology to the original sources of Christianity in the same way earlier scholars had studied the literary legacy of classical civilization.

Colet's friend and disciple Sir Thomas More followed what was to become a familiar pattern by turning his attention to the growing cries for reform of the Church. He advanced some radical views in his famous *Utopia*, which pictured an ideal society that practiced only simple religious observances and a way of life based on morality rather than involved creeds, speculative

A woodcut by Albrecht Dürer, leading Bible illustrator of the sixteenth century, portrays a scene from the Book of Revelation: an angel with the keys to heaven and hell casts the dragon into the abyss.

theology, and ecclesiastical politics. More's point was obvious; his criticism of the life of Christendom was unflinching. Eventually his uncompromising ideals brought him into conflict with Henry VIII, and he was beheaded in 1535, when the Protestant Reformation was well under way in England.

Prince of Christian Humanists

THE MOST FAMOUS and able advocate of Christian culture during the Renaissance was the "prince of humanists," Desiderius Erasmus of Rotterdam. He is one of the most fascinating figures in western intellectual history. Very few men have gained such stature among their peers as he enjoyed at the height of his powers. His scholarly and literary achievements dominated the first decades of the sixteenth century.

The circumstances of his birth remain a mystery; it was rumored during his lifetime that he was the illegitimate son of a priest, perhaps even a bishop. Educated in the schools of the Brethren of the Common Life, he was ordained priest and monk as a young man—a step he later deeply regretted. Soon after beginning his career as a minor church functionary he became known as a writer. His interests and abilities ranged over the intellectual spectrum of his age, from theology to philosophy and *belles-lettres*, from Bible translation to biting anticlerical satire.

He advocated what he called the philosophy of Christ. This he conceived as a life of balanced reasonableness coupled with deep devotion to the example of Jesus, especially his compassion and humility. Here Erasmus gave voice to an ideal which included the virtues of classical culture—prudence, moderation, courage, and reasonableness—among the "Christian" virtues of faith, hope, and love. He lampooned what he considered the extravagances of sixteenth-century popular piety, setting his acid pen against such practices as fasting, pilgrimages, the veneration of relics, the invocation of saints, and the sale of indulgences. Simple piety was good, he insisted, but it needed to be tempered by reason and sound judgment. Without sober self-discipline, piety gives way to excess, and faith degenerates into superstition.

Much of his criticism was aimed, not at the theology of the Church, but at the sheer foolishness of the practices to which he objected. He once complained dourly that if all the bits of wood that were venerated in Christendom as relics of the true Cross were gathered together, he did not doubt that a *cathedral* could be built. His satire was harsh but he remained a loyal son of the Church.

Erasmus was not a crusader, perhaps not even a reformer, for all his shrewd and observant criticism. While initially applauding Luther's courage, he came to despise the intolerance of the pioneer Protestants. A thoughtful man who stood for the delicate balancing of issues, he had a keen awareness of the ambiguity and uncertainty of all human judgments. Tolerance, reasonableness, and conciliation were his aims; he saw the value of compromise.

Dürer's portrait engraving of Erasmus of Rotterdam emphasizes the dedicated scholarship that enabled the brilliant Christian humanist to produce the first critical text of the Greek New Testament.

This attitude cost him the trust of both zealous Catholics and Protestants. Yet he saw clearly the eventual result of the Church's stubborn refusal to reform herself from within. Had he held some position of responsibility in the Church, the unity of Christendom might perhaps have been saved. At home in neither of the extreme religious parties, he seems a man out of place in his age.

In pursuing his vocation as a scholar, relatively independent of the upheavals of the early Reformation, Erasmus made a great contribution to the story of the Bible. He devoted himself increasingly to producing editions of the classic sources of Christianity, in the belief that this would further the peace and purity of the Church. His initial effort was a magnificent edition of the Greek New Testament, published in 1516. This *Novum Testamentum* he dedicated to Pope Leo X, hoping that his scholarship might in this way contribute to a restoration of Christian piety. He looked forward to a time when the New Testament would be understood by the common people—when the housewife at her cooking and the peasant at his plow would sing psalms to ease their labor. Although his hope of peaceful reform was ill-starred, his New Testament did become a working tool of biblical scholars and translators—mostly Protestant reformers, however, and not Catholic churchmen. To use a figure that circulated during his lifetime: Erasmus provided the kindling which the reformers set ablaze.

Here I Stand

A YEAR AFTER ERASMUS' New Testament appeared, Leo X presided over the magnificent closing sessions of the Fifth Lateran Council. Renaissance scholarship was flowering all over Europe. Official Christendom was at ease; all seemed well, or at least under control. Then a young (thirty-four-year-old) university professor in an obscure German city—one Martin Luther—decided that the sale and preaching of indulgences should be publicly debated. He prepared a series of propositions to serve as the basis for such a debate and nailed them to the door of the Castle Church in Wittenberg (the door served the university community as a kind of bulletin board). Luther was taking a responsible step in doing this, and certainly not a radical one; he could scarcely have foreseen the results.

But before going into the consequences of this quite ordinary action of a German professor, we must see how Luther came to be where we find him in 1517. He was the son of a miner who had become a member of the respectable middle class of the village of Eisleben. The father was ambitious for his son and sacrificed to give him an excellent education, in preparation for a career at law. He was bitterly disappointed when young Martin suddenly decided to enter a monastery, being accepted in 1505 as a novice in the venerable order of Augustinian Eremite Friars at Erfurt.

The inner scourge that drove Luther into monastic life continued to

Lucas Cranach's portrait of Martin Luther in the Augustinian habit was painted when the young monk's ideas were beginning to challenge the authority and many of the traditional practices of the Church.

deprive him of the peace of mind he had sought by taking his vows. "I was a good monk," he wrote later. "If ever a monk got to heaven by his monkery, it was I. . . . If I had kept on . . . I should have killed myself with vigils, prayers, reading, and other works." By the expectations of his Church, he should have gained peace of soul; but he was acutely conscious of his shortcomings. Much has been said about Luther's "scruples"—his sense of sin, which verged to be sure on the pathological. He knew that the gospel promised life, hope, and peace, and his spiritual crisis was provoked by a search for some way to claim these promises for himself.

Johannes von Staupitz, Luther's superior and father-confessor in the order, was a man of learning and piety whom the novice idolized and sought to emulate. Staupitz soon realized he had a problem on his hands. Brother Martin was both sensitive and gifted; Staupitz feared that the monk's zeal would upset his mental and emotional balance. He therefore offered his young charge the opportunity to pursue a career in theological education, thinking this might divert some of Luther's energies into channels promising a healthy and balanced life under the vows of the order.

Luther undertook his commission as a scholar with the same single-minded devotion he had brought to his vocation at a monk. His gifts were soon recognized, and he was invited to study for the doctorate in preparation for lecturing on the Bible and theology. He took his degree with distinction and was always proud to be addressed, as "Doctor Luther." The *Sentences* of Peter Lombard, a standard theology textbook of his day, was the subject of his first lectures. But soon his attention turned to the Bible, which he had studied diligently from the beginning of his monastic life. In facing the responsibility of teaching young theologues, he was confronted once again with his own spiritual needs, and as he worked at his lectures on the Bible he found his personal convictions being transformed.

Years later, he was able to describe the nature of his changed outlook in simple terms. He began in anxiety and terror (he wrote in the preface to his collected Latin writings); God seemed to him an angry judge who governed the universe and man by the standard of His uncompromising righteousness and justice. This image of the divine justice and retribution, he believed, led him astray. For he came to realize that the righteousness of God that had so terrified him was nothing more or less than the *loving* righteousness toward men which God had shown in Jesus Christ. The righteousness of God was that given to those who put their trust in Him. As Luther remembered it, the change was simple, yet radical.

From the vantage point of history we can see that, while it was indeed a change, Luther's personal breakthrough was neither sudden nor simple. There may have been a dramatic turning point, a moment when he first realized that he had won through to his new faith. But there was a long struggle toward a new way of grasping and expressing the faith that led to his new insight. The stages in his quest emerge in his lectures, first on the Psalms, then on the Letter to the Romans, then on Galatians, Hebrews, and Titus, and finally in 1519 on the Psalms again.

Gradually Luther abandoned the inherited theological framework and involved sacramental piety of the medieval Church for a personal confrontation with God by faith alone. In the gradual progress of his development in this direction, he was probably unaware of any radical change. Eventually he came to interpret the entire Bible in the light of his Pauline understanding of justification by faith alone. Thus, when the moment of testing came, during the indulgence crisis of 1517–1519, Luther's students were initially more aware of the radical implications of his ideas than he was. His *Ninety-five Theses*, presented for academic debate, were translated from Latin into German by his students and circulated widely. Almost overnight he became a popular hero, and the indulgence controversy a *cause célèbre*.

What was at stake in this crisis? Indulgences were part of the very complex sacrament of penance of the medieval Catholic Church; this had evolved into a form that included confession to a priest, absolution (the promise of forgiveness), and some act of repentance and satisfaction (often symbolic, such as the saying of prayers or the making of a pilgrimage). The purpose of the sacrament was to restore the relationship between God and

Martin Luther's study at Wittenberg University appears today almost exactly as it was when he wrote his Ninety-five Theses *and the many theological tracts and biblical commentaries that guided the Reformation.*

the individual Christian when it had been compromised by sin. Indulgences permitted certain carefully defined special conditions for the sacrament of penance. Sometimes the "satisfaction" part of it was forgiven. The abuse against which Luther (and many others) protested, which had become widespread during the fifteenth century, was the *sale* of indulgences, the proceeds from such sales being used to bolster the heavily burdened financial commitments of the Church.

At the center of the controversy that arose was the young, ambitious Albert of Brandenburg, who already held two powerful offices in the German Church and was seeking the highest position that Church had to offer: the archbishopric of Mainz. Ecclesiastical law forbade the holding of more than one office at a time, but Albert had already obtained permission to occupy two; he now needed further permission to become archbishop. To get this dispensation, he agreed to pay a very large sum into the treasury of the Church in return for the permission. The banking house of the Fuggers in Germany put up the money, and Albert was granted the right to sell indulgences in Germany to repay the loan, on condition that half the proceeds of the sale should go into the building fund for the new basilica of St. Peter in Rome.

Needless to say, Albert showed keen interest in the success of this venture. He commissioned the "order of preachers," the Dominicans, to be his salesmen and gave them a set of extravagant instructions which went beyond the bounds established by canon law even for the sale of indulgences. He proclaimed, in fact, that this special indulgence would grant "complete

Hans Holbein the Younger ridiculed the traffic in indulgences by showing David, Manasseh, and a confirmed sinner receiving direct forgiveness from a merciful God, while the Pope, enthroned amid worldly splendor, authorizes monks to sell indulgences to the poor and the crippled.

remission of all sins . . ." and also serve as a blank check for future sins up to an eight-year statutory limit! The young cleric intended to recoup his losses and then some.

The Dominicans fanned out across Germany. The most famous of them, Johannes Tetzel, went to Saxony and Brandenburg, where his hard-sell tactics scandalized many of the faithful. He was fond of closing his sermons with a little jingle, whose crudity even translation hardly increases: "As soon as the coin in the coffer rings, the ransomed soul into heaven springs." Luther, some of whose parishioners had slipped into neighboring Saxony to avail themselves of Tetzel's wares, was outraged. (Had he known of the devious ecclesiastical dealings behind the sale, he would no doubt have been even more shocked.) He objected to the indulgences on theological grounds, insisting that forgiveness could not be purchased with money. True penitence could come only through the grace of God working in a contrite heart. As he wrote in the first of his ninety-five theses: "When our Lord and Master Jesus Christ said, 'Repent,' he wanted the entire life of believers to be one of penitence." Thus the issue was joined; Luther would have no "forgiveness for sale" signs posted by the Church.

The young professor evidently believed that if the question of indulgences were publicly debated and the pope apprized of the abuse, the practice would certainly be condemned. Thanks to his students, the printing press, and the rising tide of German national feeling, which focused opposition to a Church authority headquartered in Rome, in an amazingly short time the issue reached gigantic proportions. Luther had dropped a spark into tinder more than ready to burn.

When the controversy broke in 1517, German politics were tangled and confused, and the lesser nobles were happy to interpose their authority between Luther and both Church and emperor as a means of asserting their ancient prerogatives. Thus his "good prince," the elector of Saxony, Frederick the Wise, willingly gave him the expert political assistance he needed to champion his cause. Without this, Luther would undoubtedly have met the fate of Hus or Savonarola; one Johannes von Wesel had already been condemned to death as a heretic for preaching against indulgences. Luther's opponents considered him a dangerous revolutionary; but, given the political situation in Germany, his supporters saw him as a crusader and courageous national hero.

Public attention was attracted by a series of debates in which Luther had an opportunity to clarify his thinking and further broadcast his ideas. In a crucial meeting with the brilliant Dominican, Johannes Maier von Eck, held at Leipzig in 1519, Luther was maneuvered into heretical statements. Eck compared him to Hus, who had died at the stake at Constance. Luther replied by asserting that Church councils could err and had erred, and that particularly the Council of Constance had erred in condemning Hus. There followed shortly the expected papal bull, *Exsurge Domine* ("Arise, O Lord"), denouncing his teachings and threatening excommunication unless he re-

Luther's ideas emphasized the rights of individual conscience and dissent, but his 1525 tract "Against the Rebellious Peasants" (title page, above) advised harsh suppression of a revolt against the German princes.

Woodcuts by Lucas Cranach illustrated the first edition of Martin Luther's great translation of the Bible into German. This scene from the Book of Revelation identifies the "harlot of Babylon" with the Papacy by placing a triple crown on her head.

canted. Leo X adamantly refused to grant the papal audience Luther now demanded; apparently the pope thought that, condemned as a heretic, he could be silenced by purely ecclesiastical means. He badly misjudged the situation. Too many people considered Luther as their spokesman for social and economic as well as religious grievances against Rome and the Empire. When news of the threatened excommunication reached Luther, he reacted violently by burning the papal bull and adding a copy of the canon law to the fire for good measure. Out of the flames arose the Protestant Reformation.

One more abortive attempt was made to silence him. The newly crowned Emperor Charles V called an Imperial Diet at Worms, an important cathedral city near the Rhine. Luther was summoned under a promise of safe-conduct. With his knowledge of John Hus' fatal journey under similar protection to the Council of Constance, it took great courage for him to appear, but appear he did. Not only so, but in the face of demands by both Church and emperor that he recant his doctrines, he flatly refused and is said to have ended his defense with the famous words: "Unless I am convinced of error by the testimony of Scripture or by clear reasons . . . I cannot and will not recant anything, for it is neither safe nor honest to act against one's conscience. Here I stand; I can do no other. God help me. Amen."

A week later Luther was allowed to leave Worms for Wittenberg. By secret prearrangement, the party in which he was traveling was intercepted by trusted friends in the Thuringian forest, and he was "kidnaped" and hidden away in Wartburg Castle for almost a year disguised as "Knight George." Five weeks after the confrontation with the young priest, on May 25, 1521 the Imperial Diet formally condemned his teachings. This decision completed Luther's break with the past. Excommunicated by the Church and outlawed by the Empire, he was forced by his conscience to defy both. After his year in hiding, he returned to his beloved Wittenberg under the protection of his prince to continue the work of reform, firm in his conviction of the rightness of his cause and with equally firm support from many influential German noblemen and friends. Luther remained at Wittenberg until his death in 1546. The flame he had inadvertently set ablaze spread throughout central Europe during his lifetime, spurring not only religious reform, but incipient nationalism as well. Luther's "reform" became the *Reformation* and his "protest" became *Protestantism*.

The Flame Spreads

LUTHER was not the only moving spirit of Protestantism. In Switzerland the reforming impulse was being given new shape by Huldreich Zwingli. In the sixteenth century the Swiss were a loose confederation of cantons differing considerably from one another yet able to preserve their relative autonomy by presenting a united front toward other Europeans. The course of the Reformation in Switzerland was shaped partly by this unusual political

Zwingli began the Swiss Reformation in 1519 by attacking the Church's views on Purgatory, the Invocation of Saints, and monasticism from the pulpit of this church in Zurich, where he was minister from 1518 to 1531.

situation. A proud and fiercely independent people, the Swiss were not inclined to accept the rule of Rome—especially with the memory of two great reforming councils at Basel and Constance fresh in their minds. Demands for reform, the new scholarship of the Renaissance, and religious dissent all found shelter among the snowcapped mountains and green valleys of the Swiss city-states.

The career of Zwingli presents a classic case of the scholar turned reformer. In the course of his excellent education he developed an interest in biblical studies, which in turn seem to have awakened in him a critical attitude toward Church abuses. From 1509, when he was ordained a priest, until 1518, when he accepted a post in the canton of Zurich, his vigorous demands for reform provoked an uproar. From his Zurich pulpit he launched an ambitious program of biblical preaching. Four years later, the Reformation began in Switzerland when a group of citizens met in the home of a printer named Froschauer to eat meat during the prescribed Lenten fast, thus setting up a test case of the ecclesiastical laws governing fasting. The expected controversy followed, from which Zwingli emerged as recognized leader of a reformation movement in Zurich, determined to repudiate any ecclesiastical authority-at-large and to determine its own faith. Two years later, on Easter of 1525, Zwingli celebrated the first Protestant Communion service in Switzerland, a radically simplified ritual in which the congregation gathered around a large table covered with a plain white cloth, and both bread and wine were simply handed around for all to partake of.

In his work in Zurich, Zwingli evolved a distinctive pattern of cooperation between civil and Church authorities. The result was a "confederation" of Church and state in which citizenship and Church membership coincided—a working theocracy under the "constitution" of the Bible. As Zwingli himself put it, ". . . We submit to the Two Hundred [the city council of Zurich] those matters which ought to be decided by the entire congregation, only under the condition that they counsel and decide under guidance of the divine Word. They are representatives of the church. . . . This position has been stated to the entire congregation." This attempt to put in practice the Bible as the constitution of a confederacy combining Church and state in a practical theocracy has become known as the "Reformed" type of Protestantism as distinct from Lutheranism. It gradually spread through Switzerland and into southern Germany, where the two forms competed.

Religious reforms and schismatic movements seemed to spring up everywhere in sixteenth-century Europe. Among the lower classes, sects that were in effect reform movements arose, often led by well-educated clerics or gentlemen. These small groups of believers voluntarily associated themselves in compacts to purify the Church of the accretions of centuries of tradition. They sought to return to the apostolic simplicity of the "original" gospel. Such "spiritual" or "radical" reform movements (as they are often called) usually gave great authority to the Bible; their members led lives of frugal self-denial and separated themselves from society in general, wanting nothing so much as to be left alone to live out their vision of the kingdom of God in peace. Many of these groups were "pacifists," as for example the disciples of Menno Simons, who became known as the Mennonites and have survived down to the present. Some radical sects espoused a doctrine of the absolute separation of Church and state. A few were violently revolutionary, as was the group led by Thomas Müntzer, thrown out of Wittenberg when he referred to Luther as "Dr. Pussyfoot, the new Pope of Wittenberg." Obviously these so-called "left-wing" reformers were a diverse lot, and their diversity was baffling and threatening to both Protestants and Catholics. Almost always looked down upon, they were often brutally suppressed; yet they survived to have an influence on history far out of proportion to their numbers. As they sought havens from the storms of abuse and persecution that assailed them, their wanderings over Europe spread the ideas for which they stood. The generally quiet (but sometimes violent) testimony of their lives was compelling. In the aftermath of the Reformation, the doctrine of the separation of Church and state which they advocated seemed a hopeful alternative to devastating religious wars. America's founding fathers wrote this doctrine into the Constitution, and some of the largest religious bodies in America today, such as the Baptists, trace their history back to sixteenth-century sectarians.

By 1534 the Protestant movement was a *fait accompli*. In that year a young French refugee appeared in Basel, Switzerland. John Calvin was of a quiet, studious bent and had been strongly influenced by the scholarly ideals of the northern Renaissance. He had been forced to flee the University of Paris when he was suspected of definite Protestant sympathies. Calvin arrived in Basel a confirmed Protestant. Within two years he had seen through the presses the first edition of his famous work, *The Institution of the Christian Religion*. The *Institutes*, as this work has come to be called, was eventually expanded into a mammoth compendium of Reformed Protestant theology and became the most influential book of the Reformation. And Calvin was just twenty-seven years old when he published it. As his fame spread, he became one of the recognized intellectual leaders of Protestantism.

If Luther was the pioneer of the Reformation and its religious genius, Calvin was its premier theologian, the creative systematizer of a Protestant theology. Already in 1536 he saw clearly what was at stake in the theology of the Reformation. Every thought was to be centered in Christ; theology was to be reconstructed on a solidly biblical foundation. Like Luther, Calvin emphasized the traditional Augustinian doctrines of election (predestination), grace, and justification by faith. Both Calvin and Luther insisted that the Bible should be both the source and the norm of Christian belief and conduct. However, Luther's concern was with the personal element in religious belief and practice, while Calvin's major emphasis fell on the formulation of a vigorous and coherent system of Reformation doctrine. Luther was concerned with the *witness* of the Bible to salvation by grace and justification by faith; Calvin sought to fix a precise theological *understanding* of these biblical themes. He intended to lay a biblical foundation for all the key doctrines of Protestantism. How well he succeeded may be seen by the generations of Protestant theologians who have been his pupils. He planted the Bible firmly at the heart of all Protestant thought to our own day.

Calvin, as an intellectual raised and educated in a climate of gentility, would gladly have avoided the rough-and-tumble of practical reform. He wanted only a study, a few books, time and peace. But fate denied him. He was forced, while returning from a visit to France in July of 1536, to take a somewhat indirect route that brought him to Geneva. There he encountered an old friend, the fiery reformer Guillaume Farel, already at work in the city. Farel constrained Calvin to stay and help by threatening him with the

John Calvin was the builder of a theocratic government and a brilliant systematic theologian of the Reformation.

judgment of God. "You are simply following your own wishes," he thundered at the young scholar, "and I declare in the name of Almighty God that if you refuse to take part in the Lord's work in this Church, God will curse the quiet life you want for your studies."

From that day on, Calvin gave his life to the practical as well as the theoretical task of reformation. He battled the hard-core issues of Church discipline through the complicated system of councils that constituted Geneva's city government. Deeply involved in the power politics of the city, he was twice forced to suspend efforts at reform. But eventually his determination carried the day and Geneva became, for better or worse, a model of what could be accomplished under the strict discipline of Reformed Protestantism. Certainly tamed down from its once dissolute habits, the city prospered economically, and its population grew as its fame spread across Europe. Protestant leaders came there to study both its theology and its civil life. The Reformed pattern was carried by like-minded reformers to the Netherlands, Scotland, England, and even to Catholic countries undertaking the work of reform. Calvinism (a term which would have been most distasteful to Calvin) became the dominant, militant force in later Protestantism.

In practice, it tended to become extremely authoritarian. Mark Twain once remarked dourly that he would rather face an armed mob than three Calvinists convinced that they were doing the will of God. There is a point in this playful rhetoric, for there was in some cases suppression—of police-state harshness and rigidity—both of religious dissent and of any manner of life thought to be in conflict with biblical standards. Calvinism made the pattern of cooperation between civil and religious authorities into a disciplined system of control for the faith and morals of an entire community. This gave it a certain inward toughness that enabled it to resist hostile governments, as did the Huguenots in France, and survive bitter persecution. Calvin, unlike Luther, permitted defiance of unjust or un-Christian laws in the name of God when the Church was convinced that a life-and-death issue was at stake. Because it could be used to justify civil disobedience, Calvinism could be at times a revolutionary ideology. This inner toughness leads to the outward appearance of harshness and intransigence that has given Calvinism a bad press in our age. All European and American history, however, has been profoundly shaped by this potent system of ideas.

The Bible for the People

THE PROTESTANT REFORMATION, emphasizing the authority of the Bible, inevitably centered Christian life and thought upon that ancient book, which was now studied as it had not been since the days of the Church Fathers. The Reformers willingly drew upon the pre-Reformation scholarship of the northern Renaissance, which had emphasized study of the Scriptures in their original languages. For they firmly believed that more adequate understanding of the Bible would foster a deeper awareness of God and a more unreserved commitment to the faith. They commonly accepted the recovery of the "original" meaning of biblical writings as a task of first importance for the Christian thinker.

It was in this spirit that Erasmus had edited and published his Greek New Testament in 1516. Another pre-Protestant reformer, Cardinal Ximenes of Spain, published a six-volume edition of the Bible in which the original Greek and Hebrew texts were printed in parallel columns beside the Latin Vulgate. This massive project, known as the Complutensian Polyglot, appeared between 1514 and 1522. In his preface the cardinal addressed a trenchant if veiled warning to the authorities of the Church, to the effect that more attention should be devoted to grasping the intention of the biblical authors; if the Church failed to undertake this as a complement to her internal reforms, he believed, she would fall on hard times.

Once the Reformation was under way, Protestant scholars took over this

The opening chapter of the Book of Genesis in the monumental Complutensian Polyglot shows Greek with Latin (left column), Latin alone (center), and Hebrew (right).

pre-Reformation program of Bible study; since Protestantism advocated a Christian faith based solely on Holy Scripture, this was very natural. So also was the concern of Protestants to make the Bible available to as many people as possible in their native languages. The reformers wanted to substitute the plain teaching of the Bible for the authority of the Roman Catholic Church.

In 1522 Luther published a German translation of the New Testament from Erasmus' Greek text. He then labored for almost twelve years over a

Robert Stephanus' Greek New Testament of 1546 became a standard text for translators, and the verse divisions he introduced are still followed today.

translation of the Old Testament, publishing it in sections as he finished them. The final publication of the complete translation of both Testaments in 1534 was a major event in the history of the Bible. His was a bold and vigorous treatment, far surpassing earlier German versions in literary quality as well as accuracy. Often it conveyed the spiritual power and insight of his own religious experience. He labored to make his native German a fit vehicle to bear the meaning of the biblical text; the Word of God must strike home to the hearts of his beloved people. So successful was he that this version virtually shaped the literary form of the German vernacular. It was an immediate best-seller. The German Bible was to that language what Chaucer had been to English: its first great literature, and the proof that vernacular

A portion of the Sermon on the Mount, including the Lord's Prayer (beginning at verse 9), from the Bishop's Bible of 1585 (opposite page) and the Geneva or Breeches Bible of 1589. The marginal commentary in the Geneva version draws practical lessons from the text.

German could be a sensitive medium of expression. Upward of 200,000 copies of Luther's Bible were printed in the sixteenth century alone, and today it is still the standard German translation.

The art of printing gave irresistible impetus to the spread of new Bible translations, as it had to the thought of the reformers. "Printing is God's latest and best work," Luther exulted, "to spread the true religion throughout the world." Bible translations, even where opposed by both Catholic and Protestant Church authorities, were irrepressible. A case in point is the career of the intrepid William Tyndale and his English versions. Tyndale was born in Gloucestershire in 1484 and educated at Oxford and Cambridge. Within five years of Luther's attack on indulgences the Protestant movement had

---

Christes doctrine.   S. Matthew.   Gods prouidence.

secret, shal reward thee openly.

7 But when ye pray, babble not much, as the heathen doe. For they thinke that they shal be heard, for their much babblings sake.

8 Be not ye therefore like vnto the: For your father knoweth, what things ye haue neede of, before ye aske of him.

9 After this maner therefore pray ye: *O our father which art in heauen, halowed be thy name. *(Luke.11.2.)*

10 Let thy kingdome come, Thy wil be done, as wel in earth, as it is in heaue.

11 Giue vs this day our dayly bread.

12 And forgiue vs our debts, as we forgiue our debters.

13 And lead vs not into temptation, *but deliuer vs from euill: for thine is the kingdome, and the power, and the glory, for euer, Amen. *(Mat.13.19.)*

14 For, *if yee forgiue men their trespasses, your heauenly father shal also forgiue you. *(Mat.11.25, eccl.28.2.)*

15 But, if ye forgiue not men their trespasses: no more shall your father forgiue [you] your trespasses.

16 Moreouer, when ye fast, be not of an heauie countenance, as the hypocrites are: for they disfigure their faces, that they might appeare vnto men to fast: Uerily I say vnto you, they haue their reward.

17 But thou, when thou fastest, anoynt thine head, and wash thy face: *(The Gospel on the first Sunday in Lent.)*

18 That thou appeare not vnto men to fast, but vnto thy father which is in secret: and thy father which seeth in secret, shal reward thee openly.

19 *Hoord not vp for your selues treasures vpon earth, where moth & rust doeth corrupt, & where thieues breake thorow, and steale: *(Luk.12.33. 1.tim.6.19)*

20 *But lay vp for you treasures in heauen, where neither moth nor rust doth corrupt, and where thieues doe not breake thorow, nor steale. *(Luk.12.34)*

21 For where your treasure is, there wil your heart be also.

22 *The candle of the body is the eye: wherefore if thine eye be single, all thy body shal be ful of light. *(Luk.11.34)*

23 But if thine eye be wicked, all thy body shal be ful of darknesse. wherefore, if the light that is in thee be darknesse, how great is that darknesse?

24 *No man can serue two masters: for eyther he shall hate the one and loue the other, or els he shal leane to the one *(The Gospel on the xv. Sunday after Trinitie. Luk.16.13.)*

and despise the other. Yee cannot serue God, and a Mammon.

25 *Therefore I say vnto you, Be not carefull for your life, what ye shal eate or drinke, nor yet for your body what yee shall put on: Is not the life more worth then meate: and the body then raiment? *(a In the Syrian tongue it signifieth money and lucre. Luk.12.22. psal.55.23. 1.pet.5.7.)*

26 Behold the foules of the aire: for they sowe not, neither doe they reape, nor cary into barnes, yet your heauenly father feedeth them. Are ye not much better then they?

27 Which of you by taking of carefull thought, can adde one cubite vnto his stature?

28 And why care ye for raimet? Learne of the Lilies of the fielde, howe they growe: they wearie not [themselues] with labour, neither [do they] spinne. *(Lilies.)*

29 And yet I say vnto you, that euen Solomon in all his royaltie, was not araied like one of these.

30 Wherefore, if God so clothe the grasse of the fielde, which though it stand to day, is to morow cast into þe ouen: shall he not much more doe [þ] same for you, [O] ye of litle faith?

31 Therefore take no thought, saying, what shal we eate: or, what shall we drinke: or, wherewith shal wee be clothed?

32 (For after all these things do þ Gentiles seeke:) for your heauenly father knoweth that yee haue neede of all these things.

33 But seeke yee first the kingdome of God, and his righteousnesse, and all these things shalbe added vnto you. *(b That is, the present day hath ynough of his owne griefe or affliction.)*

34 Care not then for the morow: for the morow shall care for it selfe: b Sufficient vnto the day, is the euil thereof.

The vii. Chapter.

1 He forbiddeth foolish and rash iudgement. 5 Hee reprooueth hypocrisie.

1 Udge ye not, that ye be not iudged. *(Luk.6.37. rom.2.1.)*

2 For with what iudgement ye iudge, yee shalbe iudged: *and with what measure yee mete, it shalbe measured to you againe. *(2.Cor.4.3)*

3 *Why seest thou the mote that is in thy brothers eye, but perceiuest not the beame that is in thine owne eye? *(Mar.25.4. luke 6.3)*

4 *Or how wilt thou say to thy brother, Suffer me, I will cast out a mote out of thine eye: and behold, the beame is in thine owne eye? *(Luke 6.41)*

5 Thou

gained a foothold in England, and Tyndale caught the fever. "I will cause a boy that driveth the plow shall know more of the Scriptures than thou dost," he once retorted to a critical cleric. In 1523 he began fruitlessly trying to find support in London for an English translation. Then he journeyed to the Continent, where he finished a draft of the New Testament in English, working directly from Erasmus' Greek text. This translation was being printed secretly in Cologne when a Catholic enemy of Protestant reforms discovered the project and managed to have it suppressed. Tyndale escaped to Worms, where he entrusted his translation to the famous printer Peter Schoeffler, who had collaborated in production of the Gutenberg Bible. Six thousand copies were printed and smuggled into England, where many were confiscated and burned. More were printed and smuggled across the Channel, only to be confiscated again. Edition after edition was pulled off the presses, some authorized by Tyndale and some pirated, in the frantic tug-of-war. Finally the English bishops formed subscription leagues to raise money with which to buy up whole editions for suppression. Tyndale, however, gratefully used the cash to support himself while continuing his labors. The story of his life and work is filled with such cloak-and-dagger maneuvers..

The general consternation and book-burning only served to increase the demand for vernacular translations. In 1535, after the appearance of sections of his translation of the Old Testament, Tyndale was betrayed to representatives of Emperor Charles V by a "double agent." But he continued to work on his translation while under arrest, until he was finally executed in October of 1536. After his death his version lived on to become a major influence on later English translations, including the King James Version, and primarily because of this, Tyndale's gifts as a translator of the Bible have left their creative hallmark on the English vernacular.

Although the Reformation in England took a strikingly different course, the Bible gradually came to assume the same central place on the sceptered isle as it had on the Continent. Tyndale's dying prayer, "Lord, open the King of England's eyes," was eventually answered. Both political and theological considerations initially dictated the separation of the Church of England from Rome, and Henry VIII—to whom the pope had granted the title "Defender of the Faith" for his earlier attack on Luther—soon declared himself to be the head of the Church in England. This Church retained many Catholic doctrines and practices, along with an episcopal form of Church government.

In 1535, Miles Coverdale had produced a complete translation of the Bible in English dedicated to Henry VIII, which he fervently hoped would be given official license. He was really more of an editor than a translator, depending heavily on Tyndale's work and on earlier German and Latin translations. By completing those parts of the Old Testament which Tyndale had not been able to finish, Coverdale gave England the first complete Bible in print. His dream of official approval, however, proved vain.

Henry did authorize the publication of an English Bible—the so-called

A painting of Frederick "the Wise," Elector of Saxony, portrays him surrounded by German Reformers, including Martin Luther (left) and Philip Melanchthon (far right). Although he did not always share Luther's views, Frederick guaranteed the Reformer's freedom and safety, hiding him in Wartburg Castle and refusing to execute the papal bull condemning him. Luther was then free to write and to work on his German translation of the Bible with other scholars (below), including Melanchthon (left), George Spalatin (standing), and Caspar Cruciger.

The Wyclif translation of 1382 (bottom) deeply influenced all later English versions of the Bible, including the translation commissioned by King James I (at left, in a portrait by Daniel Mytens). When it was issued in 1611, the King James Version (title page, opposite) was assured wide distribution because of the use of movable type, a method first applied in printing the famous Gutenberg Bible (below).

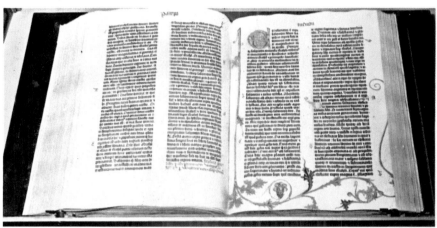

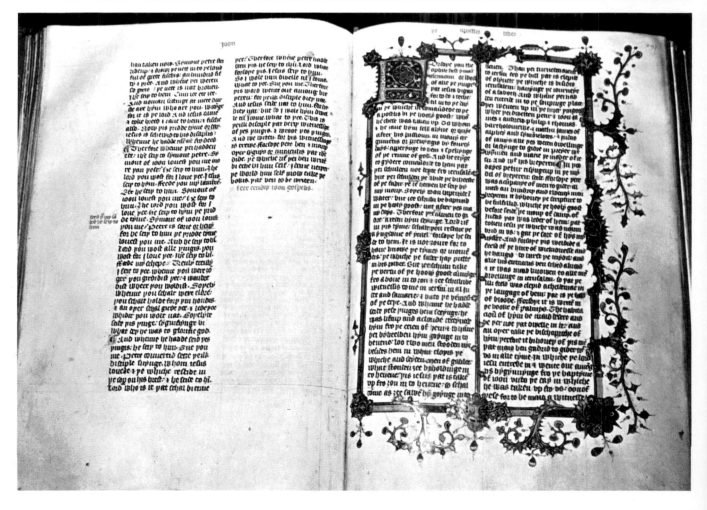

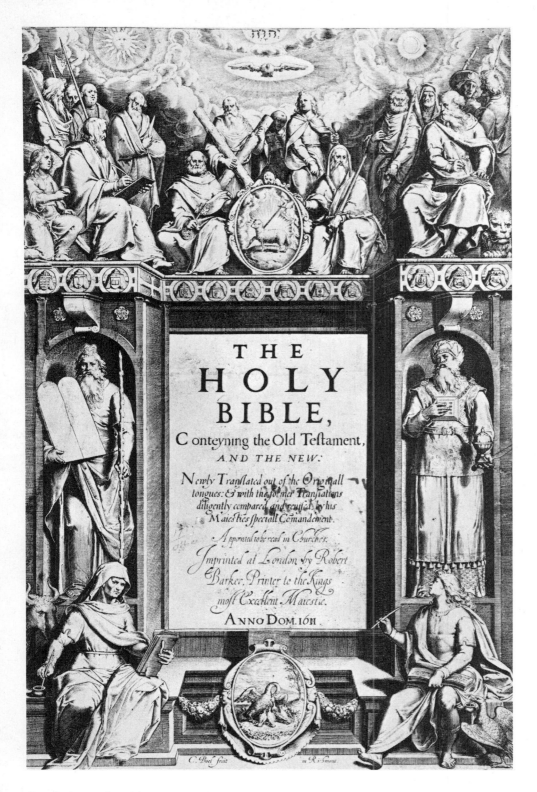

Symbols on the title page of the King James Version include the Hebrew characters for God, the dove representing the Holy Spirit, and the Lamb of God (Christ) surrounded by Apostles and Saints. Moses and Aaron flank the title.

Great Bible of 1539—with an admonition to the clergy that it be set up "in some convenient place within the churches which you have care of, so that your parishioners may have access to it and read it." The Great Bible survived, but Parliament feared and proscribed other vernacular translations, prohibited the reading of any Bible that named Tyndale as translator, and limited Bible reading to the gentry.

Protestantism was strengthened in England during the reign of the boy king, Edward VI, through the work of men like Thomas Cranmer, whose *Book of Common Prayer* shaped the piety of the Church of England, instilling a notion of the Church as "the English nation at prayers" which has survived to this day. Then came a reversal as Queen Mary, daughter of Henry VIII and Catherine of Aragon, succeeded in restoring relations between the Church of England and the papacy. Following the principle laid down by Henry that the ruler of England was the earthly head of the English Church, Mary made reading of the English Bible a capital offense and sent some three hundred Protestants to the stake, including Bishops Latimer, Ridley, and Cranmer. Many others fled to the Continent to escape the purge.

Thus it came about that a group of exiled English Protestants gathered in Geneva and there decided to produce a careful revision of the various Tyndale Bibles, under the protection and theological guidance of the Reformed Church of Geneva. The so-called *Geneva Bible*, chiefly the work of Calvin's brother-in-law, William Whittingham, and Anthony Golby, was finished in 1560 during the reign of Queen Elizabeth. The openly Calvinist notes and explanations included in this translation made it suspect to Church officials, but it soon became *the* English family Bible. It is fondly referred to as the "breeches Bible" because of the translation of Genesis 3:7, where Adam and Eve were reported to have sewn themselves "breeches" out of fig leaves to cover their nakedness.

One by one the tributaries fed into what was to become the main stream, that greatest of all English Bibles, the *King James Version*. After the Geneva Bible there were two more major translations, both products of the Elizabethan settlement of England's religious controversies. Good Queen Bess encouraged a mild spirit of reform while maintaining strict discipline in the Church from bishop down to parish priest. The Elizabethans felt the need of a new translation of the Bible. The *Bishop's Bible*, published in 1568, was intended to meet this need, but was never given official royal sanction. Printed in a magnificent folio edition, it was too expensive to rival the Geneva Bible as a family book, and the latter continued in popular use well into the seventeenth century, even after the appearance of the King James Version. While the Bishop's Bible was reprinted some twenty times over a period of forty years and served as the basis of the King James Version, somehow it never caught the public fancy.

The final tributary to the King James Version did not belong to the Tyndale family of translations, but was the work of a group of Catholics exiled to the Continent during the Elizabethan period. They first settled in

Douay, founding an English college there, then from Douay moved to Rheims, where they sponsored a translation of the New Testament which was finished by 1582. The complete *Douay-Rheims Bible* appeared in 1609–1610, shortly before the publication of the King James Version. This Bible was a translation from the Vulgate; its Latin flavor and musical style influenced the final editing of the King James Version, and it became the basis for most modern Catholic translations of the Bible into English.

By 1603, when James I ascended the throne, there was obvious need for a single authorized English translation of the Bible for the Church of England. The Thirty-nine Articles of the Elizabethan settlement had accepted the principle of biblical authority so central to Protestantism, declaring that the

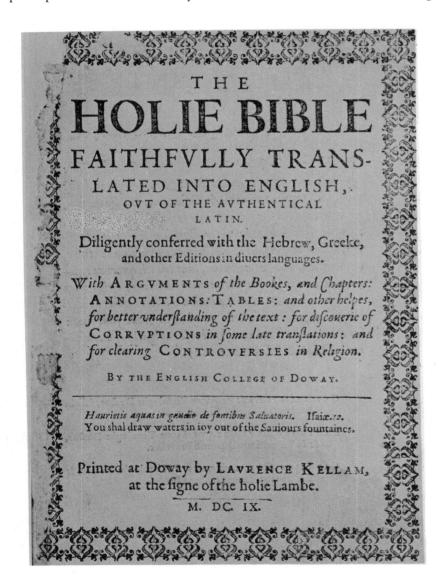

The Douay-Rheims Bible of 1609 provided English Roman Catholics with their first standard translation in the common tongue.

Bible contained all things necessary for salvation and that the creeds of the Church were dependent upon it for their authority. Yet the semiofficial Bishop's Bible was without royal sanction, and the Geneva Bible remained suspect because of its Calvinist origin. "I confess I could never yet see a Bible well translated into English," complained King James, "but I think that of Geneva is the worst." In a nation already deeply divided between Anglican and Puritan factions, James favored anything that would preserve national unity and the Elizabethan settlement. When a Puritan scholar, John Reynolds, suggested an authorized translation of the Bible, James seized upon the idea with enthusiasm. He insisted that it should conform as closely as possible to the Bishop's Bible and charged the scholars commissioned to undertake the task to avoid partisanship and preserve familiar terminology such as *priest, church,* and *charity* whenever possible. Otherwise they were left free to produce the best translation of the Bible into English they could make from the manuscripts.

By the middle of 1604, six teams of scholars were working at Oxford and Cambridge, each responsible for a section of the translation. When the basic work was finished, each team designated two members to sit on a twelve-man editorial board which reviewed the entire translation and smoothed out the style. A final revision was made by an outside scholar and one of the original forty-seven translators just before the book went to press. In sum, the King James Version was a product of the best and most careful scholarship of its age, and a labor of love as well. It had been translated from the best available manuscripts, carefully checked against the best available English translations as well as those in other languages such as German and Latin, and informed by the finest scholarly commentaries on the text. This accomplishment was all the more amazing in that it was done by a committee and was both a reforming translation and a product of inevitable haggling and compromise. It had to satisfy both a king and Church authorities who were basically suspicious of any vernacular translation. It was a magnificent achievement, of which the translators were justly if quietly proud. Remarks the preface:

> Truly, Good Christian Reader, we never thought that we
> should need to make a new Translation, nor yet to make of a
> bad one a good one . . . but to make a good one better, or
> out of many good ones, one principal good one.

So brilliant was this translation that for three centuries no major new English version of the Bible seemed called for, and so great has been its influence that, for many English-speaking Christians, the King James Version is still *the* Bible, whose language—stately, sonorous, and poetic—is a part of our Christian heritage on a deep personal level.

Thus in England as in other Protestant lands the Bible became the only necessary rule of Christian belief and practice. Protestant thought developed mainly through biblical interpretation, organized around some system or pattern. Official Protestant theology, such as Luther's catechism, used some

The elaborate title page of the Great Bible of 1539 shows God blessing the King, who is handing copies of "The Word of God" to Thomas Cranmer (left) and Thomas Cromwell (right). The Bibles are passed on to clerics and noblemen (center) and finally reach the people, who praise the King for giving them the Scriptures in their own language.

traditional scheme of organization such as the Lord's Prayer or the Ten Commandments as an outline on which to order the biblical materials. Calvin's *Institutes* was organized around the Apostles' Creed. Philip Melanchthon, the brilliant colleague of Luther, wrote a systematic theology, *Loci communes*, using the inherited "topics" or "questions" of medieval theology, themselves an outgrowth of biblical interpretation. But no matter what the organizing principle, all Protestant theology sought to establish itself upon solid biblical foundations. The Bible, according to the reformers, is "the infallible and sufficient rule, by which all that is to be believed and done by man in order to secure eternal salvation, must be examined, all controversies in regard to matters of faith decided, and all other writings adjudged." Protestant interpretation of the Bible owed its power to the spirit of the Reformation. In seeking to make a fresh start, the reformers focused on the authority of the Bible and the power of the gospel to which it bore witness: the "original" power of the righteousness of God, freely given to men in Jesus Christ.

From Wyclif on, these men emphasized the literal and grammatical meaning of the biblical texts. There was no search for novelty in interpreting obscure passages. On the contrary, they insisted on the right of the biblical text to stand by itself. The Church and its developing tradition were to be subject to the witness of Scripture, not to determine its meaning. For the most part, the reformers abandoned the complex and subtle exegesis of patristic and medieval theology and the notion of "levels of meaning" in the text. A straightforward understanding of the historical setting and the recovery of the intention of the writers were to be the basis of any adequate interpretation. Thus Luther abandoned allegorical exegesis after his break with Rome, and Calvin ridiculed the lengths to which Catholic exegesis would go to make sense of an obscure passage in the Bible.

"Christ is the point in the circle from which the whole circle is drawn," once remarked Luther in answer to the question of how the Bible should be interpreted. God made a covenant with Abraham, ran Calvin's aphorism, and Jesus Christ is the fulfillment of that covenant. According to the reformers, the inner coherence and unity of the Bible is to be found in its witness to Jesus Christ. This emphasis gives a distinctive focus to Protestant use of the Bible. The reformers insisted that if the integrity of the biblical witness to Christ is once grasped, then the Bible will virtually interpret itself.

Finally, they maintained that any adequate interpretation of the Bible must not neglect the personal relation of the faith of the interpreter to his understanding of the text. The message must be applied to ourselves. "The only truth is truth *for thee*," said Luther. "God must say to you in your heart, 'This is my Word.' " Calvin likewise insisted on the necessity of an "internal testimony of the Holy Spirit" to confirm the truth of the Bible in the heart of the believer. Given this internal witness, the message of the Bible is clear and our confidence in it will be unshakable. With this safeguard, the reformers believed that any Christian man could understand the Bible, be he scholar, cleric, or layman, without the aid of an authoritative tradition. At the very least they were certain there could be no doubt about the central and fundamental meaning of it. Eventually Protestantism, especially in its Calvinist forms, adopted a rigid and rigorous position on the verbal and infallible inspiration of the text of the Bible to guarantee the authority of the Word of God by identifying it with the *words* of the text. At this point, Protestant devotion to the Bible became as unbending as was ever Roman Catholic insistence on the authority of the Church. In response to a revived and reformed Roman Catholicism, Protestant theologians sought to safeguard the insights of the reformers by encasing them in a tight legalistic framework.

Reformation Aftermath

IN GIVING the Bible to the common man, however, the Reformation had opened a Pandora's box. Once the right of private judgment in the interpretation of Scripture was granted, the wide availability of the Bible itself meant that there was no way short of ruthless suppression to prevent the fragmenting of Protestant interpretation into competing "traditions," all the more insidious because their vocal advocates did not recognize them as traditions at all. The average Christian, then and now, often takes his own interpretation of the Bible as the plain, literal meaning of the text, and from under this banner looks upon any other view as hopelessly perverse and misguided.

The reformers would have been scandalized by the situation that later resulted from their insistence on the primacy and authority of the Bible. They had hoped that under the guidance of the Holy Spirit a single, authoritative Protestant exegesis would emerge. That hope was vain. Once the authority of the Catholic Church had been subverted—however much of its tradition the reformers might be willing to preserve in their own personal views—given two competing interpretations, there was no way to settle the question of *which* was correct, or *who* was empowered to interpret the Bible authoritatively. The stage was set for an era of schism and fragmentation, Protestants confronting Catholics, and various Protestant views confronting one another, with no court of final appeal accepted by all.

An observer of the European scene in the year 1525 would have been easily convinced that the Protestant movement was going to triumph throughout northern Europe, reducing the Roman Catholic Church to an Italian and Spanish national phenomenon, much as Lutheranism had become a German and Scandinavian phenomenon and Calvinism a product of Switzerland. Surprisingly, the Protestant advance soon slowed down and by 1530 Protestantism was confronted all across Europe by a revived and vigorous Catholicism, busily rolling back the gains of the Protestant movement and diligently engaged in internal housecleaning. The reformation of the Catholic

Church that Luther desired did come, but not along the lines he laid down. The Catholic Church's Counter Reformation took account of Protestant criticism in internal structure, and even gave positive attention to many of the distinctive themes of Protestant theology.

The Council of Trent, held in three sessions from 1545 to 1563, faced the task of reforming the theology as well as the practices of the Church. The fathers of the council met Protestant emphasis on the authority of the Bible squarely in a decree *Concerning Scripture and Tradition*, which insisted that the truth of the gospel is preserved in the Catholic Church in both written books and unwritten traditions which have been handed down from the

apostles to the present day. The Catholic Church, it said, accepted and venerated both Old and New Testament writings with equal "pious affection and reverence." Yet the fullness of Catholic truth required that the authority of the Church should complement the authority of the Bible, as it had from the apostolic period. The Church retained the right to interpret the Bible, as in earliest times it had set the canon. Thus the Church tried to save itself from the *subjectivism* it believed to be the grave weakness of Protestant interpretation of the Bible. The Catholic fathers also replied to Protestant criticism of the sacraments, as in the indulgence controversy, by reaffirming the medieval system of seven sacraments established by Christ for the hallowing of human

The Augsburg Confession of 1530, which became the authoritative standard of Lutheran faith and life, is vividly illustrated in a panel at Windsheim, Germany. Scenes in the background represent marriage, confession, baptism, communion, prayer, preaching, and teaching. In the foreground the Protestant Princes submit the Confession to the Emperor Charles V.

life. Catholicism, although it had lost important territory to the Protestants, drew a sense of triumph from its effort to "preserve Catholic teaching from heresy."

The Catholic Church, in spite of setbacks, also drew a lively sense of universality from the activities of missionaries all over the world during the "age of discovery." The post-Reformation popes, giving up some of the grandiose dreams of their Renaissance predecessors, transferred much of their ambition to a spiritual empire whose grandeur was to be reflected in the splendor of a revived Catholic art, architecture, and music. Culture was seen

The Pilgrim's Progress *by John Bunyan (below) became a classic in Protestant religious literature, dramatizing the individual's spiritual quest for salvation.*

as a vehicle of propaganda, and the arts were enlisted to establish the superiority of the Catholic faith.

The newly formed Society of Jesus founded by the dynamic and dedicated Ignatius Loyola played an important part in the Catholic revival, carrying on the battle in the ideological sphere as well as on the mission field, as a kind of shock troops of the Counter Reformation. The Jesuits centered their activities on popular preaching, education, and political maneuvering to influence persons in authority, and captured something of the reformers' spirit of personal commitment in their disciplined lives as soldiers of the cross.

In the aftermath of the Reformation, the Bible had a renewed impact on western culture beyond the Churches. Its influence seems most evident in the Protestant cultures of northern Europe. In literature, it directly affected the works of Shakespeare; in Milton's *Paradise Lost* Protestantism gave the world an epic vision which surely rivals that of Dante's *Divine Comedy*, while Bunyan's *Pilgrim's Progress* became a devotional classic to rival Thomas à Kempis' *Imitation of Christ*. In music, the polyphony of Bach, the brilliant text-setting of Handel, the hymnology of Gerhardt in the seventeenth and Wesley in the eighteenth century, all owe much to the renewed emphasis on the Bible. In Germany, baroque art and architecture may be viewed as a cultural manifestation of the Reformation. The Low Countries, too, produced noteworthy traditions in art shaped by the Reformation approach to the Bible. Peter Breughel, for example, paints biblical scenes in which the figures are costumed and set in surroundings from his own age—perhaps a result of Reformation emphasis on the immediacy and contemporaneousness of the biblical message. Nor should one neglect that "most Protestant painter," Rembrandt, whose brooding spirit of self-examination produced masterpiece after masterpiece.

Protestantism also gave to northern Europe its ideal of the "Christian family" and influenced to some extent the rapidly spreading capitalism that came to dominate the economies of the northern countries. For the so-called "Protestant virtues" of thrift and industry, plus the tendency toward self-denial that Calvinism engendered, had a potent effect on economic expansion in northern Europe.

On the Catholic side, art and architecture produced spiritual monuments. Many of the great churches and public buildings of the Vatican were completed under the impulse of the Catholic Reformation. There was a liturgical renewal symbolized by the quiet, classic beauty of Palestrina's sacred music. Catholic education produced models of scholarly excellence in the seventeenth and eighteenth centuries, such as the eminent Suarez and Cardinal Bellarmine, and Catholic culture came to be identified with southern —"Latin"—Europe, as Protestant culture was rooted in the north.

The Reformation was a cultural shock in a negative sense, too. The first "little" religious war broke out in 1529 when Zwingli of Zurich, seeking to form a confederation of Swiss and German Reformed city-states, ran into opposition from Austria allied with the Catholic cantons of Switzerland. This vest-pocket war cost Zwingli, the earliest leader of Reformed Protestantism, his life. On the larger European scene, the Catholic Emperor Charles V could not long remain indifferent to the growth of Protestantism fostering nationalism within his presumed domain of Germany. Long in coming, war finally broke out among the German countries in 1546. When strife ended, little had been settled. Germany remained a patchwork of provinces, some Protestant, some Catholic. The Low Countries were also drawn into the growing struggle: the northern sections fought a heroic war of liberation against Charles' son and heir, Philip II of Spain, and emerged late in the sixteenth century as the Netherlands, or Holland. In France, the Huguenot (Calvinist) minority, chiefly tradesmen and farmers led by a few landed gentry, fought tenaciously for autonomy but were finally crushed and suppressed, France remaining nominally *toute Catholique.*

The most savage of the religious conflicts was the Thirty Years' War (1618–1648), which began as a minor Catholic-Protestant squabble in Germany over who should wear the crown of Bohemia. Soon most of the countries of Europe were involved in a confused and bitter power struggle. Mercenary armies fought back and forth across Germany, leaving her enfeebled for generations. The war ended in the inconclusive Peace of Westphalia, which defined Protestant and Catholic boundaries on the Continent and extended political recognition to the Reformed as well as Lutheran communions. The final episode in the reshaping of Europe was the tragic English Civil War of 1642–1646, which ended in the reaffirmation of the Elizabethan settlement and in the process cost England the scandal of a king—Charles the First—sent to the block. When the second Charles ascended the throne in 1660, he was forced to issue a declaration of "liberty to tender consciences" as a condition of his coronation.

By the mid-seventeenth century Europe was divided along Protestant and Catholic lines, roughly into northern and southern halves. The rejuvenated Catholicism of the reforming Council of Trent was henceforth to be identified with Latin culture, which further alienated the north. A new form of culture had begun to develop among Protestants, and nowhere was this more evident than in England, whence a vigorous dissenting Protestantism spread to North America.

Throughout this unsettling time the Bible played a crucial role. In the end it was set firmly in the center of western thought by the Reformation. Men rejoiced in its widespread availability in vernacular translations, yet were troubled by the competing interpretations that now presented themselves for acceptance. The cultural shock of the Reformation and its aftermath produced a spiritual uneasiness to which the message of the Bible could speak powerfully, but it remained to find new ways to appropriate this message for a postmedieval, "modern" world.

6

TO THE FAR CORNERS:
THE BIBLE IN
MODERN TIMES

IN THE RELATIVELY short space of a hundred years the unity of medieval Christendom, already strained and cracking in the late Middle Ages, had been irreparably shattered in Europe. The Christian Church was rent asunder, and Christians were set at one another's throats in an unholy combination of religious differences and power politics. The conflicts sown by this upheaval were scandalous indeed. Both Protestant and Catholic parties in the religious wars were quite willing to slaughter their opponents in the name of God. Perhaps the most infamous example is the gruesome event known as the Massacre of St. Bartholomew, involving the slaughter of some two or three thousand Huguenot Protestants on the feast-day morning of August 24, 1572. The frenzied mobs of Paris, aroused in the name of religion by the Duke of Guise and the cynical Catherine de Medicis, threw the bodies of their victims into the Seine until its waters ran red. Pope Gregory XIII ordered a solemn celebration of this outrage, including a formal public prayer of thanksgiving, which was observed in the Catholic Church on the feast day of St. Bartholomew for generations thereafter. At news of the massacre the Catholic King Philip of Spain is said to have laughed publicly for the first time in his life. Although Protestants were horrified, no effective protest was registered, for the conscience of Europe, still relatively insensitive to human rights, had become in addition so scarred by the seemingly endless bloody slaughter that men expected such bestiality to serve the cause of religion.

When the fighting subsided in the mid-seventeenth century, men were spiritually and emotionally as well as physically exhausted. The conflicts of religion had given rise to debilitating scepticism and doubt. Both sides claimed absolute truth for their cause and neither could suggest a criterion acceptable to the other which would resolve their controversy. The contest ended in a stalemate; there was an intellectual failure of nerve which produced frustration and near despair. Montaigne, writing early in the century, captured the mood of his age.

> Dignities and offices are necessarily conferred more by fortune than by merit; and it is often a mistake to lay blame on rulers. On the contrary, it is marvelous that, having so little skill, they have so much luck: a most foolish procedure is often justified by its result.
>
> God preserve me from being an honest man according to the standards which I daily see every man apply to himself, to his own advantage! "What once were vices have now become custom."

Montaigne's own life is a mirror of the times. His father was Catholic, his mother a Jewess converted to Protestantism. He himself was deeply involved in the social and intellectual currents of the age. A Catholic by religion, he had friends in the Protestant camp, among them the great Henry of Navarre, whose brutal death he deeply mourned. Montaigne was also a confidant of the Jesuit controversialist, Juan Maldonat, and an adviser in the work of the Catholic Reformation in France. He had suffered the trauma of seeing his whole intellectual world dissolve into doubt, and faced squarely the problems of living in a world where there seemed no possibility of ultimate certainty. In this sense he marks the end of an era and the beginning of the modern struggle to find moral and religious landmarks in the face of recurring doubt.

New Horizons and the Bible

STRANGELY ENOUGH, the conflicts and the doubt sparked creative developments in European intellectual life. Hard on the heels of the devastation wrought by the wars of religion come the beginnings of "modern" philosophy. René Descartes published his revolutionary *Meditations* and the *Discourse on Method* in an attempt to overcome the skepticism of his age. A seventeenth-century Thomas Aquinas, he was himself seeking to renew the foundations of knowledge on a new scientific basis.

For the age of religious controversy also witnessed the rise of science and voyages of discovery in which two new worlds were opened to Europe. Martin Luther was a young man when Columbus sailed on his epoch-making voyages; by the time Luther's New Testament was published, Magellan had circled the globe. The earth began to take on a startling new size and shape. When the dust raised by the wars of religion settled, men realized to their astonishment that they were quite literally no longer living in the world inhabited by their grandfathers.

The burgeoning sciences added their impact to that of the Reformation

Thousands of Huguenot Protestants of Paris and other French cities were killed in the Saint Bartholomew's Day Massacre of 1572, here portrayed by François Dubois, who was himself an eyewitness.

and the voyages of discovery. The accepted cosmology of an earth securely
set at the center of a universe of crystalline spheres, a tiny globe on the
fingertip of God, was undermined by the Copernican world picture of an
infinite universe centered in the sun, in which man was less than an infinitesi-
mal speck. The reaction of the Church was to prohibit the teaching of his
system, and when Galileo published his *Dialogue on the Great World Systems,* he was publicly condemned and forced to recant by the Inquisition.

Intellectually disturbed and stimulated, sickened by a century of vicious
conflict, Europe concluded that religion was not worth killing over. Differing and even opposed views should be tolerated for the sake of civil tran-
quility. Rulers, too, discovered that it simply did not pay to use religion as a
weapon in power politics. If the losing side gained ascendancy, they were
only too ready to employ the same ruthless tactics as had once been used
against them. Religious grudges die hard.

Thus the seventeenth century witnessed the beginnings of a philosophy of
toleration in matters religious. This was not merely negative; its advocates
seldom meant to recommend religious indifference, however suspicious the

*John Foster's "White Hills Map of 1677," the first known map of New England,
identifies by number the settlements that had sustained Indian attacks.*

An 1836 lithograph by E. W. Clay (right) shows one of the camp meetings that drew Appalachian settlers many miles to hear "Bible preaching" by traveling evangelists. The Bible moved west with the frontier: Charles Nahl's 1872 painting, "Sunday Morning in the Mines" (below), portrays some California miners reading the Scriptures while others brawl, drink, and race.

To own and treasure a "Family Bible" has been a strong tradition in American home life. In "The Tilton Family" (1837), by New Hampshire artist Joseph Davis, the large Bible is prominently displayed on the parlor table. Verses of Scripture were also embroidered or printed and used as decorative wall mottoes, as in this 1876 Currier and Ives lithograph of the Ten Commandments.

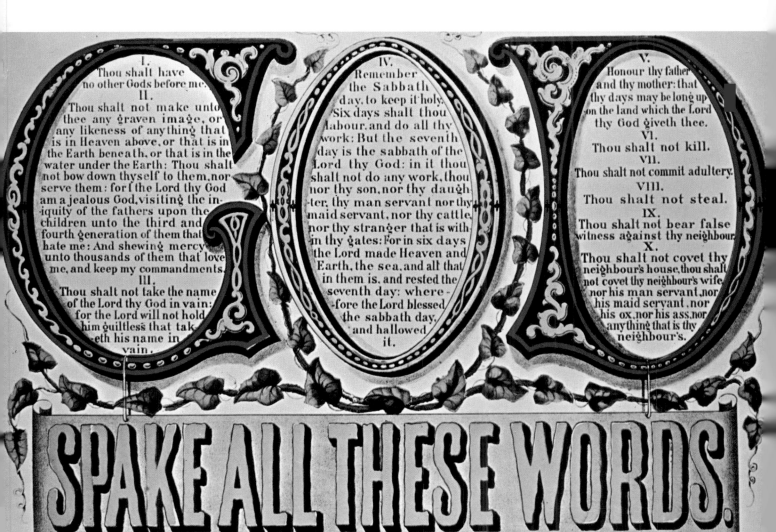

I.
Thou shalt have no other Gods before me.

II.
Thou shalt not make unto thee any graven image, or any likeness of anything that is in Heaven above, or that is in the Earth beneath, or that is in the water under the Earth: Thou shalt not bow down thyself to them, nor serve them: for I the Lord thy God am a jealous God, visiting the iniquity of the fathers upon the children unto the third and fourth generation of them that hate me: And shewing mercy unto thousands of them that love me, and keep my commandments.

III.
Thou shalt not take the name of the Lord thy God in vain: for the Lord will not hold him guiltless that taketh his name in vain.

IV.
Remember the Sabbath day, to keep it holy. Six days shalt thou labour, and do all thy work: But the seventh day is the sabbath of the Lord thy God: in it thou shalt not do any work, thou nor thy son, nor thy daughter, thy man servant nor thy maid servant, nor thy cattle, nor thy stranger that is within thy gates: For in six days the Lord made Heaven and Earth, the sea, and all that in them is, and rested the seventh day: wherefore the Lord blessed the sabbath day, and hallowed it.

V.
Honour thy father and thy mother: that thy days may be long upon the land which the Lord thy God giveth thee.

VI.
Thou shalt not kill.

VII.
Thou shalt not commit adultery.

VIII.
Thou shalt not steal.

IX.
Thou shalt not bear false witness against thy neighbour.

X.
Thou shalt not covet thy neighbour's house, thou shalt not covet thy neighbour's wife, nor his man servant, nor his maid servant, nor his ox, nor his ass, nor anything that is thy neighbour's.

SPAKE ALL THESE WORDS.

orthodox might be of their motives. Rather, the idea of tolerance was seen as a new, positive principle which allowed for the variation of the religions of mankind while seeking the rational core behind diverse beliefs and practices. Once civil authorities were persuaded to pay at least lip service to the ideal of religious toleration, it could be seen that this idea contained the germ of a truly revolutionary program. The understanding of religion would be freed from the arbitrary and irrational bonds of narrow dogmatism. Religious coercion would become unnecessary and impossible. Human knowledge and society would thus be well served, for dogmatism, not religion itself, was the threat to progress. As Pierre Bayle guardedly observed in his *Philosophical Dictionary*, "The obstacles to the progress of knowledge do not come so much from the fact that the mind is void of knowledge, as that it is full of prejudice." And in England John Locke argued eloquently in his *Letter on Toleration* that men had a moral responsibility to judge the dogmas of religion by reason, lest they fall prey to the excesses and cruelties so recently experienced. Thus the idea of toleration was intended to give men a standard by which they could separate the wheat from the chaff in religious matters on the basis of a rational morality.

One might suppose that these developments boded ill for the story of the Bible. Instead, the "new philosophy" gave new impetus to its study. For one thing, the idea of tolerating religious differences because of their underlying rational unity contained a fairly radical principle for approaching Scripture. If any reading of the Bible, however literal, violated the highest principles of morality and reason, it must be rejected as inadequate, or else that part of the biblical tradition must be seen as "defective." Reverence for the past must not be used to shield men from their duty as reasonable creatures.

Thus the Bible had now to be studied afresh, in the light of a critical reason freed from the bonds of superstition and fanaticism. A succession of pioneers devoted themselves to this task, often amid storms of criticism and abuse from defenders of traditional orthodoxies, to whom any critical study of Scripture seemed little short of blasphemy. Because of the emphasis Protestantism had placed on individual conscience, however, no study of the Bible could be effectively suppressed.

Pierre Bayle, whose *Historical and Critical Dictionary* became a gold mine for generations of succeeding thinkers, drove the opening wedge with his witty, sophisticated, and often irreverent examination of the biblical stories. His article on King David, for example, scandalized the religious by suggesting that David's conduct was, at least on occasion, immoral and indefensible. After all, had he not lied and schemed his way to the throne, ruthlessly eliminated his opposition, and even committed murder to steal another man's wife? Yet the Bible spoke of him as a man beloved of God. Bayle could only conclude that "even the greatest of saints need pardon in some respects." Bayle also went so far as to suggest that the biblical narratives, if examined as historical sources, contained numerous contradictions and ambiguities.

Other scholars took up where Bayle's hints left off. Michaelis, a German philologist, worked at applying the methods of secular linguistic study to the Old Testament. Reimarus and Lessing broadened the scope of such studies to include the New Testament, which Bayle had scrupulously avoided because of its potential for controversy. The idea that the Bible could be studied in the same way as any ancient collection of documents—that scholars might appraise these traditional materials, of varying worth in themselves—gained gradual ascendancy. In spite of opposition from those who felt that this impugned the authority of the Bible in religious matters, more and more it became a commonplace among many scholars of that day that one could not always accept at face value the claims made for the Bible by religious communities which viewed it as Holy Scripture, in every part the inviolable Word of God.

The foundations of so-called scientific study of the Bible were well established by the early eighteenth century, as Europe entered the Age of Enlightenment and witnessed the rise of a tradition of biblical scholarship outside—and sometimes in opposition to—the authoritative traditions of Judaism and Christianity. We shall return presently to the implications of this development.

Into Every Tongue . . .

WITHIN THE CHURCH there were also developments of great moment for the story of the Bible. The discovery of great non-Christian civilizations in the New World and the Orient led to a period of missionary activity unparalleled since the earliest days of Christianity. The pioneers in this adventure were Roman Catholic priests afire with the reforming zeal of the Council of Trent and eager to carry the gospel to the heathen. Perhaps the greatest was St. Francis Xavier, one of the original members of the Society of Jesus. Sailing from Europe in 1541, he traveled for eleven years through India, China, and the East Indies. Before he died on an island near Macao while organizing further missionary work in China, Xavier had conquered incredible obstacles: ancient and well-established religions, hostile rulers, strange languages and customs, not to mention the mere hazards of travel and survival.

While the Protestant emphasis on the Bible as over against the traditions of the Church had made Roman Catholics generally suspicious of vernacular translations, Xavier recognized the necessity of familiarizing converts with the basic sources of Christianity. So he did not hesitate to make translations for use in his missionary work. Among simple and uncivilized peoples, he could content himself with oral recitation, requiring the natives to repeat after him passages of Scripture and the liturgy in their own tongue. But in civilized countries such as Japan much more was needed. Xavier may have translated parts of the New Testament into Japanese himself; in any case, the

Biblical themes and images pervade the art of William Blake, as in his engravings for the Book of Job (above). Blake's mystical spirit and visionary style were alien to the rationalism that characterized many of his contemporaries.

mission he left behind completed a translation shortly after the turn of the seventeenth century, though the Jesuits were soon expelled from Japan by the government, which was becoming alarmed by the growing strength of the *Kirishitan* religion.

Other Catholic missionaries accompanied explorers of the New World and planted Christianity in the Americas. Protestants—perhaps discouraged by Catholic successes, perhaps distracted by their own intramural controversies —were slow to take up the challenge of the age of discovery. Well into the seventeenth century it was fashionable in Protestant circles to decry missionary work. Christ and the apostles had offered salvation to the world once and for all, ran the argument, and there was no point in offering it again. "If God wants to save the heathen He can do it without us." However, as trade drew Protestant shipping to the Far East and the New World, this attitude began to change. The Dutch dispatched a few pastors to the Orient with instructions to convert the natives as well as to minister to their own people. And in 1628 the renowned scholar Hugo Grotius published a book for the use of Dutch sailors in proselytizing. Around the turn of the century some English philanthropists founded the *Society for Promoting Christian Knowledge* and the *Society for the Propagation of the Gospel in Foreign Parts*. Some decades later the Moravian Brotherhood organized a vigorous program of missionary work from a base in Saxony. But Protestants did not devote themselves fully to the missionary task until the nineteenth century.

Once they took up the challenge of the missionary movement, however, their characteristic emphasis on the centrality of the Bible soon bore fruit. The Dutch produced translations of the New Testament into Malay, Taiwanese, and Singhalese. The Danish missionary Ziegenbalg translated it into the Tamil language of India, and soon there was a Tamil translation of the entire Bible. Danish missionaries translated the Bible into an Eskimo tongue. By the end of the eighteenth century Protestant missionaries had produced translations in about seventy languages.

Roman Catholic missionaries ranged widely in America, sometimes opening up new frontiers. In the late eighteenth century the Franciscan monk Fra Junipero Serra—the famous "Brother Juniper"—founded missions in what is now California. Father Jan de Smet, a Belgian, worked among Indians in the Rocky Mountain region. Other lonely priests labored in New Mexico among the Pueblo tribes, building such monuments as the church of Acoma Pueblo, which still stands, its interior bright with wall paintings of biblical scenes. Every bit of material used in building the church had to be hauled up the sheer cliff sides of the mesa by devoted Indians.

In the nineteenth century, missionary activities in America were but a small part of the worldwide missionary movement, which carried the gospel to millions of non-Christians around the globe. For the first time Protestants began to take the larger share in these activities, the United States gradually assuming leadership over the movement. In America, the missionary enterprise began in the soul-saving concern of revivalism. Eighteenth-century morality, with its emphasis on benevolence and charity, provided further motivation. But the opportunity for such missionary ventures was provided by the imperial and colonial expansion which was to plant the western presence, often by force or guile, in many a distant land. Armed adventurers often led the way, to be followed by missionaries, Bibles in hand, their songs reflecting the vision of a global Christianity, reaching "from Greenland's icy mountains to India's coral strand."

In America, the older Protestant denominations sent missionaries to the frontier. There was also interest in "Christianizing" the Indians. As always, Bible translations were a necessary means to evangelism. Thus it came to be set into the idiom of the American Indians, often requiring for the purpose that their languages be reduced to written form for the first time. Pioneer missionary James Evans worked out a set of symbols for the Cree tongue, then laboriously translated and "printed" biblical texts on birch bark, using

Spanish Jesuits established missions throughout the Southwest and California. Churches like the one shown below became the nucleus for settlements, many of which eventually grew into cities such as Los Angeles and San Francisco.

soot mixed with oil for ink. Other missionaries produced translations of biblical texts in the language of the Creeks, Beavers, Mohawks, Cherokees, Chippewas, Choctaws, Dakotas, and many others. Perhaps the most famous Indian Bible was the translation by the Rev. John Eliot, an extremely gifted man, who put the Bible into the Narragansett tongue and had it printed, section by section, with the aid of an English "Society for Promoting and Propagating the Gospel of Jesus Christ in New England." Eliot's Narragansett Bible was the first to be printed in America. His avowed purpose in translating the Bible for the Indians was to use Holy Scripture as a model—in good Puritan fashion—for setting up Christian Indian villages in the New England wilderness.

Bible translations were also done in the peculiar patois of the enslaved

Missionary efforts among the Indians began early in the colonial period. By 1641, John Eliot had translated the New Testament into the Narragansett language (title page, opposite). A century later, Charles Wesley devoted much of his visit in Georgia to preaching to Indians (below).

Negroes of America, and attempts made to convert these slaves to the religion of their masters—often, it must be admitted, as a means of encouraging docility.

Although modern biblical scholarship and missionary activity remained relatively isolated from each other, the whole missionary movement meant the dawning of a new day for the Bible. The missionaries, sometimes using the technical resources of scholarship, sometimes laboring alone against incredible obstacles, managed to produce a constant flow of translations. Over a period of only thirty years, for example, the Englishman William Carey, father of the Protestant missionary movement, along with his two fellow missionaries, Joshua Marshman and William Ward, supplied Bible translations in *thirty-four* Far Eastern languages! This amazing output included six complete Bibles and twenty-three New Testaments. Another Englishman, Robert Morrison, pioneer Protestant missionary to China, translated the Bible into Chinese between 1807 and 1819; the American missionary Adoniram Judson translated the Bible into a native Burmese dialect. In southern Africa, Robert Moffat labored *thirty years* to translate the Bible into Tswana, the language of the Bechuana—first reducing this primitive tongue into written form, then struggling to find equivalents for the biblical expressions.

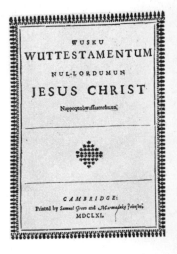

The contribution of these missionaries to the science of linguistics alone would suffice to earn them a special place in history. Imagine an African dialect with no word for "prophet," or perhaps even for "God." Because this language had never been written, it would have no word for "book." A missionary might discover that the common word for "table" referred only to a special kind of shelf-table built into the wall of a native hut and thus would not accurately translate the biblical idea. And if the language of objects presented such difficulties, imagine trying to translate *concepts* such as "righteousness," "forgiveness," or "faith, hope, and love." Finally, after the task of translation was done, there remained that of teaching the natives to read their own language.

The problems of missionaries were somewhat eased and their work greatly facilitated by the formation of various Bible societies during the nineteenth century. The infant British Bible Society, for example, supported the work of Carey, Marshman, and Ward in addition to publishing their many translations. The British society and the American Bible Society, both founded in the first decades of the nineteenth century, were closely followed by important Bible societies in Germany, Holland, and Scotland. Their common goal was to make texts widely available at minimal cost. Even today students discover that the most inexpensive source of biblical texts, whether in the original languages or in accurate vernacular translations, will probably be one of the established societies such as the American Bible Society or the *Bibelanstalt* of Würtemberg. Bible societies also cooperated—and still do—in the very important task of collating manuscripts of the Greek and Hebrew texts of the Old Testament and the Greek and Latin texts of the New. The standard critical editions of the original biblical texts used by scholars today are published under the auspices of the American and German Bible societies.

Bible translations became the tools of the missionaries' trade. But it was the Bible itself that inspired the heroic labor of these men. Although many a missionary was also an explorer and cultural emissary—as was the famous David Livingstone of Africa—he was always devoted to the spreading of the Christian gospel. Missionaries often served with their lives as fully as with their words. One thinks of the compelling witness of Father Damien, who lived and worked among the lepers of Molokai, an island in the Hawaiian chain—eventually contracting the dreaded disease himself, so that he was able to say to his charges with deep emotion one day, "Now I am one of you." Or the sacrifices of Wilfred Grenfell, who brought modern medical care to the forbidding shores of Labrador at the end of the nineteenth century. Or Albert Schweitzer at Lambarene in Africa, whose labor has come to symbolize the very meaning of faith in practice: self-sacrificing love and concern for the helpless and afflicted.

Dedicated missionaries founded colleges and schools, served as doctors and nurses, found themselves called upon to advise heads of state, introduced modern agriculture and technology into primitive cultures, and helped ease the strain of transition from ancient to modern styles of life among the people they served. At the same time they established churches, baptizing and teaching—looking toward an end to the need of their presence, when their students were able to take over. Sometimes the efforts of translators reaped unexpected rewards. When, after 1882, missionaries were permitted to enter Korea, they found Christians there ready for baptism. The same thing has happened in parts of Africa, India, and South America. In each case it was discovered that the Bible had crossed the frontiers before the missionaries— smuggled in, dropped from airplanes, or handed to individuals as they returned to their homeland. The biblical message, unaided by even the simplest explanation, had worked its own conversions.

Pietist Renewal

PROTESTANT MISSIONARY MOVEMENTS were in part a response to the new spirit of Enlightenment which was abroad in Europe during the eighteenth century. There was a concern to "civilize" the heathen which operated alongside the concern to evangelize them, spurring missionaries to bring the benefits of civilization to their charges together with the benefits of Christ. However, there were growing signs that the average western Christian found the ideas and institutions of Christianity increasingly irrelevant to much of his life. The Protestant churches found themselves struggling to devise a style of life which could motivate those caught up in the ever more secular life of the world outside the churches. For why should one be a Christian if Christianity was not relevant to life as lived?

One attempt to develop such a style of life was Pietism. This involved deep personal devotion and a concern for mystical communion with Christ. It developed on the fringes of, and occasionally outside, the established churches. In its early stages, it arose in the Lutheran churches of southern and western Germany under the influence of Swiss Protestantism, but quickly spread to Holland and England. Pietists typically formed small "cell groups" or *conventicles* which imposed some religious discipline—usually prayer and Bible study—on their members. There was a concern to relate personal faith to the social environment. In Germany the Pietists founded major educational institutions, such as the University of Halle, along with orphanages, primary schools, hospitals, and other charitable enterprises. Many laymen who could find no satisfaction in the established churches came under the influence of this movement, and through it found strength to protest against the increasing secularism and rationalism of the Enlightenment. It was also strangely appealing to intellectuals who were disturbed by the aloof rationalism of the Enlightenment and were responding to the beginnings of the Romantic movement.

One of the most important fruits of Pietism was the founding of the Moravian Brethren, already mentioned in connection with the Protestant missionary enterprise. Count Zinzendorf, who allowed a group of refugees from Roman Catholic oppression to settle on his estate at Herrnhut in 1722, gave the Moravians their characteristic spirit of communion with Christ, emphasizing the "fellowship of His suffering," lowliness, meekness, and a spirit of service and sacrifice. They spread rapidly across Europe, leaped the Channel to England and Ireland, and finally spanned the ocean to plant their gospel in the colonies.

Another fruit of Pietism was the Methodist movement in the Church of England. Founded under the leadership of Charles and John Wesley in the 1740's and influenced by the work of the Moravian Brethren in England, Methodism was in part a continuation of earlier movements. But the character of the Wesleys strongly shaped it, and when the eventual rupture with the Anglican Church came, the movement became a unique and extremely influential force, especially in American Protestantism, where it established itself as the virtual culture-religion of middle-class America. Here the Pietist spirit of Methodism was to break forth again in the nineteenth century in temperance leagues, the Salvation Army, and the founding of sectarian bodies such as the Church of the Nazarene.

By far the most important contribution of Pietism to our story, however, was its reemphasis on the Bible as the center of Protestant Christianity. In the seventeenth century Protestantism had become a system of orthodoxy that was often sterile and as doctrinally rigid and forbidding as ever medieval Catholicism had been. Pietism revived the Reformation insight that the Bible could speak anew to the heart of any man who was open to its message, rich or poor, educated or uneducated, cleric or layman. There was renewed

An illustrated report published by the Moravian Brethren in 1757 described the group's extensive missionary work among Negroes. The "laying on of hands," or "exorcism," was a traditional ceremony of preparation for baptism of converts.

interest in Bible study in the laymen's fellowships, along with renewed concern to live one's life as a visible witness to the biblical message. The combination of concern for the truth and relevance of Scripture with new methods of biblical scholarship proved a potent one. J. A. Bengel, the most distinguished German New Testament scholar of this eighteenth-century movement summed up its biblical emphasis in a trenchant motto: "Apply yourself wholly to the text; then apply the text wholly to yourself." Pietism thus lies behind one of the most important chapters in our story, because of its emphasis on the centrality of the Bible, the many translations its missionaries produced, and its importance in the founding of Bible societies whose work has made the Bible into a book for *all* men and its message one that belongs to the world.

Puritans and Revivals

AS WE HAVE ALREADY SEEN, the Protestant Reformation produced attempts to put the Bible into communal practice, most notably in Calvin's Geneva and also in the left-wing sects such as the Anabaptists. The greatest experiment in this direction occurred in the seventeenth century in the English colonies established in Massachusetts. For the Puritans of Massachusetts Bay self-consciously tried to bring the Reformation to a triumphant climax by creating a Bible commonwealth in the wilderness. Free of the "Romish taint" of bishops, altars, vestments, liturgical pomp, and ecclesiastical politics, their city would provide a shining example of pure religion that Europe—perhaps even Rome itself—would be compelled to emulate. This was the underlying motivation of one of the most audacious, highly organized, and nearly successful of all social experiments.

The holy commonwealth of New England was ruled and inspired by the Bible to an even greater degree than Calvin's Geneva. The Puritan leaders felt that the Bible gave them an unimpeachable standard by which to govern their citizens in all duties, public and private. They therefore studied it diligently and were quick to draw analogies between their own experience and that of the covenant people of the Old Testament. Their noble experiment they saw as a new Exodus: James I was their oppressing Pharaoh, the Atlantic Ocean their Red Sea, and the shores of New England their Promised Land. Their view of themselves is aptly captured in a line from an early Puritan epitaph: "O happy Israel in America!"

The Puritans embodied the Mosaic commandments in their civil and criminal law. Their children, and of course their towns, received biblical names. The Bible was the backbone of their educational system, including the curriculum of newly founded Harvard College. Even their highly prized personal liberty was defined in biblical terms as freedom "to walk in the Faith, Worship, Doctrine and Discipline of the Gospel." Their governors saw to it that the idea of the covenant was expressed in their political as well as religious institutions. Only church members in good standing were enfranchised citizens, and of course the religious leaders determined who these members in good standing were. Subtle and not-so-subtle economic sanctions were applied against dissenters and in favor of the saints, and there was stern and unbending pressure for social and religious conformity. The Pilgrim Fathers may have been rugged individualists as a group, but they had little sympathy for rugged individualists who did not fit the Puritan mold!

The Pilgrims who set sail from Holland and England in the Mayflower sought freedom to lead a communal life guided by religious precepts and unmolested by state authority. The Bible became the "constitution" of their society in the New World.

Of course there was dissent from the theocratic ideal from the beginning. Some were forced to leave the colony, like Roger Williams, who founded Rhode Island, the first colony to practice true toleration and religious freedom. Others, unlucky enough to be unable to leave, or stubborn enough to be unwilling, suffered severe civil and criminal penalties—even death—at the hands of the Puritan rulers. With growing prosperity the Puritan fervor and intolerance moderated; but it died hard, for in 1691–1692, at the dawn of the Enlightenment in Europe, it broke out again in the witchcraft madness at Salem. Twenty persons were killed before the Puritans decided—it must be admitted with genuine repentance—that their difficulties could not be blamed on witches. We today must be careful not to condemn them too harshly; there is no particular virtue in not burning witches when one does not believe in them. For all our presumed sophistication, we still have our political witch hunts and scapegoats.

In altered form, Puritanism came to permeate much of American life long after the noble experiment ended in New England. The religious dedication of the Puritans was revived in the Great Awakening of the eighteenth century. A key figure in this revival was Jonathan Edwards, inheritor of the Puritan tradition, whose uncompromising sermons, much to his surprise, sparked the new movement in the 1740's. Theologian, mystic, biblical scholar, poet, and scientist, Edwards is a towering figure in the history of American religious thought. Until the twentieth century he was clearly the greatest religious thinker America had produced. He stood for a "pure" Puritan version of Calvinism—emphasizing the absolute sovereignty of God, the inevitability of judgment, predestination, and salvation by grace alone—a total doctrine paradoxically permeated by his own warm emotional sensitivity. Gone were the sectarian intolerance, the political pretensions, the elaborate covenant theology of earlier Puritanism. Edwards appealed directly to the hearts of men, urged them to throw themselves on the mercy of God. To a generation in doubt about traditional religious values he brought a new assurance of salvation based on the experience of personal conversion to Christian faith and life.

As the "Great Awakening" spread from New England, its theology was reduced to a minimum under the demands of revivalism. A religious message that emphasized emotion rather than intellect was more suited to the frontier than the delicate balance of Edwards' Calvinism. Although the evangelists of the Great Awakening shared with the Puritans a reverence for the Bible and a horror of frivolity, luxury, and carnal pleasure, they put little emphasis on doctrine or on sectarian purity. Rather, they appealed directly to the individual. Because of the official "disestablishment" of religion in America, this afforded a solution to the problem of religious pluralism. Under the impact of revivalism, American churches affirmed the principles of "voluntary association." The main-line Protestant denominations and the sectarian groups that sprang up on the frontier became competitors in an open market for members and financial support.

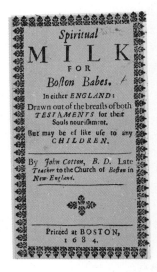

John Cotton's Puritan Primer of 1684 (title page, top) and the New England Primer of 1769 (below) are classic examples of the use of the Bible in education.

So long as an expanding frontier remained, revivalism operated effectively through the itinerant preacher or "circuit rider" and the camp meeting. The latter, with its sustained periods of gospel preaching and appeal for personal conversion, fostered the growth of small congregations dotting the countryside. The circuit-riding preacher then served these congregations—too small and isolated to support a full-time minister—by riding through the territory, staying with its local families, and undertaking pastoral duties along the way. With his rifle across his saddle and his Bible in his hand, the circuit rider became a romantic figure in the history of religion in America.

The circuit rider served the spiritual needs of frontier families by traveling hundreds of miles in all kinds of weather to preach, teach, and give counsel.

As the cultural climate of America changed, revivalism also changed. Under the impact of urbanization, the industrial revolution, and the increasing secularization of life, a new type of revivalism arose, often embracing a rigid, militant opposition to anything "modern." This type of revivalism showed even less awareness of the complexity of theological and social problems than had the frontier movements. It stressed a return to the Bible as the literal Word of God: authoritative, divinely revealed, and containing the only answer to all problems raised by the strange new urban and industrial society. The amazingly popular campaigns of new revivalists such as Charles

The artist George Bellows captured the dynamic preaching style of Billy Sunday, great revivalist of the early twentieth century.

G. Finney, Dwight L. Moody, Billy Sunday—often lasting for days at a time and resulting in hundreds of public conversions—showed the appeal of preaching which spoke directly to the individual in simple, no-nonsense terms. But the revivalists tended either to give traditional answers to radically new problems or to ignore sweeping social changes altogether. American religious life, under the influence of revivalism and other forces, came to move along in its own channels, relatively unaffected by upheavals in society and isolated from the truly revolutionary developments in European culture and thought.

The New Biblical Criticism

THE MISSIONARY MOVEMENT of the "great century"—a period extending roughly from the fall of Napoleon in 1815 until the outbreak of World War I in 1914—was responsible for transforming Christianity into a world religion and the Bible into a book for all mankind. Yet ironically, in this same period the traditional beliefs of Christianity concerning the Bible came under the severest criticism of their long history.

Once again, as at the end of the Middle Ages, conditions of life were changing drastically. Nations and national empires had emerged and the industrial revolution had given rise to great urban centers. There were vast migrations of peoples around the world. In the west, society was progressively "democratized" until any vestiges of the cultural hierarchy of medieval Christendom were almost totally obscured. World population grew tremendously; in the year 1900 almost one-fourth of the people who had *ever* lived were then alive! All fields of knowledge were expanding, and especially scientific and technical fields.

Europe, in the early nineteenth century, was entering its "golden century," an age of unprecedented intellectual and cultural advancement which produced what seemed to many the finest fruits of western Christian civilization. Intellectually, the key word was *progress* and the key idea *evolution*, understood as an upward spiral of life and culture from simple to more complex forms. What Newton's ideas had been to the eighteenth century, Darwin's became to the nineteenth. Philosophers and even religious thinkers overlooked the more sobering implications of Darwinism to emphasize the optimistic notion that nature has a built-in mechanism which guarantees that things will get "better and better"—the less successful forms of biological and social life falling by the way through the process of natural selection. Evolutionary thinking dominated the sciences, history, literary criticism, philosophy, and theology.

It was only a matter of time until such ideas had their impact on study of the Bible. Lessing, Herder, and Eichorn had already advanced historical analyses of the Old Testament amid storms of criticism from Church officialdom. Now the study of the Bible was firmly established in the secular setting of the German universities, albeit in "theological faculties." The intellectual life of Europe became increasingly secular; there was a new sense of freedom in the centers of learning. Study of the Scriptures was pursued in a "scientific" setting, with results unsettling to many. Natural explanations of biblical miracles were now buttressed by scientific data—the parting of the Red Sea, for example, seen as the consequence of prevailing winds in the area of the crossing. Similarly, developmental theories were offered to explain the growth of the diverse biblical traditions into a sacred literature. Many challenged the view that the Bible was a single, unified book containing no contradictions. Rather, it came to be seen as a collection of documents written over a long, long period developing in stages through many editions before reaching the final written form in which it has come down to us. Julius Wellhausen, one of the pioneers of modern biblical scholarship, used an already existing theory of the evolution of religion to explain the growth of the Pentateuch. Anthropologists had suggested that man's religious awareness evolved from primitive nature worship through polytheism to monotheism as the latest and highest product of human religious activity. Wellhausen argued that the "early" traditions of the Old Testament clearly showed an "early" stage of religious development, in which the Israelites freely admitted the existence of other gods than Yahweh, their God; while "later" traditions bear witness to the rise of monotheism in the religion of Israel. His theory provoked great controversy, but today virtually all scholars at least agree that there is a long period of development behind our Old Testament.

New Testament scholars were not idle either. The idea that there were also preexisting traditions behind our Synoptic Gospels was widely accepted, and the literary relationships among the Gospels, along with the process of editing they seemed to have undergone, was diligently studied. We have seen in Chapter Three how the conclusion was reached that Mark is the earliest of our Gospels to attain its present form and may be thought of as one of the sources used by Matthew and Luke.

The value of the Gospels as historical accounts of the life of Jesus was also debated among scholars. Some contended that the developing doctrines of the early Church had so colored the New Testament as to make it practically worthless as a historical source. Others went so far as to question whether Jesus had ever lived, attempting to explain the origins of Christianity by a "Christ-myth" rather than by supposedly historical events.

Thus the traditional view of the inspiration and authority of the Bible was threatened by this "scientific" study. For it seemed to many that only the scholar was competent to evaluate the literary development and historical background of the various biblical documents. And did not their religious value depend on such analysis? Scholars disparaged the accuracy of biblical accounts of such central events as the Exodus, or the resurrection of Jesus. The miracle stories, so important in earlier Christian thought, were virtually ignored. And alongside this developing biblical scholarship, the study of comparative religion was making inroads into Christian belief in the uniqueness and superiority of the Christian revelation.

Henry Ward Beecher's preaching mission through Indiana in 1840 inspired a local artist to carve this eloquent likeness of the famous pulpit orator.

New artistic styles gave new dimension to Bible passages, as in this striking 1921 woodcut by Max Pechstein illustrating the Lord's Prayer: "Our Father, who art in Heaven."

Christianity, faced with secular attitudes and a growing scepticism, challenged by the new problems of industrialized society and new revelations of science and scholarship, was forced on the defensive. The traditional literal understanding of the Bible was still very much the accepted view of the average Christian, lay or cleric, even though the new biblical scholarship had called into question almost every feature of its general outlines. The Bible was still viewed as the inspired Word of God and a reliable guide to all history—human, natural, and cosmic. Right up to the time of the Revised Version of 1885, for example, the "date of Creation" established by the Irish bishop James Ussher—4004 B.C.—appeared in the notes to the King James Version. The findings of geologists had made this ludicrous to most educated persons, and we have already seen (in Chapter One) that the discovery of other ancient religious texts with earlier versions of the stories appearing in the Old Testament showed that its authors had drawn upon a common stock of myth and legend typical of the ancient Near East. Even if one continued to defend the biblical accounts as true, they could no longer be considered unique.

The impact of these events of nineteenth-century intellectual history may be clearly seen in the rise of what has come to be called "liberal" theology, which sought to rest its case on the accepted results of modern scholarship of the Bible, the history of Christianity, the scientific understanding of nature, and the study of the religions of man. The great liberal theologian Adolf von Harnack, for example, wrote a book, *On the Essence of Christianity*, in which he argued that the central truth of Christianity was not to be found in the doctrines of Catholic or Protestant orthodoxy, but rather in the simple "religion of Jesus" which historical research could uncover *behind* the earliest literary remains. This essence of Christianity could be expressed in basic principles involving the fatherhood of God, the brotherhood of man, the infinite worth of the human person, the law of love, and the ultimate victory of good over evil. These eternal truths transcend the historical forms in which they are expressed as dogma. Even the form in which the Bible expresses them is not to be absolutized. The interpreter of the Bible must not simply repeat what he finds in his text; rather, he must ask what the relevance of his text is to the age in which *he* is called to live. The liberal theologian began by asking, "What does the Bible say?" But he ended by asking, "What must *we* say, on the basis of what the Bible says?"

Liberalism saw that modern scholarship was in process of driving a wedge between the Bible and the contemporary world, and that the wedge must be removed if the Bible was to speak to our age. This perspective dominated European theology through most of the nineteenth century, but had little impact on America until the early twentieth century. Then its advocates met with stern opposition from the churches and their spokesmen.

A major crisis was provoked in America when Charles Darwin's *On the Origin of Species* appeared in 1869, followed by *The Descent of Man* in 1871. Darwin traced man's biological ancestry to the anthropoid apes, a considerable blow to the common understanding of Genesis, that man is a special, separate creature of God. Darwin's theories, popularized by such writers as Huxley and Spencer, aroused a storm of controversy hardly imaginable today. The harvest of nineteenth-century biblical scholarship and the circulation of new "scientific" world views—including the theory of evolution—were finally making their long-delayed impact on traditional assumptions.

In America, amid cries of outrage, lurid publicity, and even a legal test in the State of Tennessee (the famous Scopes trial of 1925), the battle was fought between the old order and the new. Though some still fight on, it may be fairly said that the new perspective carried the day, as a new attitude emerged among clergymen, laymen, and scholars. This new openness to the discoveries of scholars and scientists freed the Bible and its spiritual message from older layers of interpretation and even from the cultural boundaries of the peoples who produced it. Those who found it irrelevant to the modern world were usually precisely those who could understand it in no other way than by the old literalist interpretation. Those who were viewed by the conservatives as "radical" and even "subversive" were—by very dint of their labors to understand its historical and cultural setting—able to appropriate its message afresh for the modern world. The rich heritage of a century of such painstaking study has gone into the first three chapters of this book. Biblical scholarship in the twentieth century, far from disparaging the Bible, has kept it from becoming a relic of the dead past. If the Bible should become meaningless to people of some future time, it will be only because their grasp of its message has been limited by the interpretation of a past age whose questions and situation are no longer relevant.

A satirical caricature shows Charles Darwin, originator of the theory of evolution, emerging from the jungle as a product of "natural selection."

New Versions and Translations

AGAINST THE BACKGROUND of the revolutionary developments in modern thought and biblical scholarship, it is not surprising that momentum had long been building in the English-speaking world for a revision of the King James Version of the Bible. Much of the language of this magnificent seventeenth-century translation, for all its sonorous beauty, had become archaic—and words once clear in meaning now led to obscurities and misunderstandings. Moreover, a host of extremely important ancient manuscripts had come to light since the completion of that version: the *Codex Vaticanus*, for example, had been stored away in Rome from the fifteenth century until the nineteenth. The *Codex Sinaiticus* was found in the mid-nineteenth century by an incredible stroke of luck, the great scholar Count Tischendorf discovering it in the great monastery of St. Catherine at the foot of Mt. Sinai. He also recovered a fifth-century Bible manuscript, dubbed the *Codex Ephraemi*, which had been written over by a twelfth-century scribe in search of good vellum. These and other finds enabled New Testament scholars to

reevaluate the received text of the Greek New Testament, which had been little altered since the days of Erasmus, and actually made it possible, strange as it may sound, to construct an *older* text than had previously been available. Now a critical text of the Greek New Testament was reconstructed by the British scholars Westcott and Hort as a basis for an English revision of the King James Version.

The principal biblical scholars of England worked on the revision from 1870 until 1881, with American scholars joining in the effort after 1871. The Revised New Testament was published on May 17, 1881; within a few days *two million* copies had been sold in London alone! A shipload arrived in New York on May 20, and immediately the complete texts of the Gospels, Acts, and Romans were sent by telegraph to the *Tribune* and *Times* of Chicago, while copies of the book went speeding west to arrive in time for the compositors to finish setting the whole New Testament for the Sunday editions of both papers. Inevitably, the Old Testament revision took longer, so that the complete Revised Version was not published until May 19, 1885.

While the Revised New Testament reflected the results of new discoveries and study, the revision of the Old Testament was based on the same tenth-century A.D. Hebrew text as the King James. This text, known as the Masoretic, was the oldest available. Recent discoveries show that this was a much less serious limitation than one might suspect, since discovery of the Dead Sea Scrolls (ca. 100 B.C.) has revealed that text to be remarkably accurate. But the revision of the Old Testament was very cautious, and its critics charged that it retained either too much, or in some cases too little, of the language and tone of the King James Version. The American committee, dissatisfied, continued its work until 1901, when it produced the very similar American Standard Version. Both of these revisions were competent, valuable work; but the extreme caution and conservatism of the responsible committees meant that their work would soon be outdated by the advance of biblical scholarship and the rapidly changing modern world.

In 1930 a thorough-going American revision was undertaken which has become the most popular of the modern English versions, the Revised Standard Version—generally called the RSV. When it finally appeared in 1952, the event was hailed by some 3000 solemn religious meetings in the United States and Canada, each closing with the singing of the hymn, "How Firm a Foundation." In its relatively brief history, the RSV bids fair to become as widely used as its ancestor, the King James Version. While it is not a *new* translation, as its preface acknowledges, the RSV renders the Bible into a neat, formal, simple prose which is such a happy compromise that it is rapidly becoming the most read English Bible. A joint Protestant-Catholic edition of it has already been approved and published, which means that all English-speaking Christians are able to share in the reading and hearing of the same Bible for the first time since the Reformation.

In 1961 there appeared in England a new translation of the New Testament, made from a newly constructed and attested critical text, which

The bell-banner of St. John's Abbey Church in Collegeville, Minnesota, is an example of contemporary architectural expression of religious faith and feeling.

attempted, in the words of its translators to render faithfully "the best available Greek text into the current speech of our own time," in such a way as to "harvest the gains of recent biblical scholarship." This translation, called the *New English Bible*, was suggested in May 1946 by the Church of Scotland and formally commissioned in January 1948 by the Church of Scotland and the Methodist, Baptist, and Congregationalist Churches; the Presbyterian Church of England, the Society of Friends, the Churches in Wales, the Churches in Ireland, the British and Foreign Bible Society, and the National Bible Society of Scotland. With such impressive backing, the scholars who undertook this translation did not take it to be their task to revise an already existing English Bible, but to understand the original text as precisely as modern scholarship would allow, and then to say in the translator's native idiom (modern English) what the original author was saying in his. The result was a bold and vigorous translation, remarkably idiomatic, fresh, and vivid. The overriding aims of clarity and accuracy are apparent throughout. Although the New English Bible has not yet proved as popular as the RSV, it is a distinguished contemporary translation. The committee has promised that the Old Testament and the Apocrypha will follow in the years ahead.

The Revised Standard Version, *most significant Bible translation of the twentieth century, was produced by two teams of scholars. The Old Testament committee included (from left): George Dahl, James Muilenburg, Julius A. Bewer, Fleming James, Luther A. Weigle (chairman), Millar Burrows, Harry M. Orlinsky, Herbert G. May, and William A. Irwin.*

Finally, the most recent monument to the labors of the modern translator has been the magnificent *Jerusalem Bible*, first published in French with introductions and notes in 1956 as *La Bible de Jérusalem*. The English translation appeared in 1966, avowedly intended to present to the English-speaking world the finest fruits of Roman Catholic biblical scholarship as represented by the École Biblique de Jérusalem. The *Jerusalem Bible* is an imposing achievement and illustrates the spirit of renewal which has characterized Roman Catholic biblical studies in the period of the Second Vatican Council.

Biblical Interpretation and the Modern Age

IT WOULD be extremely misleading to assume that an account of *texts* and *translations* can give an accurate picture of the twentieth-century chapter in the long, varied story of the Bible and its unquenchable vitality. For *interpretation* of the Bible has been a central and inescapable feature of the religious thought of the twentieth century, perhaps bulking larger than any other aspect of our story. Twentieth-century biblical scholars inherited a rich treasury of suggestions, tentative conclusions, and "assured results" to be assimilated.

First, the new historical understanding of the Bible brought into focus the emphasis the Bible itself places on history—the realm of time and events—as the arena in which God discloses his purposes to men. Scholars have concluded that the biblical stress on historic encounter with God is one of the unique and irreducible features of biblical religion. Other ancient civilizations have looked back, in their myths and rituals, to a precosmic "sacred time" which repeated itself in endless cycles of week, month, season, and year. But the myths and rituals of ancient Israel had as their function to recall the mighty acts of Yahweh, who delivered the Israelites from a this-worldly bondage under Rameses II of Egypt. The mystery religions of the Hellenistic world sought an other-worldly deliverance through communion with cultic deities whose death and rebirth were celebrated in elaborate initiation rites. The Christians had their mysteries and rituals too, but at the heart of their faith was belief in a Savior who was crucified "under Pontius Pilate"—that is, who lived and walked on earth as an historic person. Recognition of this strong, perhaps central biblical theme has led to a revival of biblical theology in the twentieth century.

Interpretation of the Bible has also played a central role in the development of Protestant theology in the twentieth century. Karl Barth, the dean of twentieth-century Protestant theologians, made his mark with a stirring commentary on the Epistle to the Romans in which he stressed the "strange new world" encountered in the witness of the Bible to a God who judges and redeems men in and through Jesus Christ, and within the history of human communities. His grasp of this historical witness led Barth to criticize sharply the liberal theology of his predecessors, whose "timeless truths" may be appealing, but fail to mirror faithfully the testimony of Scripture to the God who reveals himself in an individual, Jesus Christ.

Barth's great counterpart and "friendly enemy," Rudolph Bultmann of Marburg, has also fought to keep the Bible central in contemporary Protestant theology. The only way to do this, Bultmann argues, is to carry forward the nineteenth-century program of "translating" the *message* of the Bible from its cultural setting in the ancient world into our own world view, rather than simply translating the words from an ancient to a modern language. Bultmann calls this program "demythologizing," and it has become perhaps the most crucial question debated by modern theologians. Its originator has insisted that modern men simply cannot be bound by an archaic world view which includes demons, miracles, and a "three-story universe" (heaven, earth, and hell); nor, says Bultmann, can he be compelled to accept a redemption-mythology which makes no sense apart from such a world view. Rather, modern man must hear the message of the gospel in a form that speaks to his condition and can transform his *own* self-understanding rather than impose an archaic and unscientific world view upon him. Bultmann has challenged the preachers and theologians to strip away the "false stumbling blocks" and confront modern men with the true gospel which has the power to transform men's lives through encounter with Jesus Christ. His critics have argued that he gives away too much of the biblical world view to an uncritical "modernizing"—that, in fact, he throws out the baby with the bath. This debate has continued in Europe and America for thirty years.

Roman Catholic theology has also experienced a biblical revival. In 1942 Pope Pius XII issued an encyclical letter, *Divino Afflante Spiritu* ("Inspired by the Holy Spirit"), which has become the Magna Charta of modern Catholic biblical scholarship. For the first time since the Reformation, Catholic and Protestant biblical scholars have entered into serious dialogue, taking account of the views of their colleagues not as "opponents" but as partners in the task of interpreting the Bible. The decree of the Second Vatican Council concerning revelation, *Dei Verbum* ("Word of God") has caused great excitement, since it seems to move toward healing the breach between Protestants and Catholics by emphasizing the authority of the Bible and its unique place in Christian teaching. In fact, there have recently been expressions of concern from the Catholic side that perhaps the document may go too far and compromise the fullness of Roman Catholic teaching on the authority of Church tradition. But such a development would have been unthinkable in the climate of nineteenth-century Roman Catholicism.

Jewish religious thought has also experienced a biblical renewal in the twentieth century. Virtually every leading scholar and theologian of Judaism in our time has taken it as a major calling either to further biblical scholarship or to appropriate this rich heritage for the Jewish people. Names such as Franz Rosenzweig and Martin Buber, whose lyrical paraphrase of the Torah was published in German beginning in 1926 and republished as recently as 1954, or Yehezkel Kaufmann, whose scholarly achievements have domi-

The dense black outlines and bold contrasts of Georges Rouault's "Miserere" prints have given powerful contemporary expression to biblical events.

nated a generation of students at the Hebrew University in Jerusalem, spring immediately to mind. Others, such as America's Abraham J. Heschel or Will Herberg, Cyrus Gordon, and Theodor Gaster, must also stand high on any list of twentieth-century scholars and interpreters of the Bible.

Twentieth-century religious thought is in ferment. There is a restless demand for new forms of worship, service, and belief and an impatience with old, outworn patterns dating from the sixteenth century and earlier. Of course old ways are not necessarily bad ones, but it is often difficult to see them in the light in which they developed and became vital.

Everywhere there is evidence of a spirit of reform and renewal in

The Shrine of the Book, in Jerusalem, houses many priceless manuscripts, including many of the most important Dead Sea Scrolls.

241

twentieth-century religious life; often meeting with stern opposition but never defeated. Ministers, priests, rabbis, and nuns march together in defense of common humanity and of human rights. Laymen in the various religious communions show new concern for the meaning and relevance of their inherited faith. Provocative ideas pour forth from pulpit and publishing house. Often the glare of publicity obscures the fact that Christians and Jews are concerned to bring their faith once again into the midst of life—and that means modern life with all its complexities and enigmas. And once more, the Bible is playing a central role.

It is common knowledge that the Bible has remained first on the best-seller lists for as long as there have been best-seller lists. Modern vernacular versions, such as those by J. B. Phillips, or Ronald Knox, or James Moffat, continue to satisfy a demand for fresh approaches to the Bible, which is now being printed and distributed in an amazing number of languages. Remarkable pioneers such as Frank Laubach, the Wycliffe Bible Translators, the Bible societies, and other dedicated missionary groups have served the twin causes of world literacy and Bible distribution through translating efforts in less developed cultures. By 1967 there were translations of some major part of the Bible in more than a thousand languages and dialects, including 240 different renderings of the entire Bible and 301 of one or the other Testament. Translations of one or more books of the Bible had appeared in 739 additional languages. It has been estimated that no less than four-fifths of the world's population can today obtain all or part of the Bible in their own language.

The sheer presence, the availability of the Bible, is phenomenal. How great its actual influence is, how much it is read and studied, may remain an open question. It of course continues to nourish the life of the Jewish and Christian communities. Biblical scholarship makes new strides with new methods. For example, textual criticism and the comparing of manuscripts has been partly "computerized." Archaeology has filled in some major gaps in our understanding of Old and New Testament backgrounds through discoveries such as the tablets of Ras Shamra mentioned in Chapter One and the Dead Sea Scrolls mentioned in Chapter Three. All these developments are reflected in a deeper understanding and interpretation of the Bible in church and synagogue.

The Bible has also played a role in the vigorous and growing ecumenical movement of our time. Where once it divided Catholic from Protestant and Christian from Jew, today the fragmented communities are being drawn together in the common task of appropriating and witnessing to their shared heritage. Renewed interest in the Bible among Roman Catholics has led to increased numbers of laymen participating in Bible study programs. American Catholics now hear the Epistle and Gospel readings of the Mass in the direct modern English of the Confraternity translation—an official version based on the original Greek rather than the Vulgate. A milestone of interfaith cooperation on the scholarly level is the multi-volume Anchor Bible now being produced by a group of Protestant, Catholic, and Jewish translator-commentators, several volumes of which have already appeared.

It is hard to foresee precisely what the latest chapter in the story of the Bible, begun in the dark shadows of the dawn of history, may include. This three-thousand-year-old giant of a Holy Book still inspires and strengthens men today as it did in ages past. It sustained the ancient Hebrews in their national calamities; it challenged Jesus, Paul, Luther, and a host of God-fearing men and women over the centuries. In every renewal of western faith and culture the Bible has been a dynamic source of inspiration and a vital witness to man's long struggle to find God. And men of faith remain confident that "God will yet cause more light to break forth from His Word."

And what might be the nature of that light? The great crises that confront men in the revolutions of the twentieth century sometimes seem to have little to do with religion. Future judgments on the significance of our time will probably focus on the snowballing technology that has advanced us to the threshold of a "postindustrial, postliterate, postcivilized age." Mass communications have combined with automation and advanced electronics to produce a baffling style of life, radically secular, increasingly urban, and incredibly complicated. It has been suggested that such an age will inevitably be "postreligious" as well, that the inherited religious view of life seems less and less relevant to the new era. Of course religion will continue to influence the behavior of persons for generations to come, we are told; but basically, it belongs to the childhood and adolescence of the human race, and the time has come to put away childish things. Even religious leaders sometimes offer such comments, to the shock or dismay of the man in the street.

Contemporary religious thinkers are discovering, however, sometimes to their surprise, that there are resources in the Bible to meet this challenge. The biblical affirmation that God is the Creator of *this* world and that He had a purpose in creating it, along with the insistence that God pronounced His creation *good* and thus not to be despised, seem to demand that we not turn our backs on the creative possibilities of even the most radically secular styles of life. The biblical faith that God is at work to redeem His world demands that the struggle for genuine humanity, justice, and love in our age not be abandoned. However complex and baffling the problems that confront us, there is a biblical foundation for hope and service in the cause of God.

Inevitably our understanding of the Bible will reflect our human situation in the mid-twentieth century. So it has been in every age. Today the Bible is the world's possession, the gift of the Judeo-Christian heritage, but far more than a sectarian document, more even than the sacred scripture of one or many religious communities. Increasingly, biblical scholarship has reflected this fact; increasingly, so must our understanding of the Book itself. Read as a whole, and understood in its broadest perspective, interpreted by faithful and responsible men, the Bible will remain a vital witness to our common humanity under the sovereignty of God. Through this witness it may supply the power for all men to be partners in a creative and redemptive work.

Illustration Credits

The publisher gratefully acknowledges the following sources for permission to reproduce illustrations on the pages indicated:

ERRATA

Illustration Credits listed on pages 243 and 244 should be corrected to read: **Page 123. Hirmer Verlag, Munich. Page 124. Top: Giraudon; bottom: Bibliothèque Nationale, Paris. Page 125. John C. Trever. Page 126. Top: Hirmer Verlag, Munich; bottom: The Cleveland Museum of Art, Mr. and Mrs. William H. Marlatt Fund. Page 143. Top: The Cleveland Museum of Art, Mr. and Mrs. William H. Marlatt Fund; bottom: John C. Trever. Page 144. Top: left and center, H. T. Frank; top right and bottom, John C. Trever. Page 145. Top: Cleveland Museum of Art, purchased from the J. H. Wade Fund; bottom: National Gallery of Art, Washington, D. C., Samuel H. Kress Collection. Page 146. Harriet-Louise Patterson.**

Legend on page 143 should read: **The Dome of the Rock, opposite page 147.**

Index of Names